PORTFOLIO / PENGUIN

THE VIRGIN WAY

Sir Richard Branson is an international entrepreneur, adventurer, icon, and the founder of the Virgin Group. His autobiography, *Losing My Virginity*, and his books on business, *Screw It, Let's Do It* and *Business Stripped Bare*, are all international bestsellers. He is also the author of *Reach for the Skies*, *Screw Business as Usual*, and, most recently, *Like a Virgin*.

THE VIRGIN WAY

If It's Not Fun, It's Not Worth Doing

RICHARD BRANSON

PORTFOLIO/PENGUIN

PORTFOLIO / PENGUIN
An imprint of Penguin Random House LLC
375 Hudson Street
New York, New York 10014
penguin.com

First published in the United States of America by Portfolio / Penguin 2014
This paperback edition published 2015

Published by arrangement with Virgin Books Limited, part of The Random House Group Limited

Quotes on pages 31, 32, and 86 reproduced with permission of Curtis Brown, London on behalf of the Estate of Sir Winston Churchill. Copyright © Winston S. Churchill.
Quote on page 79 from *A Soldier's Way* by Colin Powell, Published by Hutchinson. Reprinted by permission of The Random House Group Ltd. Published in the United States as *My American Journey* by Random House, Inc.
Quote on page 287 from *See You at the Top: 25th Anniversary Edition* by Zig Ziglar. Copyright © 1975, 1977, 2000 used by permission of the publisher, Pelican Publishing Company, Inc. www.pelicanpub.com.

THE LIBRARY OF CONGRESS HAS CATALOGED THE HARDCOVER EDITION AS FOLLOWS:
Branson, Richard.
The Virgin way : everything I know about leadership / Richard Branson.
pages cm
Includes index.
ISBN 978-1-59184-737-3 (hc.)
ISBN 978-1-59184-798-4 (pbk.)
1. Leadership. I. Title.
HD57.7.B72743 2014
658.4'092—dc23
2014021086

Printed in the United States of America
1   3   5   7   9   10   8   6   4   2

'Try everything once.
Except incest and folk dancing.'

Sir Thomas Beecham

CONTENTS

Part Four – LEAD

LIFE'S TOO SHORT

Don't enjoy it? Don't do it!

From my very first commercial venture at age sixteen with *Student* magazine, right up to today's far loftier adventures with such things as Virgin Galactic and space tourism, I have always had one paramount philosophy: if a new project or business opportunity doesn't excite me and get my entrepreneurial and innovative juices flowing, if it's not something with which I sense I can make a difference while having a lot of seriously creative fun, then I'd far rather pass on it and move right along to something else that does excite me.

This same line of thought flows into my attitude towards writing books: if I don't enjoy writing them, then the chances are pretty good that nobody is going to be too happy reading them. The simple fact is that if you don't enjoy what you're doing and the people with whom you're doing it, then there is no possible way that you are ever going to do it as well as something that you do enjoy. As some wise person once said, '*Life is not a dress rehearsal.*' This is it! So unless you plan to give it a better shot in your next life – assuming you are lucky enough to get a second chance – then why risk wasting any of your limited time on this earth doing stuff that doesn't light your fire?

I am constantly amazed at how many people appear to live their lives either always looking in the rear-view mirror or talking about how things are going to be different in the future. There is nothing wrong with cherishing and enjoying memories and hopefully learning from past experiences just as planning for the future is something we obviously all have to do as well – but what about today? All too frequently 'now' gets lost in the frenetic shuffle to rush ahead to tomorrow. Face it: these are 'the good old days' that you'll be looking back on twenty years from now – so why not move heaven and earth to enjoy them while you've got them?

Mahatma Gandhi is one of my all-time heroes, and a quote from him that I think I first read in a school history lesson has stuck with me ever since: 'Live as if you were to die tomorrow. Learn as if you were to live forever.' This good advice has been popularly abbreviated to, 'Live every day as if it were your last', which is a wonderful sentiment even if it has frequently become a worldwide rallying cry for never-mind-the-consequences hell-raisers. I remember well the one time (as an apprentice hell-raiser) I tried using the latter version on my mum as an excuse for some mischief or other. 'But Mum,' I implored, 'I was only doing what Gandhi said I should do.' Unimpressed, she gave me a straight-faced reply of, 'Pull that trick again, Ricky, and today could very well be your last!'

Actually the best quote on living every day like it's your last belongs to Steve Jobs, who in a commencement speech he made at Stanford University in 2005 said, 'If you live every day like it's your last, someday you'll almost certainly be right.' It would be funny but for the fact he courageously gave the address just twelve months after he had been diagnosed with the cancer that would kill him six years later.

As fallible human beings we all make our share of mistakes and get ourselves into the kind of predicaments that result from making the wrong choices, but in the vast majority of such situations we all have the ability to pause, take stock and say, 'Sorry, but I'm really not happy with this so I'm out of here.' I recognise that in a lot of instances – particularly when friends and family are involved – this may be easier said than done and taking any such drastic action usually calls for a lot of courage. However, as the old adage goes, when you make mistakes at least try to make them quickly.

I have often had people say to me, 'Well, sure, Richard, all that stuff is easy for you to say when you've built your business and you've pretty much made it in life.' To this my response is always along the lines of, 'Yes, that's true – to a degree. But why do you think I have all those companies? They almost certainly wouldn't be there had I not repeatedly dug my heels in and refused to spend my time on things I recognised as just not right for me.' One of the earliest examples of a situation in which I felt off-kilter was my time at school. When I shocked my parents as well as friends by dropping out of the prestigious Stowe School at age sixteen, I did it with my young eyes wide open in order to pursue a dream of starting my own magazine publishing business. In my heart of hearts I knew that making *Student* magazine a success simply didn't necessitate me spending any more of my precious time sitting in stuffy classrooms. The idea of spending another couple of years memorising mind-numbing facts from textbooks, wrestling with the joys of calculus and defining little-known Latin verbs seemed totally irrelevant to my future life and so I had to escape or risk losing my sanity.

Please don't misinterpret this as some kind of 'burn your books', anti-education tirade – quite the opposite. Availing yourself of the best education you can get is an imperative particularly in today's ultra competitive commercial world. When I went to school, however, learning was much more of a memorisation and regurgitation process than it seems to be today. The old way was particularly challenging for someone like me with dyslexia and borderline ADD – attention deficit disorder. There were several excellent teachers who did make their subjects come to life, but with my early-stage entrepreneurial juices starting to flow I had mentally moved on already. The paradoxical twist is that ever since I dropped out of school I have spent the balance of my life with a thirst for learning about new things, businesses, people and cultures. The big difference, of course, is that my learning process has involved experiencing all these things first-hand as opposed to reading about them in books or third-hand from someone who frequently had never lived outside of academia.

Although I had serious trouble tuning into teachers in school, when I struck out on my own I had to quickly set about honing my dubious listening skills. One of the first of many tasks I took on at *Student* was that of 'cub reporter' so when interviewing someone, I had no option but to listen intently while scribbling down notes that sometimes were almost completely indecipherable. Whether it was with John Lennon or John le Carré, I had to rapidly acquire the art of simultaneously listening, writing and thinking about my next follow-on question. It was somewhat of a 'Chinese plate trick' as you had to keep all the components spinning or you found yourself helplessly adrift. But the ability to lock in and listen is a skill that has served me well in life. Although it seems to be somewhat of a dying art, I believe that listening is one of the most important skills for any teacher, parent, leader, entrepreneur or, well, just about anyone who has a pulse.

What's become known around our various companies as 'the Virgin way' is something that has evolved since day one. When someone who has just joined us from outside comes out of their first, usually highly informal, strategy or product meeting and says, 'Wow, you folks certainly do things differently, don't you?' the response is often, 'Yup, that's the Virgin way', usually said with a smile and a knowing wink.

As you will (I hope) understand, one of the keys to 'the way' we do things is nothing more complex than listening – listening intently to *everyone* who has an opinion to share, not just the self-professed experts. It's also about learning from each other, from the marketplace and from the mistakes that must be made in order to get anywhere that is original and disruptive. And perhaps most importantly, it's about having fun with a capital F while we're doing it. Leading 'the Virgin way' often has quite unpredictable consequences and takes us to places where other 'more sensible' operations might fear to tread. And with a brand that is now as visible as it is, this means leading from the front and sticking your neck out in ways that a lot of leadership styles might not consider 'prudent', a word that I do not use on a frequent basis.

I don't profess for one moment to have some kind of secret formula or a panacea for the challenges of business in general. What I write about in the coming pages is simply what, in my wide-ranging experience, has served me and, by extension, Virgin extremely well – the vast majority of the time at least. Having what we like to call 'serious fun' is at the core of 'the Virgin way' and that's something for which I will never apologise. Being passionately engaged and enjoying every minute of what you do is an attitudinal thing – a spark – that cannot be mandated, trained, put in a job description or an employee manual. It's something that's either in a person's DNA or not, and as such has to come from within.

If you're someone who believes in going your own way and having a lot of fun doing it, then you're already on the right track and there's probably very little anyone can say to modify your course more than a few degrees. I'd just urge you to do a lot more listening than talking, don't be afraid to wear your passion on your sleeve for all to see, and when in doubt trust your instincts.

I only mention all of this in order to be totally transparent on how I have lived my life and to put my, perhaps somewhat less than traditional, take on listening, living, laughing and leading in the proper context. There are a lot of slightly crazy things I have done with boats and hot-air balloons, jumping off tall buildings and more that certainly had the potential to shorten my life expectancy. Some may call it recklessness but I prefer to call it taking 'calculated risks'. One way or the other, though, I'd certainly put many of my past adventures in the category of 'Don't try this at home'. What I do believe to be an essential, however, particularly for anyone with entrepreneurial aspirations, is an unfettered willingness to trust their instincts and to follow their own star, even if at times it might appear to be leading them towards the edge of the precipice.

My star has certainly led me over quite a few cliffs and in some pretty wild and woolly directions and so I should also confess that from an early age, my idea of 'having fun' might not be the same as a lot of other people's. Whether the challenges are physical or financial – or sometimes both – fun, aka excitement, has for me always been inextricably linked with taking risks and sometimes perhaps some pretty insane ones. The problem is that being told 'You'd have to be crazy to even think about doing that' has to me always been like the proverbial red rag to a bull. Whether it's starting a Christmas tree farm, a capital-intensive business like an airline, kite-surfing across the English Channel in my sixties, fighting to reduce the suffocating carbon blitz that is killing our planet, or seeking to commercialise space travel, I love nothing better than what appears to be an outlandish challenge. As any of my colleagues at Virgin will attest, in my vocabulary the phrase 'seemingly impossible' is defined as 'something that should be a lot of fun disproving'.

After a Laser dinghy ride around the island with me, one frequent guest on Necker (who wishes to remain anonymous) once laughingly commented, 'Wow, Richard! After that experience I now understand what makes Virgin different: you really take the "shortest distance between two points is a straight line" thing very seriously, don't you?' When I asked what exactly he meant by that, it turned out that the thrill I get from sailing at high speed through, and frequently right over the top of, the island's encircling jagged rocks was clearly not what he'd had in mind when I suggested we go sailing. The way I see it, though, just about anyone can chart a safe course and laboriously pick their way around a field of obstacles – but where's the fun in that?

My approach to sailing around Necker is perhaps a pretty good analogy for my view on leadership in business. If your vision is to reach a distant beach where, because of the reefs surrounding it, no one has ever set foot, then the chances are that reading the same old charts as everyone else has used isn't going to get you there either. And the readily available excesses of data on just about every subject tends to give most people more ammunition on why *not* to pursue any even slightly off-the-chart objective. I have spent my life trying off-the-chart things and going places that friends and colleagues have told me were bad ideas. Does that make me nothing more than a contrarian? Perhaps. However, pushing the envelope and zagging when everyone else zigs is something that just seems to be part of my DNA, and to date it has worked pretty well for me – most of the time, at least.

I didn't take any business courses or read any books on leadership to figure out how I would make it in life, so be warned that some of the pages ahead probably aren't for everyone. While I wouldn't necessarily categorise this as a 'leadership book', on a whim I decided to search the term on Amazon and was more than a little blown away by the results – on the day I checked, I found a mere 93,467 matches! Not only that, but I have to confess I don't believe I have read a single one of them. As a result I have no idea what the other 93,467 authors have to say, but I doubt that few if any of them can have had a fraction of the fun I've had in the forty-plus years I have been leading the charge with the Virgin group of companies.

Then I had a thought that perhaps 'leadership' simply isn't the right word for what I have been practising? So when I went back to Amazon and searched, *'Having a great time while building a highly diversified global business with an extended family of simply wonderful people'*, guess what? There was not a single match – at least not until now!

PART ONE

MONITOR
PICK UP ON
HEAR OUT
TUNE IN
MONITOR
GIVE HEED TO
BE ATTENTIVE LISTEN HEAR

LISTEN

GIVE HEED TO
MONITOR
PICK UP ON
ATTEND
BE ALL EARS
TAKE NOTICE
LISTEN
PICK
UP ON
LEND AN EAR
HEAR OUT
ATTEND

Chapter 1

OLD BLOCKS AND YOUNG CHIPS

Leadership lessons begin at home

Sometimes the greatest leadership lessons can come from the most unexpected places. Some elements of leadership are almost certainly genetic and there is no escaping the fact that we are all products of our upbringing and our environment. As the saying goes, 'An apple never falls far from the tree that bore it'. Well, as anyone who knows my mother Eve or my late father Ted will testify, I am certainly no exception to the rule. I recognise a lot of traits in myself that I have clearly inherited from my parents – mostly good – although just a few of the things that drove me nuts about my mum and dad when I was a kid almost certainly had the same effect on my own children.

From my first memories of her, my mum was always on the go, buzzing around the place. She had a seemingly limitless imagination for coming up with new business ideas. I don't recall her ever considering herself an entrepreneur – that was probably only because I don't think the word existed back then and if it did nobody knew what it meant – but she was certainly the definition of 'enterprising'. Eve is a human whirlwind. No matter what the latest big thing was, she'd always manage the whole process by herself from developing the ideas to crafting the products, to making deals with distributors, delivering and selling the goods. Nobody else could get in her way, it was her show and hers alone! I remember being very impressed by one of her more successful ventures, which was building and selling wooden tissue boxes and wastepaper bins. This one made it to some fairly swanky stores but they were generally more local ventures. She was absolutely tenacious, and taught me never to cry over spilt milk. If an item didn't sell, she'd just write it off, learn from the experience and quite dispassionately move on and try something else. My sisters and I were always being dragged in as unpaid child labour, 'a labour of love' she'd call it, or the household chores would be delegated to us while Mum was in manufacturing mode. Obviously I didn't realise it at the time but there was unquestionably a lot of osmosis going on in that house that would stand me in good stead later in life.

Eve hasn't changed much even though she is now… oops. As she was the one that taught me never to talk about a woman's age let's leave it at 'she is rather well into her eighties'. In her early life she had a spell as a West End dancer, and later became a stewardess for

British South American Airways – that was in the really glamorous days of flying when they had to don oxygen masks to cross the Andes. To this day she just never stops moving! I don't exactly lead a sedentary life myself but I swear that sometimes I have trouble keeping up with her.

One recent example was when quite out of the blue she casually announced her intention to organise a charity polo match – not exactly the kind of thing one expects from an octogenarian! But this wasn't going to be something on the village green near her home – she was planning to do it in Morocco! Surprised but far from stunned, I told her in no uncertain terms that I thought it a really crazy idea; not only would it be a huge amount of work but it would probably end up costing her money rather than raising it. She listened intently to what I had to say and then went ahead and did it anyway. Not only did it happen but it was a huge success and raised about a quarter of a million dollars. So while I was denied the opportunity to say, 'See, Mum, I told you so', I really had to admire her tenacity and so instead simply said (a very quiet) 'Well done, Mum.'

Another of those family signature characteristics that I am told I have inherited is forever insisting on getting the last word in on any given subject. Well, just to show how flexible I can be on such things, I am going to let Eve have some of the first words in this book so (as a published author herself) I invited her to write a few thoughts. Based on what I've just told you about her, see if any of the following sounds familiar? 'Apples and trees!'

Dear Ricky,

If you're really going to let me say something in your next book, then here it goes.

We saw it in you from virtually the first moment you began to talk. But even before that, when you learned to walk we realised we were going to have our hands full; you were just a toddler but you were clearly someone who liked to do things his own way and on your own terms.

To make matters even more interesting, as you grew you perpetually had some crazy new scheme or other up your sleeve that you were convinced was either going to change the world, make lots of money, or both! On a few such occasions we would say things like, 'Oh don't be ridiculous, Ricky! That's never going to work.' More often than not, however, your father and I instead opted to give you plenty of scope to learn by your mistakes and so left you to get on with your Christmas tree growing, bird breeding and all the other weird and wonderful enterprises you came up with. Almost without exception they all ended in some form of a disaster with us picking up the pieces – literally and metaphorically – but we'd soldier on and just kept hoping that one day the lessons learned would help you in life.

And that certainly would seem to have turned out to be the case. After a rocky beginning, once you and Virgin had become an established success, Ted and I would often ponder on just how differently you might have turned out had we been more controlling, or some might say 'better', parents. What if we had insisted that you not take so many silly risks and, rather than allowing you to drop out of school at sixteen, forced you to buckle down and complete your education? Like your headmaster at Stowe, who famously (now) predicted that by twenty-one you would either be in jail or a millionaire, we too shared some very serious misgivings about what the future might have in store for you.

As we now know, of course, we needn't have worried. What we saw as being a pig-headed little boy who was utterly determined to do his own thing, turned out to be nothing more than the growing pains of a budding entrepreneur. If only we had been able to recognise that at the time we might have had a lot fewer sleepless nights!

Love, Mum

I read that some wag once said of me, 'That Branson chap is the luckiest person I know. You just watch – if he ever falls off a high building he's almost certainly going to fall upwards!' Please don't hold your breath on this one as it's not a theory I intend to test any time soon! Others have suggested that I was simply 'born lucky'. Perhaps!

In my opinion 'luck' is a highly misunderstood commodity. It's certainly not something that drops out of the heavens, you really can work at helping it along – but more on that later. For now suffice it to say that I came into this world a lot luckier than most people. I had the good fortune to be born into a wonderfully loving family where I enjoyed a safe and 'sensible' childhood in post-war England. I grew up in a home where there were few if any excesses, but at the same time my two sisters and I never really wanted for much of anything, especially affection and guidance from our parents.

Looking back on that period of my life I have to heap praise on the stalwart efforts of my mother and father, as I certainly was not the easiest child to bring up. Apart from being dyslexic I was blessed with an indomitable spirit that, whether she wants to admit it or not, unquestionably came from my mother Eve's side of the family. Perhaps she recognised this kindred spirit in me as she was constantly taking the lead in trying to keep young 'Ricky' (that would be me) in line. At the same time it was also very much a team effort with my father Ted, even if the two of them didn't always realise it at the time.

There are many examples of this. Like one Sunday in church when I point-blank refused to sit next to the son of a friend of my mother's simply because I didn't like the child. Despite my mum's loudly whispered protestations, I instead sat with a friend on the opposite side of the aisle. I really didn't think it was that big of a deal, so I was utterly shocked when I got back home and, for what might have been the first time ever, my mother insisted that Dad should spank my bottom. She loudly proclaimed that, 'The boy has to learn that such behaviour will simply not be tolerated in this house.' As I was thinking, 'But I didn't do it in this house', Dad dragged me out of the room by the scruff of the neck and then, just loudly enough to ensure that Mum would hear him, proclaimed, 'Okay, young man. It's time for me to teach you a lesson that you'll never forget!'

And he certainly did. Following his quickly whispered instructions, I squealed in an appropriately pained manner as my dad proceeded to loudly clap his hands together half a dozen times. In a conspiratorial whisper he then told me to go back in to see Mum and apologise while looking 'suitably chastised'. It was all I could do to keep my face straight when mid-apology Dad gave me a huge wink from behind Mum's back.

Dad was really just a big softy at heart, but I am convinced that the way he handled the situation after church that day taught me a far more lasting lesson than a severely bruised bottom (and ego) could ever have achieved. I'm not sure if my mother ever knew about the fake spanking – if she didn't then when she reads this she certainly will – but there was another more serious occasion when Ted's parenting skills have stuck with me forever. On the odd occasion I had been guilty of helping myself to a few pennies from the loose change that Dad used to unload from his pockets into the top drawer in his bedroom wardrobe. To my childish amusement I had also discovered it was the same drawer where Dad kept his secret stash of what we used to call 'dirty books', but I digress. Helping myself to his change was never something I saw as 'stealing' per se. In my juvenile mind I was just kind of 'borrowing' it and we'd simply never established the repayment terms or structure.

As it turned out, however, I was the one who was about to get repaid by getting myself into a lot of trouble. We lived just around the corner from a sweet shop and I'd been using my ill-gotten gains to buy chocolate, with Cadbury's fruit and nut being my particular favourite. One day, though, I'd taken a much bigger 'loan' than usual from Dad's wardrobe bank and promptly done my part to boost Cadbury's shareholder value. The 'old lady' who owned the shop, who at the time was probably all of forty years old, quickly smelled a rat. She said nothing to me, but the next time I was in her shop in the company of my father she staggered me by blurting out, 'Now I don't want to get him into any trouble, Mr Branson, but I don't know where young Richard's getting all his money from. He's becoming quite my best customer – so I do hope he isn't stealing it.' I remember her words like it were yesterday and thinking, 'Did she really have to put that zinger on the end?'

But then, just as I was thinking, 'Oops, I'm really in for it now!' my dad staggered me by putting his nose right up to hers, looking her straight in the eyes and loudly declaring, 'Madam, how dare you accuse my son of stealing?' I was even more surprised when, after we'd marched out of the shop, he never said another word about it. Sometimes, though, the power of the unspoken word can be a frighteningly powerful thing and my father's studied silence with me for the rest of that day spoke volumes. In addition, the fact that he'd immediately jumped in and vehemently defended his light-fingered son's integrity made me feel more guilt-ridden and miserable than if he had berated me in front of her.

Dad's handling of the situation certainly taught me a hugely effective lesson. Not only did I never pinch another penny from my parents, but it also taught me a life-lesson on the power of forgiveness and giving people a second chance. I'd like to say the incident also taught me the importance of 'giving the benefit of the doubt', except in that particular case my father was in no doubt whatsoever as to precisely what had been going on.

Some business leaders have built their personal brand images (and businesses) around their quirkiness and outspoken eccentricities, be they hard-nosed, authoritarian or just downright crotchety. Michael O'Leary, CEO of the Irish airline Ryanair, once described his ideal customer as 'someone with a pulse and a credit card' and in the same 'Lunch with the *Financial Times*' interview referred to the British Airports Authority as the 'Evil Empire' and the UK's Civil Aviation Authority as a bunch of 'cretins and twerps'. While nobody can question Ryanair's incredible financial success (last time I checked the low-cost carrier had built a market cap of over $13 billion), being voted Europe's 'least liked' airline by TripAdvisor subscribers is something that would not sit well with me no matter how good the bottom line looks. American property magnate Donald Trump is another controversial character who seems to be either loved or hated by the consumer and is perhaps most famous for his 'You're fired' line, something he seems to delight in telling people on his TV show *The Apprentice*. Unlike both these very successful gentlemen I have always believed there are tremendous upsides to a more conciliatory approach to life and business – an attitude that even Michael O'Leary is now publicly proclaiming he wants his much-maligned airline to assume, although it remains to be seen whether or not this particular Celtic Tiger can change his stripes. I'm not a betting man, but if I were, I'm not at all sure I would put money on this one!

While I wouldn't be foolish enough to pretend that Virgin's three airlines have never had passengers with valid complaints or that I have never fired anyone, I can honestly say that, unlike Mr Trump, the latter is not something I have ever taken the slightest pleasure in doing. On the contrary, I will usually move heaven and earth to avoid letting someone go, as when it comes to such a last resort I feel both sides have somehow failed each other. It's so much better, where possible, to try and forgive offenders and give them a second chance, just like my mother and father did so often with me as a child.

I had a very similar incident to my sweet shop experience much later in life only this time it was me who got to play the role of my dad. One day while sitting at Virgin Records I took a phone call from the owner of a nearby record shop who wanted to tip me off to the fact that one of our employees, whom he named, had been offering him piles of brand-new Virgin Records at suspiciously low prices and on a cash-only basis. When he signed off with the words, 'I just hope he's not stealing them', I had a definite déjà vu moment as my mind flashed back to my identical sweet shop indictment as a boy.

Sadly, the person that the record shop man named happened to be someone we considered to be one of our brighter young A & R people and, much as I dislike these kinds of confrontation, on this occasion I had no option but to haul him into the office and repeat what I had just been told. The poor guy went bright red and was clearly horribly embarrassed but he made no attempt to deny or defend his actions, opting instead to simply apologise profusely and say there was really no excuse for his behaviour. Rather than firing him on the spot, however, as he had every right to expect, on the spur of the moment I opted instead to tell him that although he had let himself and the company down very badly we were going to give him a second chance. The look of stunned amazement on his face said it all, and from that day on he worked his socks off for us and went on to have a stellar career, personally discovering some of Virgin Records' most successful artists along the way – Boy George being just one of them.

When it comes to needing a second chance, however, nobody needs it more than ex-prisoners who are looking to restart their lives after they have served their time. The sad thing is that if they are honest and tick the 'criminal record' box on an employment application form they'll seldom get an interview, let alone a shot at landing the job. Ironically, the result tends to become one huge self-fulfilling prophecy. When they can't find employment, statistics show that fifty per cent or more of ex-offenders take the seemingly easy way out and resort to crime as the only way to support themselves, and then quickly end up back inside.

My good friend and Comic Relief creator Jane Tewson was the one who first drew my attention to the sad plight of ex-cons. In the process, Jane even succeeded in doing something I have worked long and hard at avoiding – she had me put behind bars. Actually, it wasn't the first time, but we don't need to go into that right now! Suffice it to say that Jane encouraged me to see first-hand the challenges prisoners face when attempting to re-enter the workforce by voluntarily spending a day in jail with them. In late 2009, I duly served my day in a high-security prison in Melbourne, Australia and it certainly opened my eyes to the problem ex-prisoners have re-entering society, something about which I had never given a moment's thought.

While down under I also met with an inspiring group of leaders from The Toll Group, Australia's largest transportation company. I learned how they had been trying to do their bit to improve the lot of recently released prisoners and had hired almost 500 of them over the previous decade – a number that represents about ten per cent of the company's workforce. The truly inspirational part of what they told me, though, was that not one of their former inmates had, to the best of their knowledge, ever reoffended!

I have since constantly encouraged all of the Virgin companies around the world to work hard at following Toll's example. In the UK we have been cooperating closely with the charity Working Chance, which since 2007 has taken the lead in working to place female ex-prisoners back into gainful employment thereby breaking the cycle that can turn one little mistake or bad decision into a life sentence, whether in or out of prison. Last time I checked, Working Chance had placed almost 200 female ex-prisoners with Pret a Manger, Sainsbury's and a variety of Virgin companies like Virgin Trains and Virgin Management.

Perhaps the biggest irony here is that in 1971, but for the good graces of a British magistrate, I might well have had a prison record myself. I was caught red-handed by Customs and Excise officers in the act of ingeniously (or so my naïve teenage self had thought) 'manipulating' purchase taxes on the export and import of record albums. It was only by way of my parents generously posting the family home as collateral for my bail and then my fully paying off the hefty fine I'd been given that I managed to avoid being stuck with a criminal record. Had I actually done time and been branded as an ex-con, then the chances are very real that Virgin might never have happened and the tens of thousands of jobs we have created would never have existed. Had I gone to jail for my stupid teenage error of judgement I would have been the same person as the one who (luckily) did not end up behind bars, but I would almost certainly have been stigmatised by society and almost certainly have led a *very* different life as a result.

SPEAK NO EVIL

In our living room at home my mum and dad used to have one of those peculiar little statues of the 'Three Wise Monkeys' – you may have seen them – that embody the proverbial principle of 'See no evil, hear no evil, speak no evil'. Well, while there wasn't a lot they could do about the 'see no evil' part, they went to great lengths to teach me to never think or speak badly of others.

They encouraged me to always look for the good in people instead of assuming the worst and trying to find fault. If they ever heard me gossiping or talking someone down they would have me go and look at myself in a mirror for five minutes, the idea being that I should see how such behaviour reflected badly on me. I was also taught that fits of pique or any outward displays of anger or rudeness never serve any useful purpose and if anything play only to your disadvantage. It was a lesson that stuck, and to this day I frequently have people say things to me like 'I really don't know how you could be so pleasant with those people' or 'If I were you I'd have been really angry about what they just did', when in fact I had just bottled up my emotions. The thing my parents didn't make any effort to teach me was how to keep my obvious delight at something under wraps, the downside of which is that it doesn't help my poker game very much.

Whether we like it or not, however, we are all very much the product of our upbringing and our environment. After my little church incident, had my father handled the moment differently and put me across his knee, I would probably still remember the spanking but would have long forgotten what it was for! The importance of the leadership lessons we absorb from our parents and in due course pass along to our own children and those with whom we work cannot be understated.

I have always viewed the maturation of companies as being very much like that of young people. When they are newborn or toddlers they tend to get away with all kinds of stuff on the basis that they are just finding their feet and so they generally enjoy a higher forgiveness factor. If companies survive this stage (many do not), like teenagers they then start to develop acne and other character blemishes while they get a little bit cocky and know-it-all.

After that there comes a more mature stage: they have hopefully learned from their mistakes and settled down, but this period is filled with very different kinds of risks, with complacency possibly being the biggest. And once a company reaches the mid-life crisis stage it easily gets lazy, overweight, set in its ways and, like adults, can spend more time looking in the rear-view mirror than forging new ways forward and trying to see what's around the next corner.

From a leadership perspective, shepherding a company through each of these various stages of growth is not that different to bringing up a child. Just as raising a toddler is very different to keeping a teenager on track and the skill sets may change a little as the company gets older, the fundamentals of parenting and corporate leadership are very closely intertwined. I was reminded of this fact when I recently overheard a friend of mine, who has three incredibly rambunctious young sons, playfully threaten his youngest, eleven-year-old, Charlie that if the going ever got tough, on the basis of last in, first out, he'd be the first one to be let go. I laughed out loud, but it was the boy's immediate response that really struck home with me. With a big impish smile, he looked his father right in the eye and retorted, 'But Dad, why would you do that? If you think about it I am much cheaper to keep because I don't eat nearly as much as my older brothers do.'

The inescapable fact is that learning and leadership are two-way streets and even the oldest and wisest block can pick up a lot from the most junior of chips. Sadly, my father and best friend Ted Branson passed away in early 2010 at the grand old age of ninety-three, leaving a huge hole in his family's lives. He certainly left his mark on me and but for his wisdom and restraint on more than one occasion, those marks could quite deservedly have made sitting down a very painful process!

Having given my mum the chance to chime in earlier, I am also going to let her have the last word – something she always enjoys! I very much doubt that she will remember saying it, but I certainly have never forgotten the sage advice my mother gave me after a school cricket match. I loved cricket and was generally pretty good at it, but this had been a game in which I had an uncharacteristically timid outing with the bat and before I'd contributed a single run I was clean bowled without so much as a 'wave of the English Willow'! Driving home afterwards Mum surprised me with her cricketing wisdom when she said, 'Ricky, as I'm sure you'll agree, that wasn't really one of your better performances out there this afternoon. In future just remember one thing: you're guaranteed to miss every shot you don't take.'

It was years later before I realised she had probably been talking about a lot more than just cricket!

Chapter 2

THE DYING ART OF LISTENING

Listen – it makes you sound smarter

When I was a boy my parents never let me spend my time watching television. I well remember one time when my mum turned the TV off and asserted that it was going to be 'the death of conversation', which immediately provoked a twenty-minute argument with her TV-starved son. After we'd agreed to disagree, Mum couldn't resist getting the last word in: 'You see, if you'd been watching TV we wouldn't just have enjoyed that interesting discussion.'

And, while I may not have appreciated it at the time, as usual, my mother was absolutely correct. Although I may have been denied access to the small screen, I did get to watch my fair share of stuff on the big screen where I was (and still am) a big fan of Westerns, especially those starring the late great John Wayne. Despite all the memorable visual moments in Wayne's films it was one line that has stuck with me from the movie *Big Jake*: 'You're short on ears *and long on mouth.*' Even without the classic John Wayne drawl, it is such a great way to describe one of the most common human failings – listening too little and talking too much – that I have been borrowing it ever since.

L-I-S-T-E-N

One thing I do remember from an English class at school was when a teacher pointed out that if you want to play anagrams with the above letters they also form the word SILENT. As an ardent Scrabble fan and being a little more tuned in than usual that day, I recall precociously pointing out that the letters could also spell ENLIST. This led to a class discussion, which has clearly stuck with me: if more of us could 'enlist' the art of remaining 'silent' in order to 'listen' we would, in one fell swoop, dramatically improve our ability to learn and get a lot more out of our time at school.

Maybe the class discussion was too little too late for me as within a year or so of that English class I had left Stowe in order to launch *Student*, my own magazine, and soon found myself putting that teacher's words into practice. I remember as if it were yesterday, interviewing novelist John le Carré whose 1963 breakthrough novel *The Spy Who Came in From the Cold* was an instant bestseller. I was as nervous as a kitten as I frantically scribbled down notes on his responses to my carefully prepared list of questions. I often carried a big old reel-to-reel Grundig tape recorder, although it was more to give me the appearance of being a professional than anything else as half the time it never worked. That was when I took up what was to become a lifetime habit: I began capturing my thoughts, observations and just about anything of interest that someone said or did in my hard-backed lined notebooks.

In the forty-odd years that I have been in business – wow, just writing that makes me suddenly feel ancient – those now hundreds of notebooks have served me incredibly well. And I am not talking about just their day-to-day aide-memoire uses, but in four major lawsuits with British Airways, G-Tech, T-Mobile and most recently with our run-in with the UK Department for Transport on the West Coast train franchise renewal. Listening is a wonderful skill, but given that the average human brain tends to store a very small percentage of what, at the time, may seem like insignificant statements and ideas, those books fill in a lot of what otherwise would be blank spaces in my memory bank. Acquiring the habit of note-taking is therefore a wonderfully complementary skill to that of listening. Please write this down right now so you don't forget it!

Unfortunately, as leadership skills go, listening gets a bit of a 'bum rap' – that may also have been a John Wayne line. It's such a seemingly passive thing that many people misguidedly see it as almost a sign of weakness – as in 'Did you notice Harry hardly said a word in the meeting, I wonder what his problem is?' Such a viewpoint is almost certainly fuelled by the historical association between great leaders and great orators being powerful people. Ask a Brit of my generation whom they would consider to be history's greatest leader and like me they'd probably name wartime prime minister Sir Winston Churchill. Ask for a speech and they'd almost certainly reference his 1940 'this was their finest hour' broadcast. Had I grown up in the US, the chances are that I would probably put John F. Kennedy on the same pedestal and perhaps justify the choice by referencing his famous 'Ask not what your country can do for you' speech.

Don't get me wrong, both these men were iconic leaders and the importance of having the ability to express one's thoughts in an articulate and compelling manner is a tremendous asset – and certainly in our video clip/sound-bite driven world, a lot more newsworthy than being a great listener; news footage that features 'and here we see the president listening intently as only he can' is hardly going to move the opinion polls! Oratorical excellence, however, is just one of a compendium of leadership skills and not the be-all and end-all that some would believe it to be. Apart from anything else, the majority of world leaders and captains of industry don't actually write their own speeches – Churchill being one highly notable exception to this rule – so it is dangerous to judge them by words that are not their own but rather the work of highly paid speech writers. Winston Churchill was, however, renowned for his ability to sit down and listen to anyone and everyone, and his view on the importance of listening is evidenced by another quote often attributed to him, 'Courage is what it takes to stand up and speak; courage is also what it takes to sit down and listen.'

Could it be that his skills as a listener might have been one of the things that made him such a great writer and speaker? I would venture to submit that it is no small coincidence.

LISTENING IS NOT HEARING

If there were ever a dead giveaway that somebody is not listening to a word of what you're saying, it's when they repeatedly use the annoying phrase, 'I hear you, I hear you.' Unfortunately, hearing is not listening. On a recent long-haul flight I could most assuredly hear the infant a few seats behind me that cried incessantly for the whole night, but I didn't care to listen to it. I can hear the wind in the trees but I don't take as much time as I should to listen to that either. And I don't believe it's entirely a matter of semantics. When someone says, 'I heard every word he said', in a strictly literal sense they may be telling the truth, but fifty per cent of the time they could probably just as truthfully add, 'although I didn't absorb one iota of it.' Paradoxically, while I have always prided myself on being a good listener, I may have had an unfair advantage on most people. Having grown up with dyslexia I learned very early in life that if I wanted to take anything in then I had to force myself to listen intently. Not only that, but in order to have any chance of remembering what I was listening to, I also had to make the effort to take copious handwritten notes: a habit that I still diligently practise to this day.

As an adult in business I have used this lesson to great advantage. I've also discovered that, as an adjunct to listening to what people have to say, my now infamous and utterly low-tech notebook is one of the most powerful tools I have in my bag of business tricks. Apart from helping me remember little things I want to bring up with one of our airlines, like 'Add cold – not hot towel service' as I am travelling, more importantly I can't begin to count the number of times when referring to my notebooks has given me a clearly unexpected advantage on much bigger issues. A typical situation would be when someone says, 'Well, Richard, as I recall when we last spoke in early March, we agreed to get a draft proposal to you by the end of April', and they are totally discombobulated by a response of, 'Well, no, at least not according to my notes of our last conversation. At 3.15 p.m. on 7 February you promised you were going to have the complete business plan to us by 31 March at the latest.' Nailed! I even had someone once suggest that I had been illegally recording my phone conversations with him – like some kind of a Nixon White House tapes deal – but shut him down by saying, 'Yes, I do record a lot conversations but with a pen and a notebook!'

I suspect that over the years 'Richard's thing about taking notes' has become legend around the Virgin family of companies as I always detect a much higher percentage of note-takers at internal meetings than with outside parties. For example, I recently had a day-long series of meetings on Necker with a group of about twenty senior people and I couldn't help but observe that our own people seemed to be the only ones taking any serious notes. I don't know if the senior executives present were accustomed to having an assistant to take the minutes, or if they somehow felt it was beneath them to take notes – or maybe they all felt they had photographic memories – but I was distinctly unimpressed. One of the outside executives did peck away at his iPad on a regular basis, but based on the semi-furtive way he went about doing it, rather than taking notes I suspected he was responding to emails or playing Words With Friends.

Call me old-fashioned if you will, but the all-too-common practice of texting or emailing under the boardroom table in the middle of a meeting is something that I find extremely irritating and downright disrespectful to everyone else in the room. I am not a big fan of lengthy meetings at the best of times, but is it really asking too much to have someone's undivided attention for an hour without them having to constantly demonstrate their self-perceived indispensability by electronically tuning out every few minutes? I think not.

Since my children were little, I have always kept notes on the funny things that they have said over the years. I always suspected these would come in handy some day and when twice in the last couple of years I've had to prepare speeches for their weddings it turned out I was correct. One of the best ones came from a five- or six-year-old Holly when she triumphantly announced, 'Daddy, Daddy, I know what sex is! And you and Mummy have done it twice.' Another time, Holly hysterically expressed her frustration at something by loudly proclaiming, 'I don't know what I want, I don't know what I want, but I want it.'

But back to the business world and another story I like to cite as to the benefits of listening combined with note-taking that goes back to a speech I delivered in Greece about twenty years ago – I honestly can't remember what the occasion was other than the fact we did have some short-lived airline activities in the country. In any case, I couldn't help but notice one very bright young man in the audience who kept asking me excellent, mostly aviation-related and clearly very well-prepared questions. In fact, over the course of the day he must have asked about 50 per cent of all the questions and 90 per cent of the really good ones! Not only did he ask good questions, but he listened intently to my responses and wasn't afraid to zing me back with a tough follow-up when my response fell short of fully addressing his question. He was clearly an excellent listener and given my 'thing' about it, I was equally impressed by his ferocious note-taking. At the end of the day I asked one of the organisers if they happened to know the name of the young man who had so dominated the Q&A sessions – I had it in my mind that maybe he was someone who could work for us some day. Their response was one of, 'Oh yes, we most certainly know him!' and they proceeded to tell me that Stelios Haji-Ioannou was the scion of a wealthy Cypriot shipping family, and clearly not someone who was looking for a job. Sure enough, it wasn't long before his name was all over the news in the UK as the founder of easyJet, a low-cost European airline that would go on to be a huge success: in fact I believe that, by passengers carried, they are now the largest UK-based airline. I like to use this story as a light-hearted example of the incredible benefits that can accrue from listening intently and taking notes when I am speaking – something that will invariably draw a chorus of groans from our people who have heard the line one too many times. But, all joking aside, listening and taking notes are clearly habits that have served Stelios well... oops, correction, make that

Sir Stelios; he was knighted by the Queen in 2006 for 'services to entrepreneurship' – and note-taking.

I can't promise knighthoods for everyone, but if you're still not convinced let me suggest you try a self-imposed crash course in listening more and talking less and I promise you will be amazed at the immediate benefits you'll observe.

SAY LESS – CONTRIBUTE MORE

While the late Nelson Mandela was a man of innumerable talents, one that always impressed me the most about him was his unfailing willingness to listen to what others had to say. Even during his long years in prison he took time to listen to what his jailers had to say about life, so much so that he made them the first people he publicly forgave when he was released. Whenever I spent time with Madiba I was amazed at his ability to make you feel like the only and most important person in the room through his desire to hear what you had to say and, of course, his willingness to act on those things he believed in. Few other people could have galvanised the formation of the Elders in the way that Madiba did and yet few people were better qualified to appreciate the critical role the ability to listen plays in diplomacy, business and life in general.

Another remarkable human being and listener par excellence is Archbishop Desmond Tutu, who as a close friend of Nelson Mandela's was a founding member of the Elders and chaired the group from 2007 until 2013. Seldom in history has a nation put more faith in the healing power of listening than post-apartheid South

Africa did with its Truth and Reconciliation Commission (TRC). President Mandela named Desmond Tutu to chair the historic commission's work, the primary focus of which was on those who had suffered human rights abuses as a result of apartheid between 1960 and 1994. As stated in the Promotion of National Unity and Reconciliation Act the TRC was convened in order to address 'a need for understanding but not for vengeance, a need for reparation but not retaliation, a need for *Ubuntu* [human kindness] but not for victimisation'.

The commission reportedly received more than 22,000 statements from such victims and held thousands of public hearings at which they testified on the atrocities they had suffered. Under Archbishop Desmond Tutu's compassionate but no-nonsense leadership the commission received in excess of 7,000 amnesty applications, held some 3,000 amnesty hearings and granted more than 1,500 amnesties. As with any such polarising issue, the TRC's work had its critics but was considered by most to have been an unprecedented success in healing wounds that, if left untreated, could have become festering sores for generations to come.

Among the Elders, two equally remarkably listeners whom I have been lucky enough to get to know, are former US president Jimmy Carter and Mary Robinson, the first woman president of Ireland and UN high commissioner for human rights. No matter what the subject, they both possess an incredible talent to tune in intensely to what's being said – I am a firm believer that the kind of wisdom such people manage to accumulate and dispense is directly attributable to their extraordinary listening skills. What they have said and done is what the history books will post as their legacies, but their greatest achievements are all down to what they were able to absorb by the simple act of listening.

'AS I WAS INTERRUPTING...'

When you start trying to become a better listener the first difference you'll notice is similar to how you see things after you've lost some weight. It's only once you manage to successfully drop fifty pounds that you are suddenly aware of all the people around you who could benefit from doing the same thing. Watching others, one of the first things you will be aware of is that listening while keeping your mouth shut and saying nothing is a whole lot smarter than not listening, speaking up and saying nothing. As opposed to really listening, a lot of people get totally hung up on frequently interjecting with comments and questions they mistakenly think make them look smart. This is seldom the case as, on the usually flawed assumption that they know what the speaker is going to say, instead of listening their focus shifts entirely to trying to formulate 'smart' questions. In addition to the sheer rudeness of their constant interruptions, such people usually only succeed in looking foolish. It all comes back to note-taking. Rather than constantly interrupting a speaker with self-serving questions, it is a whole lot smarter (and better table manners) to note down comments and questions and save them for later – if indeed the issues haven't been covered by the time everyone gets to ask questions.

A wonderful Mark Twain quote is: *'There is nothing so annoying as having two people talking when you're busy interrupting.'*

Interruptions when speaking are unfortunately a fact of life and we have to learn to live with them. I must confess, however, that when I am trying to express my thoughts to a group of people I find constant interruptions really exasperating. I have tremendous admiration for our CEO and president at Virgin Galactic George Whiteside's uncanny ability to handle interruptions. Perhaps he learned the art in his previous position as chief of staff at NASA where he was accustomed to dealing with highly opinionated politicos much of the time, but one way or the other he is a master at it.

If someone rudely interjects when George is speaking, it is a thing of beauty to watch. He will stop mid-sentence, smile and listen politely for as long as it takes them to get their point across. George will then acknowledge the person's point of view or question and either respond there and then or say he will come back to it later before seamlessly resuming where he left off with his presentation. It can sometimes help to try and ward off interruptions by asking for questions to be held until the end, but George's technique certainly beats any other approach – particularly the popular one of simply ploughing ahead at a higher volume while totally ignoring the interruption from the floor.

THE UNSPOKEN WORD

A really skilled listener not only takes in what has been said but will also hear what has *not* been said. One of the easier results of this can allow questions such as, 'I was intrigued to note that you failed to make any mention of XYZ. Does this mean you don't consider it relevant to your proposal?' A more interesting spin on the unspoken word, however, can be recognising when someone is deliberately avoiding an issue that they should really be addressing. In a one-on-one chat with a mid-level manager, for example, if they painstakingly steer the subject away from any mention whatsoever of their divisional vice-president's role in a failed initiative when they would seem to be a logical part of the dialogue, it may be enough to confirm concerns about there being a cover-up going on.

An actual example of such a 'deafening silence' was to be seen in the UK Department for Transport's bungled handling of Virgin Trains' 2012 bid to retain the West Coast franchise. More on this later, but suffice it to say that in this context the government's silence and disinclination to address cold hard numbers that showed our rival's bid to be far riskier than the government believed and it set alarm bells ringing in my head that all was not well with the process.

Similarly, paying close attention to not just what someone says but the way in which they say it can help you to read between the lines – a place where the real story is often dramatically different to what the casual listener might understand is being said 'on the lines'. While what a speaker says can have several layers of meaning, how it is said can also be a giveaway to various subtexts. I have always found it hugely interesting to closely observe a speaker's body language, facial expressions, the enunciation of certain words and all sorts of subtle innuendo, which can put a very different spin on what the words alone might convey. I remember vividly watching British Airways chairman Lord King responding to a TV interviewer on the so-called 'Dirty Tricks' case. When he asserted that no one on BA's senior management team had sanctioned, or had any knowledge of, the unauthorised misdemeanours of his airline's lower-level employees, the way he looked away from the camera as he said it made me seriously question the veracity of his statement.

LISTENING DOESN'T GO UNNOTICED

When you take the time and effort to improve your listening skills by growing that extra pair of ears, you will be pleasantly surprised by how much your people will appreciate the new you. It is a strange facet of the human condition but invariably when you engage in a thirty-minute dialogue with someone and manage the conversation in such a way that you get the other person to talk for twenty-five of the thirty minutes, the person who you allowed to do all the talking is highly likely to go away impressed by what a great conversationalist you are. If on the other hand you yourself had spoken for twenty-five of the thirty minutes, that same other party would most likely be thinking, 'What a talker! I couldn't get a word in edgeways.'

Actively creating meaningful ad hoc or semi-formal opportunities to speak *with* rather than *at* your people, and then actually listening attentively to their responses, achieves some incredibly positive outcomes. In addition to what you'll hear straight from the horse's mouth that you'd never be able to find in a management status report, the fact that a senior person (you) cares enough about their opinions to actually ask for them –

time and attention to listen to them – is of un

all concerned. It may be hard to believe but I'd even su

such an event contributes much more for most people's morale than

giving them a raise! Show me a company where such interactions

are a comfortable feature of the daily routine and you'll be looking

at a company with a culture that works better than most – in every

sense of the word.

HOW VIRGIN VIEWS VIRGIN

Our top company, Virgin Management, recently conducted a major piece of research throughout all the Virgin Group companies around the globe, the purpose of which was to try and gain a clearer understanding of how our people define leadership in the Virgin world. This was not some type of '360' review session, but more of a wide-ranging, in-depth review of the leadership styles our people are experiencing presently and what they expect to see from their leaders going forward. To avoid any misunderstandings, I should make it very clear that this was not about me – it was focused on leadership at every level throughout the Virgin companies. By sheer coincidence the project was titled 'The Virgin Way'.

We believe that one of the key differences that makes Virgin such a special place to work is the fun and freedom of expression that results from the absence of employee handbooks that read like some kind of a corporate penal code. There are, of course, some people who require and enjoy the disciplines and order that stems in a highly regimented work environment, the kind of people who are governed by 'the book' and where the role of management is to enforce the rules and regularly throw the said (heavy) book at anyone who dares to deviate from the corporate dogma. Such people would *not* enjoy the Virgin way.

Along with all the top people from almost every company in the group, I attended a day-long review of the first cut of the research and as expected it was filled with some utterly fascinating takes on the inner workings of what makes Virgin tick. Before going into this session had anyone asked me (which they didn't) what I would list as the top Virgin leadership attributes, I would likely have said, not necessarily in this order:

- integrity
- a sense of humour
- an entrepreneurial spirit
- they have to be ultra-gregarious
- they should truly care about their people
- be able to delegate work (and credit) where it's due

As it turns out I was almost spot on as the employee list, although longer, fell under the broad categories of:

- they should embrace individuality
- have an entrepreneurial spirit
- empower their people

- inspire trust
- be 'in it together'
- be genuinely caring
- be energisingly passionate
- be accessibly informal

The day was spent going through the wealth of employee-generated feedback that had built these categories and in the process I couldn't help but notice that there was one common denominator that ran like a golden thread through every one of these headings, as you may have guessed based on the theme of this chapter. The key to almost every one of these leadership attributes was the vital importance of a leader's ability to listen.

Here are some direct quotes on listening that we received about our leaders in just a few of the companies. They are representative of recurrent themes that we were delighted to see ran through every business unit.

From Virgin Mobile Australia:

'He can have a conversation with you on a personal level but you can also challenge him and give your opinion without feeling like he isn't listening or it's a career-limiting move.'

I especially like this one as I believe that good employee relations should stretch beyond purely work topics. You cannot fully understand colleagues if you don't know anything about their life outside of the office. As described here, a broader relationship can make both sides more comfortable expressing their feelings openly and honestly.

From Virgin Trains:

> '*He obviously has interests to do with the shareholders and the financial side of things, but he also wants to hear what I have to say, wants to hear what the cleaners have to say. He wants to see the whole picture and he has all of our interests at heart.*'

This is great to hear as sometimes feedback from the most unlikely places can be the most valuable and I believe that, as the old saying goes, 'God is in the details' – details that often go unseen if only viewed from the corner office.

From Virgin Media:

> '*She's out there, she's on the ground, she listens, she acts on feedback.*'

More of the same – getting out and about and keeping an ear to the ground on a daily basis works wonders for any leader and the culture.

From Virgin Active UK:

> '*I don't care if you're the managing director or whoever, somebody that you feel you can talk to, I think embodies Virgin.*'

Rank simply isn't part of the Virgin way of being. A hierarchy is always a huge obstacle to good workplace relationships, especially when elitist managers hide behind their desks and their titles. I go by plain old 'Richard' – Mr Branson was my dad!

From Virgin Limited Edition:

> *'He's always fair. He always listens to suggestions. He's always got time for you in anything really, if it's eleven o'clock at night or whenever he'll always listen, that's important.'*

Getting around the company is important but only if you make the time to listen to your people. Lines like, 'That sounds really interesting but I'm afraid I have to run to a meeting right now' can do irreparable harm.

LOCATION, LOCATION, INTIMIDATION

In the research there were a group of attributes that were locked in with the importance of listening. One of the most frequently mentioned was 'accessibility'. Clearly there's little value to being a great listener if people can't get to you – or worse, if you can't get to them. Visiting your staff in their 'natural habitat' as often as is practicably possible is huge for you and for them. I often find this to be one of the biggest gaps in the make-up of otherwise very accomplished leaders. They are all busy-busy people, with big important things to do, big important people to meet and big decisions to make and big... well, you get the picture! To close this top priority circuit, though, making the commitment every week to spend some quality time with your most important assets – your people – is every bit as critical as any other entry in your diary. A tall order, perhaps, but it is a discipline that, if you can pull it off, brings huge paybacks on multiple levels, often in the most remote places where you probably never imagined you had levels of influence.

I have always enjoyed a bit of an unfair advantage when it comes to my appreciation of the need to visit one's employees in their own workplaces. It is almost certainly a by-product of the fact that I have never really worked from anything remotely resembling the conventional perception of an office. I started out in a church crypt before moving to *Duende*, a houseboat in London's Little Venice, on which I also lived with my wife and newborn daughter. Next I inhabited what would usually have been the living rooms of our various family homes and then in recent years I have moved into a rattan chair or a hammock on Necker Island. I can put my hand on my heart and say I have never sat in the corner office!

At one point my hectic business activities, the perpetually ringing phones, the battery of assistants and constant stream of visitors totally overwhelmed our family home in London's Holland Park. It got so bad that sometimes my young kids were the ones opening the front door to all kinds of high-flying visitors coming to meet me in my 'office'. It finally got so silly that my wife Joan quite rightly declared, 'Richard – enough is enough!' and insisted that I find an office somewhere else. Much as I empathised with her annoyance, I really didn't want to uproot all my business stuff, so we came up with a rather ingenious compromise. We purchased an almost identical house just two doors up the street and moved the family into that one, while my office clutter and I stayed put. It was tough for a while, but I eventually got used to the grind of my four times a day 100-foot commute – only twice a day if I didn't go home for lunch. Now of course Joan and I have settled on our beloved and utterly glorious Necker Island in the British Virgin Islands. Necker is such a fabulous spot that of all the home-offices I have ever had it is possibly the hardest to spend time away from. Despite that I still manage to spend more than half my time on the road, or perhaps more accurately in the air: according to my diaries, in 2013 I was travelling an average of seventeen days a month.

So as you can see my unfair advantage comes from the fact that since the very early days at Virgin, whenever I've wanted to see the people I work with, I have always been obliged to go to them. Even when the Virgin Group's head offices were located in London's Notting Hill Gate, a stone's throw from my Holland Park home, I still steadfastly refused to accept a dedicated office there. When a well-meaning Trevor Abbott (at the time the most senior director at Virgin Group) once suggested they really should set up an office there for me saying, 'It'll just be somewhere for you to hang your hat when you come in, Richard', I was quick to (politely) point out that as I never wear a hat it wouldn't be necessary.

Trevor's well-meaning gesture might also have been intended to give me somewhere else to set myself down other than in his office when I came in for a few hours. Generally, however, I find that visiting staff on their own – or at least neutral – turf is a lot less intimidating for them than if they have to come to you. I still break out in a cold sweat just thinking of the words I used to dread hearing at school. 'Branson – the headmaster wants to see you in his study. Now!' Even if it were to impart some positive news – which was seldom the case – just stepping into that musty oak-panelled room used to put the fear of death into me. The business equivalent is, 'The CEO wants to talk to you in his/her office as soon as possible' – particularly if it's on a Friday afternoon! But even if the meeting is for an amicable chat on some good idea that made it 'upstairs', for the junior employee, the intimidation factor of going through that door can often be enough to completely tongue-tie even the most confident of staffers.

The obvious solution, therefore, is to stop issuing edicts to 'come unto me' and instead get out there, walk about and change a few lives. It's hard to imagine the impact of a 'C' level heavyweight showing up unannounced at a mid-level manager's or front-line staffer's workplace and saying, 'Hey, it's Mario, right? I'm Maggie Cohen, the chief information officer, and I just came down here to see if you can spare me a few minutes to talk about your great idea for the new distribution software' – and then sitting down and listening and taking notes. I assure you such a transformational moment is priceless. A simple twenty-minute exercise such as that goes way beyond 'accessibility'. But I firmly believe it's these types of seemingly insignificant little moments that go unrecorded on HR files and balance sheets that distinguish the true leader from the mediocre and, over time when multiplied by hundreds or thousands, help to build the kind of stand-out corporate culture that differentiates a merely good company from a truly great one.

The simple fact is that nobody has ever learned anything by listening to themselves speak. At the same time, sitting in a top-floor corner office may afford some wonderful views of the surrounding scenery but until you get out of there on a regular basis you are never going to get a proper view on what is going on in the company. Get your extra ears strapped on, get out there and take note – literally – of what your people will be anxious and excited to discuss with you. And if they find it odd that you're suddenly mixing with 'the madding crowd', just tell them that Richard sent you!

Chapter 3

MIRROR MIRROR

How do you look to your customers?

My lovely wife Joan was born and bred a Glaswegian and as with many of her fellow Scots she loves to quote the great Scottish poet Robert Burns. By osmosis, therefore, I too have become familiar with some of the works of the bard. 'Rabbie' Burns is possibly best known as the author of 'Auld Lang Syne', which most of us sing every New Year in various states of inebriation.

Of all the words he wrote, however, the ones that have always resonated with me come from his somewhat unlikely titled poem, 'To a Louse', in which he wrote, 'O would some power the giftie gie us, to see oursels as others see us'. Simply stated this does of course mean, 'If only we had the power to see ourselves in the same way that others see us.' Of all the mantras one might adopt in life, this is surely one of the better ones and for anyone in a leadership role it should be an essential part of the checks and balances that are built into a company's standard operating procedures. I suppose the corporate version of Burns' famous line would read something like, '*Always try to look at what we are doing from the customer's perspective.*'

IF IT WALKS LIKE A DUCK...

Like it or not, in the eyes of our customers, employees, friends, whoever, perception is very much reality. Or as the old saying goes, 'If it walks like a duck – it usually *is* a duck'. The ability to see one's own actions either personally or corporately through the eyes of others is a skill that takes practice and ideally one that should be applied well in advance of making public statements or policy decisions that might be open to ambiguity or question. We are all consumers and yet I am constantly amazed at how many business people seem to dwell in some kind of subjective blinkered cocoon instead of looking objectively at their own products and services.

Even more amazing is the simple fact that we are all surrounded by highly objective, ready-made focus groups. You don't have to go outside and pay them to sit in a mirrored room – they're around us every day and go by the name of family, friends, employees and acquaintances. In my experience some of the harshest and most valuable sounding boards you will ever find can be found around the family dinner table. I cannot begin to tell you how many times what I thought to be a really good idea never made it past the tough audience of Joan and the kids. I will never forget her no-holds-barred response to one new idea in particular that I casually announced over dinner with her one night. Never!

It was during the height of the HIV/AIDS epidemic in the late eighties and I was thrilled to see how fired up everyone at Virgin was about doing something positive to help tackle this dreadful disease that was destroying the lives of millions. In typical fashion we brainstormed to try and come up with some practical contribution we could make and before long someone had the great idea of setting up a company that would manufacture and sell condoms for a fraction of the price being demanded by Durex, the UK's dominant condom manufacturer. Nobody stopped to consider any potential disconnects on the branding front and we simply set about turning the idea into a reality.

Flash forward to my excited dinner table announcement that we were planning to introduce a new product line that would go by the name of 'Virgin Condoms'. I remember seeing Joan choke on her food before exclaiming in her wonderful Glasgow accent, 'Condoms! Virgin Condoms? Oh come on, Richard, pleeeease tell me you're joking. Cos if you're not, you're soon going to be the butt-end of a hell of a lot of jokes.' And of course she was absolutely correct!

As is often the case, with the best will in the world, one can simply get too wrapped up in the creative process and forget to step back and see how whatever you're working on is going to look from the customer's perspective. In this instance we were all so fired up with the big idea that nobody had given a moment's thought to how nonsensical it would be to offer a product called 'Virgin Condoms'. I mean, it would be almost as crazy as starting a company by the name of 'Virgin Bride' – oops, well, maybe even crazier! In any case, following Joan's astute observation we went straight back to the drawing board and quickly came up with a clever solution. Our first venture into the latex-wear business would instead be branded as 'MATES' – which if you think about it is really quite appropriate – and the M on the front of the logo was cleverly crafted using an inverted version of our signature Virgin 'V.'

IF IT AIN'T BROKE, BREAK IT

Not everyone, it seems, has access to a pragmatic market expert like my wife – or more likely they do, but they clearly are not making very good use of them. Imagine for instance how differently things might have turned out for Reed Hastings, CEO of video-rental company Netflix, had he polled his family's or friends' reaction to the question, 'Okay, folks, how would you feel about a new Netflix offer that will give you the same service you enjoy today but for twice the price and with double the complexity?' Now, as I've said, I'm not a betting man, but I'd have put money on the response to that one! Clearly, however, such a conversation never took place.

In July of 2011 Netflix was flush with success. It had twenty-three million subscribers, its stock price was riding at an all-time high at around $300 and new members by the boatload were signing up every month. And then in September, for reasons that no one can fully explain, the DVD rental giant shocked Wall Street analysts and its employees and customers alike by announcing it was revamping its highly successful business model. They announced that a new spin-off company, Qwikster, would take on the mailbox DVD rental side of the business, while those customers who preferred streaming video would buy that separately from the newly pared-down Netflix. What had been working just fine for them – a single monthly fee to Netflix for both services – would now be payable to two separate entities – doubling the complexity and forcing customers to lock into choices they didn't really want to face.

The attempted transition was so badly executed on every front that it quickly turned out to be an exercise in 'united we stand, divided we fall'. Some analysts speculated that the company may have been foolishly attempting to fast-forward evolution by trying to wean its client base away from the old-fashioned business of having DVDs delivered by mail with all the associated logistics, warehousing complexities and costs – none of which existed with the rapidly growing online streaming mode of video delivery. Everyone agreed that video streaming was indisputably the way of the future, but such a monumentally dumb move was certainly not the way to get there. The customer reaction was instantaneous and furious: within a month almost a million of them cancelled their subscriptions and the company's stock – which in July had been trading above $300 – had fallen to around the $100 mark by early September.

It was way too late for the publicly embarrassed Reed Hastings to have that dinner table chat with the family, but to his credit he did at least react quickly by instantly hitting the brakes before the ill-conceived new structure ever took effect. Qwikster was 'qwikly' gone and in what was described in one report as a 'tear-stained apology' to both the remaining and recently departed Netflix subscribers, Hastings openly admitted, 'I messed up and I owe everyone an explanation.' What that explanation didn't say, however, was, 'If only I'd talked this over with my friends and family, none of this fiasco might have happened.'

While Netflix almost managed to 'snatch defeat from the jaws of victory', happily the company has recovered well as a predominantly online provider, although the dinosaur-in-waiting of DVDs by mail still contributes significant revenues. A lesson to be learned from this story is the importance of leaders displaying the courage to own up to and accept responsibility for their mistakes then act to quickly fix them and move on. Last time I checked, Netflix stock was in the region of $450, so its shareholders' pain was a temporary thing as a result of the quick actions of a CEO who wasn't afraid to admit that, like all human beings, he was fallible.

HOW TO SHOOT YOURSELF IN THE CAN

While the Netflix story is one of the more recent examples of failing to look at a business from the outside in, in the annals of blinkered decision-making it is by no means the most incredible. That honour must surely belong to the Coca-Cola Company. 'Coke' is not just one of the world's biggest selling and most recognisable brands but it has fiercely loyal customers – as we discovered when we tried to go up against them with Virgin Cola – or 'Virgin Coke' as I was prone to calling it until several of our lawyers suggested I might be wise to cease and desist!

Unfortunately for us, Virgin Cola never succeeded in wreaking one tenth of one per cent of the damage to Coca-Cola that they managed to inflict upon themselves in the mid-eighties. I am usually a believer in the 'if it ain't broke, fix it anyway' school of thought, but what happened with the ill-fated introduction of 'New Coke' was, as someone described it at the time, 'Like trying to improve the Mona Lisa's smile by painting over it.' On 23 April 1985 – a date that will forever ever live in fizzy drink infamy – Coca-Cola surprised the planet by suddenly introducing their 'New Coke' and simultaneously ceased production of the original formulation. This was no ordinary drink they were messing around with – I read somewhere once that 10,000 Cokes are consumed around the world *every second* of every day! With that kind of a following it was hardly surprising that the reaction around the Coke-drinking world to the New Coke's coming was nothing short of seismic.

It was a textbook case of just how flawed a strategy it can be to place too much reliance on assuming the customer knows what they want. The guys in the white lab coats at Coke had conducted extensive blind taste tests with existing customers and others, all of whom had apparently indicated a strong acceptance (if not necessarily a preference) for the planned New Coke's slightly sweeter formulation. Of course, these tests had been conducted in somewhat of a vacuum and none of those contributing to the shocking result had been asked, 'We are glad you like this, now how would you feel about it replacing the Coca-Cola that you've loved all your life?'

The stunned consumer response was, to put it mildly, 'not pretty'. The company HQ in Atlanta was deluged with hundreds of thousands of calls and letters expressing utter disgust from global Coke drinkers. To a person they not only didn't like the new taste but also felt betrayed that the decision to go ahead and change their favourite drink had been taken without any open consultation process. Many felt that at the very least the old and new versions should have been offered side by side on supermarket shelves for a time so that consumers could have made their own choice.

As a fan of well-written complaint letters (even when addressed to me) I have to say that some of those received by Coca-Cola should be enshrined in a 'Hall of Shame' somewhere. Coke's CEO Roberto Goizueta was inevitably singled out as the villain of the piece and 'Coca-Colass CEO' and 'Chief Dodo' were two of the more polite forms of address taken by angry letter writers. One missive even asked the embattled executive for his signature on the grounds that 'The autograph of one of the dumbest executives in American business history will likely become valuable some day'. Even a few offshore fans chimed in – from Cuba, life-long Coke drinker Fidel Castro dubbed the misadventure as, 'A sign of American decadence'. Of course, he was probably thinking, 'How can I have a Cuba Libre without Coke?'

It turned out that Castro's much-publicised comment only served to get CEO Goizueta into more hot water, this time from his own father. He later recounted how his dad, a Cuban who had fled his homeland to get away from Castro, told his son in no uncertain terms that he had screwed up big time. But the classic capper to this story was when he reportedly said, 'Roberto, I think this is the only time in my life that I have agreed with something Fidel Castro had to say.'

Now I am not suggesting that soliciting the input of foreign dictators is necessarily the way to go, but when you have family and friends who are also consumers, it is downright foolish not to take full advantage and listen to their outside-in points of view.

THE CUSTOMER IS ALWAYS... RELEVANT

Please don't think that by promoting outside-in vision I am suggesting that the customer is always right – far from it. In fact, in my experience, particularly with anything that represents a really game-changing innovation, I believe that most consumer opinions tend to be overly cautious and tempered by what they have or have not experienced in the past. If they cannot envisage what you are talking about because they have never experienced anything like it, then they are likely to be overly guarded in their comments.

For a variety of reasons – and as the New Coke taste-test fiasco demonstrates – I have always had trouble accepting the validity of the kind of consumer feedback that is garnered from formal focus groups. This is the kind where they all sit down in a room and pretend they don't know they're being watched and recorded by the people behind the mirror. Not only does it frequently bring out the prima donna in some members of the group, who see it as an opportunity to perform for the cameras, but most groups behave like sheep.

Usually one dominant participant will have the most boisterous opinions and the others will meekly get in line behind them. Now while there is always a similar risk within a family group, at least you know a little bit more about the people involved and they also aren't walking away at the end of dinner knowing their comments will never come back to haunt them. For example, if I had chosen to ignore my wife Joan's 'Virgin Condom' comments and gone ahead with the name anyway, I suspect I might have chosen to eat out for a while.

The approach we have taken in deciding what our new Virgin Hotels should look like is a good example of the Virgin way of taking advantage of family input. Certainly the women in my life, my wife Joan and daughter Holly, have had their say but in this case the 'family' I am talking about is the extended Virgin family of companies, their employees and our fifty million or so customers around the world. The Virgin Hotels input in question was not by way of any formal research but by leveraging our years of acquired understanding as to what our customers like and expect from Virgin-branded products and services. It is vital that our new hotels exude all the same elements of unrivalled personal service and design excellence tempered with user-friendly functionality that have evolved by trial and error with our three airlines, at Limited Edition (our resort/luxury escapes division), at Virgin Active and other family member ventures.

As Allie Hope, the head of development at Virgin Hotels, likes to put it, 'It's all about stylish functionality – about leveraging what works and transforming what doesn't.' An example of something we know works extremely well for our Virgin Atlantic Upper Class customers is our Clubhouse Lounges. As anyone who has ever visited our flagship London Heathrow Clubhouse will tell you, it is just an amazing oasis of pre-flight calm in which to relax, enjoy a meal, play pool, have a massage, a haircut, a shoeshine or – if you must – work! Everything we have learned over the years with the steady refinement of our Clubhouses will be incorporated into Virgin Hotels, which will all have a 24/7 Clubhouse-like space for guests to make their own. It will also make for a very seamless hospitality experience for our airline loyalists who we fully anticipate will be the first ones in line for our new hotel offering. After all, they already sleep with us in the air, so why not do it on the ground as well?

And when it comes to 'transforming what doesn't work' in the hotel space, as with every one of our businesses, we have found there to be no lack of amazing opportunities for us to ring the changes. One big-little facet we have focused on is the needs and expectations of our women guests – where lots of little details that are easily overlooked can make the difference between an 'okay' stay and a, 'Wow, I can't believe they thought of that' experience. And again we have an abundance of female executives within Virgin – many of whom travel incessantly – so we have gleaned a wealth of input from this travel-savvy sorority within the family.

Raul Leal, the highly experienced hotel professional that we brought in to head up Virgin Hotels, won me over the instant he told me that his vision for our hotels was one of 'exclusivity for all'. While the big legacy hotel chains might be classified as 'reliably boring' and some of the more established 'lifestyle' hotel brands take a slightly holier-than-thou/red-rope view on the world, our hotels will bridge the gap between the two. We'll be neither 'ladies and gentlemen serving ladies and gentlemen' nor 'too cool for school'. Instead we'll be fun, slightly cheeky and irreverent, and everyone, whether a guest or an associate, should feel better for the experience. We have done an equal amount of work in ensuring both groups feel treasured and we know that creating raving fans in our guests will only happen if we can achieve the same level of engagement from our own people.

What's happening at Virgin Hotels is just an extension of the tried and true belief in trusting your own consumer-based instincts. This is, of course, considered a very pragmatic investment strategy – if as a consumer you really like using a particular product and purchase it over other choices every time, then presumably lots of others do the same, so it may be a stock worth acquiring. The ultimate example of such consumer behaviour is the tale of American entrepreneur Victor Kiam, who made a fortune from his company Remington Products. As the story goes, his wife bought him a Remington electric razor and, as he famously said in their advertising campaigns, 'I liked the product so much, I bought the company.'

CHECK YOURSELF OUT

So the simple fact is that any business leader worthy of their paycheque should, at every possible opportunity, be playing the role of a consumer of their own company's goods and services. It has never been the Virgin way to put too much credence in the findings of third-party customer satisfaction ratings when so much more can be gleaned from testing your own product first-hand at every possible opportunity.

Despite living in an online age, when things go amiss consumers should be able to talk to someone – a real someone, not an electronic avatar. So when you're playing customer, one of the first things to do is to try and locate a phone number to call on your website that will enable you to get through to a real human being. If you can find the number – most organisations foolishly bury a contact number in some deep dark corner of the website after 'Contact Us' has led you nowhere except back to the webpage you started on – try calling it and count how many recorded options, pre-screens and hand-offs you are forced through before you (perhaps) get to a real person. Once you get to that human voice, have a reasonable problem ready, one that they should be able to fix, and see how well they do and how pleasantly they go about it. If they do it really well you might want to consider identifying yourself at the end of the call and praising their efforts. If they get it hopelessly wrong you are better off taking the story to their supervisor so the failing can become a training subject.

Or for some real fun – play-act the part of a dissatisfied customer and try and call yourself just to see what happens. Do you get an incredulous, 'No, I can't possibly put you through to Mr Smith's office.' Or, if you are put through (don't worry, you aren't there to take your own call), how much grief are you subjected to in order to get there? Are you (the irate customer) deflected to someone who can genuinely take an interest and help you with your problem or are you just headed off at the pass?

I tried pulling this stunt myself once but it didn't work out too well. I am so pathetically bad at imitating someone else's voice that Penni, my trusty assistant for many years, sat there and let me make a complete fool of myself with some trumped-up complaint before saying, 'Well, thank you so much for sharing all that with me, sir. Let me see if Mr Branson is available to take your call.' She then kept me hanging on for what seemed like an eternity – it was probably a couple of minutes – before coming back on the line to say, 'Sorry, Richard, but you appear to be out of the office at the moment, can someone else help you?' before dissolving into howls of laughter. But give it a shot – I am sure you'll be able to make a much better job of it than I did.

I had greater success on the phone when I was based full-time in the UK and used to frequently cold-call Virgin Atlantic passengers who had just arrived at Heathrow. Our Upper Class (business class) passengers could easily be tracked down on their way into London as they were in the limos we had supplied for them. The drivers were primed to expect this and to simply pass the phone back saying, 'It's a call for you, sir/madam.' Needless to say they were surprised at getting a call and so would usually start out with a very suspicious,

'Hello, who's this?', to which I'd typically answer with a cheery, 'Hello, this is Richard Branson, I'm just calling to welcome you to England and ask if everything went well on the flight.' Needless to say I got a lot of 'Yeah, sure it is! Who is this really?' -type reactions (some in much less printable language) but when we did finally strike up a conversation it was always time incredibly well spent on my part. Complaints, or 'observations' as I prefer to call them, are usually unsolicited and with too many companies not particularly welcome, so a senior person reaching out and inviting honest input really wins a lot of points as well as bringing in some interesting insights.

In the case of my calls to the limos, the results were almost always a win–win–win. The passenger was impressed that I'd made the effort to contact them, I got a lot of excellent hot-off-the-press feedback that I could immediately address with the airline and I was also able to pass along any specific compliments to the cabin crew or airport staff, who were never that surprised to take my calls. It was also a great way to say thank you to our most frequent fliers. I liked to be tipped off when a passenger was going through milestones, like say 100,000 miles, and would call to congratulate them and say how much we appreciate their loyalty. A little 'thank you' goes a long way.

I have always found it to be one of the more intriguing idiosyncrasies of the human condition that a problem that is handled quickly and effectively will almost always serve to generate more long-term customer loyalty than when the original service was delivered satisfactorily. That said, I am a huge believer in the old customer service mantra of, 'First to know, first to handle.' If someone can fix a problem on the spot it saves all kinds of angst for the customer plus time and expense for the company – just as importantly, an on-the-spot resolution more often than not will also keep a customer in the fold.

Call it leadership in reverse if you like, but any company that views their business's level of performance strictly through the optic of the bottom line is living very dangerously. That kind of blinkered 'view from the boardroom' thinking was what cost Steve Jobs his job at Apple and history very quickly showed where that took the company – almost to the point of extinction. So rather than sitting in a gilded cage believing what the financials and customer surveys seem to indicate, effective leaders have got to set an example and get out there kicking the tyres on a regular basis. I am probably one of the biggest (constructive) critics of every Virgin company, always balanced with praise where appropriate, of course. Whenever I experience our services, as good and trendsetting as they might be, there is nearly always a way to improve upon them. Yes, I can sometimes be accused of nit-picking when I travel with my notebook in hand but it's invariably the small details that combine to make memorably good – or bad – customer experiences. Like why were we handing out hot towels to our newly boarded passengers on a boiling hot Las Vegas day? Wouldn't cold towels make a lot more sense?

I have always found that having senior people who demonstrably care enough to pay attention to customer-focused nitty-gritty details

– as opposed to just the stock price – serves to encourage everyone in the organisation to get into the habit of seeing what you look like from the outside in. A domino benefit is that middle managers don't want a senior officer to be the first to tell them how their part of the operation looks from the other side of the fence, especially if they've never troubled to set foot over there themselves!

As an example of continually attempting to 'see yourself as others see you', now that Virgin Hotels is opening its doors I will be encouraging our hotel managers to regularly spend (unannounced) nights sleeping in random empty rooms in their properties. Just spending a few minutes inspecting a room during the day doesn't give any clue as to what paying guests experience while sleeping there for the night. If you want to fully grasp what you are selling then you have got to see it from the customer's perspective – or in this case when you've made the bed then you've got to sleep in it too!

While on the subject of hospitality, perhaps the boldest management initiatives I've ever witnessed was in a Florida property used by Virgin Holidays. The manager there had put his picture, name and phone numbers – office, cell phone and home – inside every elevator. The note with it read something along the lines of, 'If there is any problem during your stay that is not resolved to your satisfaction by our staff, please feel free to give me a call.' When I asked him if this hadn't been a problem, his response was, 'For me – not at all: for my staff maybe. I made sure they know how much I dislike getting disturbed when I'm at home with the family.' He then added that in the year the signs had been in place he'd maybe received a couple of calls a month – a great example of the senior person putting themselves on the front line 24/7!

When I was hands-on CEO at Virgin Atlantic I did something similar with our staff. I'd write them a letter every month with an update on how things were going and – before cell phones and email – gave them my home address and home phone number if they wanted to get in touch with me. And, as with the Florida hotel manager, on the rare occasions they did I was always delighted to hear what they had to say.

C YOURSELF AS THE COMPETITION SEES YOU

Running a business would be a lot easier if finding a leader were as simple as handing out impressive titles like CEO, president, managing director or whatever. A fancy corporate title with a 'C' in front of it might open doors (once at least) or get more people to take a phone call, but it doesn't guarantee the levels of respect and influence that are the marks of a real leader – those who earned the position as opposed to merely having it bestowed upon them. To this day, too many businesses still view the top job as being the prerogative of the 'next in line' who has diligently put in their years as the number two person in the corporate pecking order. That *might* work in royal families but it certainly doesn't always get it done in a lot of business situations.

Middle management can make or break a company so having good departmental leaders at all levels is vital to any business – but not every good manager is going to naturally grow into a senior leadership role. It certainly happens in a number of cases, but it's no given. Too often when the number two person is moved up it is done to ensure continuity in the way the firm is run, which usually translates to 'business as usual' or protecting the prior incumbent's legacy. This may make sense with some highly successful companies, but even there I've always found a transition at the top is a perfect opportunity to get a fresh perspective on where the company is going (or not) and if necessary then a little shake, rattle and roll never did anyone any harm.

Clearly when considering candidates for leadership positions their resumes/CVs have to come into play, but they really should be judged equally on their vision for the future as on what they've achieved in the past. If a company is to move forward, hiring clones of the previous incumbent will rarely generate much in the way of positive change. No matter how good the previous person in the job might have been there is always room for improvement so my favourite question with internal applicants has always been, 'So if you get the job, what are the first things you are going to change around here and why?' Much as we like to hire from inside at Virgin I have no aversion to bringing in new blood from the outside – a pair of fresh eyes (and ears) can often see latent opportunities that long-term employees have simply come to accept as the norm.

THE INSIDE ON THE OUTSIDE

As it happens, over the last few years we have put new CEOs in charge of our two biggest airlines, Virgin Atlantic and Virgin

Australia, and in both cases I believe we may have surprised a few people by replacing the long-term incumbents with senior executives from two major legacy airlines.

In Australia we most certainly shook the industry a little by hiring John Borghetti to take over from the airline's outgoing founder Brett Godfrey. As a thirty-six-year veteran of Qantas, Australia's dominant carrier, John had quite literally started in the mailroom and worked his way up to the second highest position in the company. When he came to us he was more than a little bit bummed because he had just been passed over for the top job there. In my opinion this was a huge mistake on Qantas's part, but we remain eternally grateful to them for letting someone like John escape their clutches. So much so, in fact, that after we'd had John on board for a couple of months I was sorely tempted to send Qantas's chairman a 'thank you for the wonderful gift' note, but managed to resist the urge.

My first meeting with John to discuss the possibilities of joining us was in Singapore after the F1 Grand Prix and I have to confess I was incredibly impressed. I'd been extremely doubtful that a career (thirty-six years is a long time in any one place) big airline guy could ever be a good fit at our somewhat funky little Australian operation but he proved that I was way off the mark. John came totally prepared with strategies for everything he thought needed to be done to take Virgin to new heights and was clearly our man. While all the dating books say you should never get into a relationship with anyone who's on the rebound from a failed marriage, I felt there was a lot more than a revenge motive in John. Yes, he was angry, and justifiably so, that he hadn't been offered the top job at Qantas after spending his entire career there, but it was as if he was desperately seeking an outlet for all the things he hadn't been able to get done while at his former employer. When I asked him why he had not put a particularly smart initiative he'd suggested in place while he was at Qantas, he simply replied, 'Because I wasn't the CEO and didn't have the board's support. Here I already get the feeling that's not going to be a problem.'

Suffice it to say that if we had a cloning machine and the ability to replicate our best and brightest Virgin leaders, John would be one of the first ones we pushed in there. He is a highly strategic thinker and yet he also has outstanding people skills, which is a must-have for any CEO in a Virgin company. One big bonus, of course, is that he certainly knows how to read the mind of our biggest competitor in Australia – on a couple of occasions I have been convinced that he knew what they were going to do next before they did – I suppose thirty-six years in one place will do that for you. But equally importantly he had been carefully observing everything that had been going on at Virgin Blue (later Virgin Australia) and had a competitor's perspective on how we were not quite as smart as we thought we were in a few areas. In other words, he brought that all-important ability to 'see ourselves as others see us' and to act accordingly upon a few minor course corrections.

It has also brought with it a new energy that the staff has named the 'NBO' – the 'New Borghetti Order'. John makes it part of his routine to do what the Australians call 'going walkabout' around the company. When he does this, one of many things that make the NBO different is John's habit of not just saying 'Hi, how are you?' but instead taking the time to get into deep impromptu discussions with all level of employees and, importantly, acting on their feedback rather than telling them he'll 'consider it' and moving on.

One interesting observation John made right up front was that he felt we had maybe been too intent on driving the brand as opposed to the business. Having observed what we were doing for years through the eyes of a competitor, he told me – and I wrote it down in my notebook – that he felt the brand image we had developed was 'misrepresenting some of the airline's richest qualities'. By this he meant that the kind of 'party central, super-laid-back' image that Virgin Blue had developed in Australia had led to a lot of potential customers – particularly older, more straight-laced business flyers – failing to see us as a serious-enough player to be deserving of their business. Funnily enough, this was exactly the same identity crisis we'd once had to confront at Virgin Atlantic many years earlier when we were initially perceived as the 'rock and roll airline'.

Conversely, John also – quite bravely I thought – expressed his thinking that our aircraft liveries (fuselage paint jobs) needed a little bit of tweaking for the Aussie market. He felt that Virgin Atlantic and Virgin America's applications of the Virgin logo were overly conservative and that they needed something a little more contemporary. I say 'bravely' because for many years in Virgin the logo was sacrosanct and something that should not be tampered with under any circumstances.

Anyway when John raised the subject in front of all the airline heads I was probably expected to be the one to quickly put this Qantas interloper in his place and say something like, 'Sorry, but that is one area where we cannot go.' On the contrary, other than John, I think I was the only one in the room who thought it made sense and so said, 'Screw it, if that's what you think you need then let's do it.' The result was a very different-looking sideways rendition of the logo that, in all honesty, some love and some don't, but the updated treatment freshened up the brand and got us lots of media and consumer attention in the process.

But just to show that nothing is truly sacred, another more outlandish 'modification' of the Virgin Atlantic brand was to be seen in Los Angeles when the airline sponsored a big joint promotion with the 1999 Austin Powers' movie *The Spy Who Shagged Me*: billboards all over LA featured 'Virgin Shaglantic' and a variety of somewhat bawdy one-liners from the Mike Myers' character. When, after the fact, the 'logo police' (as the group's custodians of the brand are affectionately known) in London found out about this mangling of one of our biggest brand names, they were suitably appalled. When they tackled the US marketing team as to whether they had asked for approval, the response was a no-nonsense, 'No, of course not. We decided this was one of those occasions when it was better to ask for forgiveness than permission.' When I found out about it, all I could do was smile and do a lame 'Ooh baby!' impression of Austin Powers.

Back in Australia, though, there are still a couple of things on which John Borghetti and I have not completely come to terms as yet. First of all he expressed a concern that we spent too much time and money on staff parties – that's one that I think we will win him over on after he's been to a few more of them. The other one is his proclivity for tie wearing – something borne out of all those years at stuffy old Qantas, I'm sure. This is another part of the 'Virginisation' process that I am confident will also get sorted out in time: so far I think I have only snipped off a couple of his expensive silk ties with my ever-ready scissors. With other chronic tie-wearing cases such as John, I've found it can sometimes take as many as three or four 'tiectomies' before they are completely cured of the habit.

Our second 'imported' airline CEO is Craig Kreeger at Virgin Atlantic who, like John in Australia, joined us after a very long time at a legacy airline. In Craig's case he put in twenty-seven years at American Airlines, but despite this it appears he won't be too difficult to 'untie'. I met Craig for the first time when he came to Necker Island as the last stop on the selection process bandwagon. When I asked him what his greatest concern was about coming to work for Virgin he surprised me by saying, 'Well, to be perfectly honest, Richard, probably knowing what to pack to come down here to meet you. I figured that I wouldn't need a tie but after that I hadn't got a clue as to what the dress code was going to be!' I think Craig must be the first person ever to have worried about 'dress code' when meeting me, and I am sure it will never again be a problem for him.

As with John in Australia three years earlier, Craig's hiring may have been a surprise to a few people who had thought Steve Ridgway's successor (Steve had been Virgin Atlantic's CEO for twelve years) was probably going to come from within the airline. Again, though, like in Australia, we opted to take someone from a big legacy carrier – it wasn't the first time we went fishing at American, having hired David Cush from there to head up Virgin America some years earlier. From the get-go I was impressed with Craig's easy-going manner and one part of his CV also jumped off the page: his role at American several years earlier in London had included putting together American Airlines' big alliance with British Airways. As we were just about to announce that Delta Air Lines had acquired the 49 per cent stake in Virgin Atlantic that Singapore Airlines had held for a number of years, we needed someone to mastermind that new relationship on our behalf. Singapore had always been a very passive partner, but the Delta relationship was going to be very different and maximising on every ounce of the many transatlantic synergies the new relationship would present was going to be critical to the on-going growth and profitability of the airline we had built from scratch in 1984.

So Craig was our man and while at the time of writing he is still relatively new to the job he is already making his mark and has established a highly comprehensive two-year plan against which everyone can measure their own and the company's progress. Both John and Craig are demonstrating my long-held belief that everything can always be improved upon and often only someone who has seen your operation from the outside in can bring the required perspective and willingness to upset even a pretty sturdy applecart.

So don't spend all your time obsessing over what the competition is up to – divert some of that energy to looking in the mirror to see how you appear to your employees, your competition and your customers. And you shouldn't wait until the tyres start falling off before you get out there and kick them; do it while the going's good if you want to keep it that way. Getting into the habit of looking at your business from the outside in will tell you a lot about how long those good results are likely to continue – or not!

Chapter 4

K-I-S-S AND TELL

Simplicity wins every time

'Great leaders are almost always great simplifiers, who can cut through argument, debate and doubt to offer a solution everybody can understand.'

✳ *Colin Powell* ✳

The key to this statement by Colin Powell is that great leaders are not just simplifiers but that they can communicate to their entire audience in terms that are universally understood. You can't always be listening to your people as sometimes they need to be listening to you. Whether he falls into the 'great leader' category or not may be debatable, but one of Powell's contemporaries, former US president Bill Clinton, is certainly a good example of a politician with a gift for delivering understandable, no-nonsense messages. In fact, after Clinton had delivered a masterful address at a 2012 Obama election campaign event, I had to chuckle when I heard the White House incumbent jokingly say that maybe he should appoint Clinton as 'the Secretary of Explaining Stuff'.

KISS is an acronym for 'Keep it simple stupid' that is believed to have originated in the US Navy in the sixties. It was directed at system designers in recognition of the fact that most battle systems work better when kept as simple as possible, whereas complexity builds in nothing but problems. Unfortunately, however, the KISS principle is something to which a lot of business leaders and politicians do not seem to subscribe.

In my own case, having grown up facing the challenges that come with dyslexia, simplicity in communications has always been more of a necessity than a nicety for me. But whether in our professional or private lives, developing the art of simple clear speech is something that every one of us, and everyone with whom we associate, can only benefit. For some people, like Bill Clinton, the 'gift of the gab' comes with an innately intelligent and concise delivery; for others, however, it can be anything but concise and frequently utterly unintelligible.

One such aggravating example is to be found in BBC Television's brilliant comedy series, *Yes, Prime Minister*. I don't watch much television, but this show has long been a favourite of mine – it was reportedly also one of the late prime minister Margaret Thatcher's few 'must watch' TV programmes. There is one wonderful character in the show, Sir Humphrey, who is the absolute antithesis of everything KISS stands for. Paradoxically, my old English teacher at Stowe School would probably have described Sir Humphrey as 'the quintessence of verbosity and polysyllabic pomposity', which we always joked would have been a fair description of that particular teacher as well! In simpler terms, however, Sir Humphrey is a perfect caricature of the kind of person who loves to talk at great length but does so without actually saying anything remotely intelligible.

In case you're not familiar with *Yes, Prime Minister*, here is a snippet of Sir Humphrey at his best – or perhaps more accurately – at his worst.

'Questions of administrative policy can cause confusion between the policy of administration and the administration of policy, especially when responsibility for the administration of the policy of administration conflicts with responsibility for the policy of the administration of policy.'

SHORT AND SNAPPY WINS EVERY TIME

Whenever I run into a real-life Sir Humphrey, it's all I can do to prevent myself from grabbing them by the collar and yelling, 'Life's too short! Get to the point, will you.' When the person in question happens to be a revered diplomat or captain of industry such an 'in your face' approach isn't always the smartest way to go. But you can take steps to avoid falling into similar bad habits yourself, and in my own case this has meant trying my best to live by the simple old mantra of, 'Say what you mean and mean what you say' – and preferably in as few well-chosen words as possible. There are a lot of Sir Humphrey types in business who mistakenly feel they have to assert their authority by continually interjecting with some kind of a comment on anything and everything that's being discussed, when the fact is that if they don't have anything intelligent to add to the debate they'd come across as much smarter by shutting up and saying nothing.

When going into print, the art of distilling one's thoughts into as few words as possible is something that takes practice as well as that often rare commodity of time. The French mathematician Blaise Pascal summed up this conundrum when he famously wrote, *'I am sorry this letter is so long, I didn't have time to make it shorter.'* Twitter wasn't an electronic option when Pascal was around, but with its 140-character limit, tweets have become the champion of economy in words and, as a man of few words, I must say that I love it. In anything I write I now make a conscious effort to condense the point I want to make into a Twitter-like format. Even if I only manage to get it down to a couple of hundred characters, I can still count on getting my message across much more effectively than if it were ten times the length.

So, a word of advice here to anyone writing an initial pitch document or for that matter any written communication – and certainly if it's coming in my direction – anything longer than a 'one pager' is way too long. In fact, even an email that is longer than a couple of hundred words is not going to hold my or many other people's attention. There are only so many hours in a day and nobody has the time to wade through long, Sir Humphrey-like missives. My friend Larry Page of Google told me that his colleagues all know that sending him anything that is much longer than a tweet exponentially increases the likelihood that he will never find time to read it. Capturing someone's attention in writing is like the process of mooring an ocean liner. First the thin lightweight rope (the tweet) gets tossed to the dockhand, this leads to a larger stronger line (the email) that eventually pulls in the big heavy mooring hawser (the full presentation). Try throwing out the heavy line first and, like a five-page email, it will likely sink without a trace.

I LOATHE MAKING SPEECHES

Coming from someone who does a lot of it, such a statement must come as a surprise, but it's almost as true today as it was when I first spoke in public fifty-odd years ago. I remember being scared half to death when I had to stand up in front of my school to make a speech. It was a contest where we had to memorise a fairly short speech and present it to the school. If you stumbled at any point you were 'gonged' and that was it. You were out. I had actually worked very hard at getting it down pat and despite my sheer terror I managed to start out quite well but a couple of minutes into it my mind momentarily blacked out. Within a split second the G-O-N-G brought me back to reality. I still break out in a cold sweat just thinking back to the excruciating experience.

Quite apart from the nervousness, the simple fact of the matter is that I have never particularly enjoyed public speaking and as with everything else in my life that I don't enjoy doing I didn't do it terribly well. Over the years I have become much more comfortable as a speaker but it still makes me nervous. It is some comfort that

I am not on my own with this, as the fear of public speaking – or 'glossophobia' as it is clinically known – is right up there with the fear of flying as one of the most common human fears.

One inescapable reality of business life is that the more successful you become and the higher up the corporate ladder you climb, the more frequent the requirement for you to step up to the microphone. Unlike in government circles, where the ability to deliver a great stump speech gets a lot of otherwise distinctly mediocre politicos elected, in the private sector, as helpful a talent as it may be, I doubt that too many people ever got hired or promoted strictly on the basis of their public-speaking abilities. The other sad irony is that while teleprompters are a wonderful crutch for those really big speeches – with a teleprompter, a few beta-blockers and the ability to read, just about anyone can turn in a reasonably respectable performance – those little glass screens are not something you can easily swing with smaller audiences. The more intimate atmosphere that is found with groups of fewer than a hundred makes for a much higher incidence of interruptions and questions – which are not a good idea with a teleprompter!

And a word of warning: over-reliance on technology can be dangerous in lots of ways but never more so than when it is a teleprompter and you are standing in front of an audience. Things break! I always make a point of having a printed version of my presentation at hand just in case there are problems. I have, however, seen several people over the years that clearly had not rehearsed their speeches sufficiently well to be able to wing it when they experienced technical problems with their electronic scripts – something that *Transformers* director Michael Bay clearly didn't do at a Consumer Electronics Show press event for Samsung. When his teleprompter went on the blink mid-presentation, he looked flustered, stopped speaking mid-sentence, said something to the effect that 'the type is all off' then turned on his heel and walked off the stage, never to return! He later apologised with the understatement that 'I guess live shows aren't my thing.'

I remember the very first time I used a teleprompter being asked by the technician if I was familiar with them and, not wishing to appear a novice, I nodded and made like I was an old hand – which turned out to be a big mistake. Within a few minutes of starting my speech, I found myself talking faster and faster in a frantic effort to keep up with the darn thing. It was only after I finished and the same technician who had run the teleprompter said, 'Wow, you're a fast talker! I had trouble keeping up with you,' that I figured it out. His job was to run the teleprompter at my speed of talking – not vice versa.

Having seen that I was a very nervous speaker, the late Gavin Maxwell, author of *Ring of Bright Water* and other successful novels, gave me some wonderfully helpful advice on speechmaking that has served me well over the years. It takes practice, but it can be done. Close out your mind to the fact that you're on a stage with hundreds of people staring at you and instead imagine yourself in any personal comfort-zone like your dining room at home where you're telling a story to a group of friends over dinner. I know it sounds a little corny but try it – it has certainly worked for me.

I am a huge fan of Sir Winston Churchill – how can you not love someone who, in a 1948 House of Commons speech, could say, '*For my part, I consider that it will be found much better by all parties to leave the past to history, especially as I propose to write that history.*' Somewhat ironically, his words have been 'massaged' by history and the reinvented quote most often attributed to the great man is now, '*History will be kind to me for I intend to write it.*' One way or the other it is an approach that I may well decide to follow myself some day! Churchill is universally recognised as one of the greatest orators of all time, but he only achieved this status on the back of a lot of hard work: he claimed that he averaged an hour's preparation for every minute of a speech. Few if any are better equipped to give advice on the subject of public speaking as these two classic, funny but right-on-target quotes serve to illustrate – my absolute favourite being the following quote which is often attributed to him:

'*A good speech should be like a woman's skirt: long enough to cover the subject and short enough to create interest.*'

Take this advice to heart. Even highly gifted speakers like Churchill would never push an audience into listening to him for more than twenty-five minutes or so. Extending a presentation beyond thirty minutes is really stretching the attention span of any audience.

I put Mark Twain right up there with Ernest Hemingway as one of my favourite American authors. Twain was also a highly acclaimed public speaker who, like Churchill, seemed to enjoy speaking about speaking. He was obviously aware of the common misperception that to be a great speechmaker you have to be able to make off-the-cuff deliveries. Twain addressed this perfectly in 1899 when, speaking at a dinner given in his honour at London's Whitefriars Club, he said:

> 'But impromptu speaking – that is a difficult thing. I used to do it in this way. I used to begin about a week ahead, and write out my impromptu speech and get it by heart.'

Another piece of astute advice to speakers from Twain speaks to the tendency nervous speakers have of taking a deep breath and then – like me with the runaway teleprompter – rushing through it like an express train. It's almost as if, as is usually the case, they just can't wait to be done with it and get off the platform. Addressing this very common affliction, Twain spoke about a rightly timed pause being every bit as critical and effective as choosing the right words. 'The right word may be effective, but no word was ever as effective as a rightly timed pause.'

Before the teleprompter arrived on the scene, I always used to work from index cards. David Tait, who would usually write my speeches for Virgin Atlantic in the US, used to take delight in sticking in the odd strategically placed card that in big letters would just say 'PAUSE' to ensure I stopped long enough to let a point sink in with the audience – low-tech, for sure, but highly effective nevertheless.

Twain's other statement on the subject of speaking that made me feel a lot better about my qualms was, '*There are only two types of speakers in the world: 1. The nervous and 2. Liars.*'

The strange fact is that nervousness is good. The best and most experienced public speakers still get nervous, so don't fret about it. A touch of the jitters sharpens the mind, gets the adrenalin flowing and helps you to focus. At least that's the theory, and as easy as it is to say, 'Don't sweat it', for some people, of whom I used to occasionally be one, the fear of public speaking can be absolutely debilitating. The best way to mitigate it is quite simply, practise, practise, practise and practise some more. Go through it until you are saying it in your dreams and it will be a lot easier on the day.

THE NO-SPEECH SPEECH

So you can – and should – heed all this wise advice, or you can also consider adopting an approach that I find very helpful when it comes to making speeches to large audiences: I don't do it any more! Well, maybe that's not strictly true, I do have to make formal speeches every once in a while, but before accepting any speaking engagements I will always try and get them to switch the format to a question and answer session.

Not only do I feel a lot more relaxed and comfortable with a Q&A format but I also believe that the audience gets a lot more out of it. With a standard twenty-five-minute speech, you might sometimes manage to fit in a few questions from the floor at the end, but it's usually rushed and seldom very productive. With a well-orchestrated Q&A format, however, the audience gets to lead the dialogue (or at least thinks it does) and so I always find myself covering a much wider range of topics than I could ever jam into a prepared address. At the same time, if there is some topic I especially want to discuss, then a pre-planted question or two can always discreetly accommodate such things!

Interestingly, since I have adopted this non-speech approach to 'speaking engagements', I have become (so I am told) one of the world's more highly paid 'speakers' and as a result have been raising around $10 million per year for charity.

Have you ever noticed how after any formal speech the audience often spends more time discussing all the things that were *not* covered by the speaker than those that were? 'I wish she'd taken some time to explain XYZ' or worse still 'And did you notice how he studiously avoided mentioning XYZ, which is what I really wanted to hear about.' Even with a good Q&A session you obviously don't always get to discuss everything you or your audience might like to cover, but at least they have an opportunity to become participants rather than just listeners.

And the number one question that I still get asked by audiences almost every time I take part in a Q&A is that old favourite: 'Richard, can you please tell us how you came up with the name Virgin?' I suppose I should be grateful, though – they could be asking a lot more difficult ones!

WORDS AND PHRASES BEST AVOIDED

Whether you are making a formal speech in an amphitheatre, a Q&A in a ballroom or talking with a group of twenty staff in the boardroom, you should work hard to maximise on your audience's attention level while minimising the chance of any ambiguity and subsequent (potentially damaging) misunderstandings. To this end here are a few popular words and phrases (and sounds) that, in my experience, are best avoided:

Uhmms, ahhs, 'you know' and 'like'

Nervous public speakers tend to be even more terrified of public silence. As a result they rush to fill in every blank that should be a pause (remember what Mark Twain had to say on this) with all kinds of uhmms, ahhs, grunts and filler words. My generation used to favour sprinkling 'you know' into every other sentence, while today's favourite (English language) filler word is 'like'. Some Generation-Yers can get like more 'likes' into every like sentence than like all the other like words combined. But whatever your predilection, any and all such verbal fillers are best avoided – all they do is drag out the speaking time while adding zero value.

I learned a painful lesson on this subject after my first-ever radio interview when, but for the good graces of the late Anthony Howard, I could have made a bit of a fool of myself. Howard was an esteemed journalist, broadcaster and writer when, for BBC Radio 4, he conducted a pre-recorded interview of a very young and very nervous me talking about the nascent *Student* magazine. After the taping I felt the interview had gone surprisingly well, if maybe a tad on the long side. Anyway, before the show aired Mr Howard was kind enough to send me two different tapes of my performance. The first tape I listened to was the ten minutes that would be aired, and I recall smugly thinking how polished, confident and to-the-point I sounded. Then I listened to the second tape and came down to earth with a major bump. To my horror it consisted of nothing except all the 'uhmms', 'ahs' and 'you knows' and throat clearings that had been edited out of the full interview. And what really depressed me was that the outtake tape was by far the longer of the two!

'That's not a bad idea'

Any use of double negatives such as this is an open invitation to mass confusion within the audience. Add the word 'maybe' and it gets even more problematic. The take-away from anyone hearing the CEO saying such a thing can vary from, 'He loves it – let's push ahead with the project' to a diametrically opposed 'He hates it – he specifically avoided saying it was a good idea.' So, be definitive. If you approve or disapprove of something be assertive and make your position absolutely clear, making sure you explain why.

'You're not going to like this but...'

Avoid any such negativity whenever possible. Rather than immediately sowing a seed of doubt with the audience it's far better to say something like, 'This may be a tough nut to crack but I'm sure we'll get it done.'

'That's certainly different!'

A statement such as this could be anything from a ringing endorsement to a stinging condemnation or even an admission of 'I have no idea what the heck this is all about'. Differences, like 'change', can be good or bad and for every company that differentiates itself by its excellence there's at least one other that achieves it by mediocrity.

'We've had better years'

This kind of negative half-statement is yet another often-heard cop-out of a comment. People want the truth, not some sugar-coated version of it. 'Unfortunately last year was a bad one' followed by an honest explanation as to what is going to be done to learn from it and ensure next year will be better is a much more positive approach.

'Let me get back to you on that'

When you truly don't know the answer to a question, rather than making something up and possibly looking foolish in the process, this is absolutely the correct response, *but* only if you take a note of the question and then make certain that you do indeed get back to them with an answer in a timely manner. Even better, make a commitment that, 'I will get back to you by X date.'

'That said...'

Put at the front of just about any sentence, these two little words form what is quite possibly one of the most destructive phrases in the

English language. I am constantly amazed at how people can unwittingly shoot down everything they have been saying by using these two words. To most people's ears, 'that said' immediately invalidates everything that has gone before and can breed instant resentment in the listener who may have been buying into the subject matter before 'that' was 'said'. As a verbal bridge from the pros to the cons, try using something like, 'Of course, we shouldn't overlook...'

'No comment'

I know everyone knows this, but it's still surprising how often this sure-fire PR disaster phrase seems to slip out! Even if you find yourself in the unenviable position where your legal advisors have said, 'We can't tell them [the press] anything at this time', please avoid the 'no comment' at all costs. 'I'm really sorry but until we gather all the facts we are not in a position to issue a statement' will play much more favourably on YouTube and or the evening news! A stark 'No comment', on the other hand, tends to come across like, 'We're guilty as hell and don't want to talk about it until our lawyers have come up with a plausible alibi.'

'Okay'

Apparently this is the most universally recognised word on the planet next to Coca-Cola and yet it is one of the most ambiguous. The original meaning is rumoured to have come from 'Oll Korrect' but in popular usage it can mean a wide range of things. One person's 'okay' *might* mean 'good', another's 'it's adequate' and to yet another's 'barely acceptable'. It is a word that is also used in a dismissive manner when you really mean to say, 'Okay – just don't bother me now.' Avoid it! Don't be lazy: if you mean 'This is an excellent idea' then say so. If you think the idea sucks then tell them (nicely) that 'I don't like it' and give them a few reasons why so they can learn from it.

And lastly, one that may surprise you, but it is a word that can cause as much trouble for Americans visiting the UK as it can for Brits in the USA: the word is 'quite'. To an American, 'quite good' means 'very good' whereas to a British ear it can mean anything from 'reasonably good' to 'barely acceptable'. If in doubt it's best to avoid it on both sides of the Atlantic as – using the American connotation – the results can be quite dangerous!

LITTLE WORDS THAT GO A LONG WAY

So having listed some of the words and phrases I recommend are best avoided, here are a few everyday words and phrases that I strongly suggest using as often as possible. The first consists of seven little words that I sincerely believe might constitute one of the most powerful sentences a business leader can utter: 'I'm not sure – what do you think?'

The upsides to popping this question every once in a while are almost innumerable. First of all, if you truly aren't sure of your answer, admitting it will usually spare the other party from a lot of Sir Humphrey-like blather – or 'blether', as the Scots like to call it. I only know that because my wife Joan has on more than a few occasions said, 'Oh come on, Richard, spare us the blether, will you.' And when this comes from my lovely wife I usually do – quickly!

There will, of course, be some bombastic 'I'm in charge and I'll make the decisions around here' types that will see any admission of uncertainty on their part as an utterly unacceptable sign of weakness in front of their 'underlings'. As far as I'm concerned, however, quite the opposite applies. When a leader displays the self-confidence to effectively say, 'Hey, I can't be expected to have all the answers, so I'd love to hear your thoughts on the subject', it not only has a very humanising effect, but it also tells the employees that their opinions are respected and considered to be of value. Even without the 'I don't know', frequently asking simple little questions like, 'So what do you think?' or 'Are we missing anything here?' will yield all kinds of highly positive rewards. At school we always knew which teachers made a habit of asking questions and which would just drone on and on and on without asking one question per term. The same applies in the office – if your people know that their opinions may be sought at any moment they will pay much closer attention and also have to have an opinion at the ready.

SPEAK AS YOU WOULD BE SPOKEN TO – PLEASE

Now what I am about to say may not be something you've heard from anyone since your parents used to say it to you when you were growing up. Many of you did actually listen and learn from them and so this is not directed at you, but at the same time I'll bet you'll be the first to concur with my position here. I apologise if this comes across in any way as condescending but there are two tiny but hugely important words that tend to be grossly underused by a lot of people, and quite often the higher up the totem pole you go, the less you tend to hear the words *'please'* and *'thank you'* spoken.

We were all brought up to say please and thank you. My mum and dad's rule was a very simple, 'No please, no get.' So why do so many people seem to grow out of the habit? I don't know if it's some kind of a misbegotten status thing or if it's just sheer bad manners, but I am frequently saddened at how many people just don't seem to use these words any more. Perhaps today's kids just aren't being taught the social value of such things but as far as I'm concerned, whether in emails or face-to-face, you simply cannot overuse these two words. It's not just a question of politeness, it's about recognition and respect for your colleagues at every level. Just consider what a difference it makes leading off a conversation with, 'Thank you so much for all your hard work on this report and...' as opposed to, 'I got your report and...' In the same way a simple 'please' can make a world of difference. 'I need this by Monday' is much less likely to get you there than, 'Can you please try and get this to me by Monday.'

If you listen to experts like McKinsey & Co. on the subject of motivation and 'employee recognition', they are generally in agreement that, contrary to popular perceptions, money is seldom the prime motivator. In a report titled 'Insights into Organization' McKinsey agreed that while being fairly compensated is important, so are a lot of other more subtle factors, one of which is pride in one's work. People take a lot of satisfaction from knowing that they're doing a good job, and that their efforts are appreciated – and the simplest way to stoke this passion is for leaders to use ample doses of gratitude. A simple 'thank you' when coming from a senior person can go a long way, particularly if they have made a trip to the employee's desk to express it. And if there is an opportunity to extend the thank you into something a little more meaningful then that will make an even more lasting impression.

In addition to the frightening reduction in face-to-face conversations, another casualty in the wake of emails and texts is the handwritten thank you letter. Given their rarity nowadays, however, a well-crafted, handwritten thank you note – which in case you've forgotten involves the use of paper, pen and ink and sent in an envelope – is something that really stands out. I send them several times a month to say thank you for something special, offer condolences, congratulations on a newborn baby or sometimes even to try and sway a business deal that looks to be getting away from us. I remember dropping a line to Mick Jagger in 1991 when we were pursuing the Rolling Stones for Virgin Records, but perhaps the oddest one I have ever sent was when we were trying to sign the Stereophonics to the V2 label. I was told the deal was slipping away, so on a whim I sent a handwritten note to the mother of the band's singer Kelly Jones. I had been told that Kelly still lived at home, so I implored his mum to have her son make 'the right choice' – which he did; they signed the deal a few weeks later. As Kelly told me later, 'It's quite amazing what a handwritten note from "that nice Mr Branson" can do!'

In recognition of outstanding performance I occasionally like to surprise employees (and their significant others) by saying thank you in somewhat grander style than a note in the mail and invite them to stay with us on Necker Island for a few days. One time in 1997 we entertained an entire twenty-plus Virgin Atlantic crew that had performed in exemplary fashion when faced with an emergency landing at Heathrow. One landing gear had failed to extend properly but our captain made what was described as a textbook landing – it maybe helped that Tim Barnby, the captain in command in question, was also a former aerobatic champion! Anyway, as much as the crew will always remember the frightening experience on the airplane, I am sure they will also treasure the few days we enjoyed on Necker together. But as the old saying goes, 'It's the thought that counts' – taking the time to make the gesture is much more important than its size. So if you don't have a private island to share with your people, try something like giving them a surprise day off, take them out for lunch or give away those seats you have for a sporting event that you probably weren't going to use anyway. At the very least, walk over there, shake their hand and say a heartfelt 'thank you'.

So whether communicating via the written or the spoken word, try and make 'keep it simple stupid' your mantra and while you're at it you should also work on adding a third 'S' for 'short'. If you can rigorously adhere to the K-I-S-S-S principle in all your communications, you will not only have much better informed and more engaged employees, shareholders and customers but you will also save yourself and your company a lot of heartache.

Chapter 5

BURN DOWN THE MISSION

Mission misstatements

At some time or another, particularly in the early days of every start-up company, it is almost inevitable that some investor or job applicant is going to ask, 'So, what is your company's mission statement?' It's the kind of question some people think is impressive to ask in an interview, although I beg to differ.

In fact, I will be totally up front and admit that I have never been a fan of corporate mission statements, many of which I find to be utterly blah truisms and anything but inspirational. With very few exceptions they are something that have next to no bearing or influence on a company or its employees and in many cases can in fact become a bit of a laughing stock. After all, if you work for the XYZ Widget Company, do you really need to be told that, *The mission of XYZ Widgets is to make the world's best widgets while consistently delivering excellent customer service*'? Frankly, if that's the best the company can come up with, they'd be better off working without the thing! Rather than inspiring one's people, such ho-hum statements only serve to draw a reaction of 'Why do they waste their time producing stuff like this?'

Before anyone even tries to come up with a mission statement, however, there is the little matter of actually considering your company's commitment and ability to live up to it. If neither of these conditions is present then there's no point in trying to 'put lipstick on the pig' by means of a fanciful, pie-in-the-sky mission statement. When a business puts out some highfalutin mission statement that draws a roll of the eyes and a 'Yeah right!' reaction from every employee who reads it, then clearly the time and effort would be better spent righting the problem instead of writing the cover-up. The classic example of a major disconnect in this regard was evident in 2001 when the Enron Corporation went bankrupt, destroying the lives and savings of hundreds of thousands of employees and investors. At the time of its demise Enron proudly sported the specious mission statement: *'Respect, Integrity, Communication and Excellence.'* Maybe the less said the better!

IT'S ALL LATIN TO ME

My first contact with anything approaching mission statements was as a boy growing up in England. At the time my greatest real-life hero was the Second World War Royal Air Force fighter pilot Douglas Bader. After seeing the movie *Reach for the Sky* (several times), which told the legless Bader's incredibly heroic story, I remember asking my father about the RAF motto of 'Per Ardua ad Astra'. When Dad told me that it meant, 'Through Adversity to the Stars', my impressionable young brain seized on to it as the most inspirational thing I'd ever heard. There was something incredibly compelling about the notion of battling one's way to the stars no matter how difficult the challenge. Much to the astonishment of my pals, I remember barrelling along on my bike and bellowing 'Per Ardua ad Astra' to the heavens – probably in much the same way as today's kids might use the wonderful *Toy Story* character Buzz Lightyear's mantra of 'To Infinity and Beyond!' Something I know the Virgin Galactic crew think is really pretty cool.

A few years later, at Stowe School, I came across my second mission statement of sorts in the school's motto of '*Persto et Praesto*'. As every new student had to learn on day one, this means 'I Stand Firm and I Stand First'. I need hardly point out how much silly giggling the first half of this motto generated among a group of pubescent schoolboys, but nevertheless it was an excellent mission statement for young 'Stowics' to take forward into adult life – and although I may have forgotten most things from school, this still resonates with me.

It was also at Stowe where an English master, displaying zero sensitivity towards my dyslexia, once told me that I had 'the attention span of a gnat'. He then amused himself further by adding, 'But there again, Mr Branson, I'm probably being grossly unfair to the average gnat.' It wasn't long after this that the same teacher was utterly taken aback to find me totally engrossed in Ernest Hemingway's classic, *The Old Man and the Sea*. What I am sure attracted me to Hemingway was his crisp, punchy writing style with its short, easy-to-digest sentences; a technique that almost certainly stemmed from his days as a journalist. One way or the other it certainly seemed to work well with my limited attention span. In fact, one of the only pieces of prose I have ever committed to memory was a whole short story often attributed to Hemingway. Okay, maybe this is a bit of a reach, as it was after all only six words long, but it does support the point that shorter is more memorable. The story goes, that in the 1920s colleagues of Hemingway's bet him that he couldn't tell a complete story in just six words. They had to pay up on the bet after they read what some consider to be his finest work. What he wrote was the heartrending:

'For sale, baby shoes, never used.'

Had he told this same story in even twenty words, I doubt it could have been anywhere near as poignant as it is in six, and I for one certainly wouldn't still be talking about it fifty years after I first read it.

Inspired by the recollection of this mini-classic, I recently ran a contest on my blog soliciting my online 'followers' (sorry but something about that term always sounds so incredibly pompous) to write a short story. And, being the generous soul that I am, I even gave contestants one more word than Hemingway had to play with:

they were given seven days to write a seven-word story with the winner getting a pair of tickets on a (very short) flight on one of our Virgin airlines.

The level of response we received was incredible. Quite a few of them were brilliant but regrettably not suited for reprinting in a book that might be read by children. There were also a lot of really fun ones like LC Moningka's wonderful, 'The vegetarian butcher entered. The chicken cheered' – you can just see it happening! The winner, however, came from Sarrah (sic) who, like Hemingway before her, chose to tug at the emotions with the tragic, 'Holding hands, they laughed. Watching, I cried.' Sob!

While inventing these ultra-short stories makes for a really fun dinner party game, you can also try it on your mission statement writing team. 'Okay, now please go back to the drawing board and reduce this 560-word mission statement to just ten!' When they've picked themselves up off the floor you can always back down and show your conciliatory side by saying, 'Okay what the heck – I'll give you twenty-five!' In all seriousness, though, it's not just mission statements: the PowerPoint culture in which we live has got completely out of hand. The hours that people take putting the things together with all kinds of charts, graphics and illustrations would be much better spent boiling the presentation down to its essence that they could put on two rather than thirty-two slides. So practising what I preach, let me summarise in seven words: *'Keeping it short goes a long way.'*

CRIMINAL NEGLECT

There is a lot to be said for the sheer simplicity of these old heraldic mottoes. Of course, the practical reality that they had to fit across the bottom of a coat of arms ensured they were always concise and punchy. While Hemingway's six words may be pushing it, brevity is certainly a key to a good mission statement. As such, Twitter's 140-character template is a good place to start drafting that inspirational message. Not only will a long drawn-out diatribe fail to inspire and motivate employees (if they ever even read it) but, as one UK police chief recently discovered, it may also attract a lot of attention for quite the wrong reasons. The UK's Warwickshire Police outsourced the job of coming up with a new mission statement and the result was so outstanding that the piece was soon nominated for a national award. Unfortunately however the UK's infamous 'Golden Bull Award' exists to recognize 'excellence in gobbledygook' and as the nominating committee pointed out, not only was the rambling 1,200-word epistle filled with buzzwords and jargon but, somewhat surprisingly, the word 'crime' was conspicuous by its absence.

ONE MISSION FITS ALL

Another pet peeve of mine with mission statements is their tendency to be totally interchangeable between competing companies, with no differentiating characteristics whatsoever. For example, pharmaceutical giant Bristol-Myers has (or at least had) a mission statement that reads, *'To discover, develop and deliver innovative medicines that help patients prevail over serious diseases.'* Well, you certainly can't argue with that. At the same time, however, couldn't the identical mission statement be claimed as their own by just about every drug company on the planet? Just swap out Bristol-Myers for Pfizer or Bayer and before you know it you have a 'one-sentence-fits-all' industry-wide mission statement, but not something that is unique to any single player.

At the opposite end of the scale is the company that tries too hard, only to fail by dint of what I'd describe as 'flowery waffle'. An example of this would be, *'Yahoo powers and delights our communities of users, advertisers and publishers – all of us united in creating indispensable experiences, and fuelled by trust.'* Sounds wonderful, but what does it actually mean? Whoever writes the mission statements at Yahoo would have done better to listen to their own CEO Marissa Mayer, who in a recent speech said, 'Yahoo is about making the world's daily habits more inspiring and entertaining.' Far from perfect but at least it would be a step in the right direction.

Writing an effective mission statement is not an easy task but, as my late dad used to love to say, 'If a job's worth doing, it's worth doing well.' One of the primary roles of a mission statement has to be explaining the core purpose of a company and outlining expectations for internal and external clients alike. Finding the right tone, content, balance and length – ideally somewhere closer to a motto than an employee handbook – can be a daunting task. I have seen an amazing number of mission statements that might start out on the right track but then succeed in blowing the whole thing by saying stuff like, '*We must provide services and products that consistently match our customers' expectations.*' Are they serious? While the whole subject of defining 'expectations' can be a tricky one, why would any right-minded company strive to merely 'meet' customer expectations? Shouldn't they be pulling out all the stops to *exceed* them each and every time they interact with a customer?

AN ACTIVE MISSION

An example of precisely this latter approach can be found at Virgin Active, our international chain of health and fitness clubs. Powered by the inspirational leadership of Matthew Bucknall and his incredible team all around the world, Active is one of our greater success stories in the way it has managed to encapsulate all the very best things the Virgin brand stands for. In other words, every Active club is a living, breathing mission statement for the customer service excellence the Virgin brand delivers in all its many incarnations. And as statements go, living up to it every day is a lot more important than writing even the cleverest words and then locking them away in a drawer.

Virgin Active set out with an extremely simple business plan that doubled as a mission statement of sorts. It read, '*We want to create the first global comprehensive consumer-led branded health and fitness facility – readily accessible to a wide socio-demographic group at a price consumers are willing and able to pay.*' Feeding off the back of this, Matthew and team put together a document they dubbed 'The Guide'.

This is not some kind of employee manual to take home and forget, it is very much a (dare I say) active working document that is designed to inspire new and existing Virgin Active employees to dive into the deep end and totally immerse themselves in the brand expectation pool. It does talk to a few slightly airy objectives like enriching people's lives through '*activeness*' (a word coined by Matthew and team) but it's the 'Thou Shalt' and 'Thou Shalt Not' sections that really delineate the gospel to which Active employees aspire.

The 'Thou Shalt' section implores Active's people to:

- Be genuine
- Be yourself
- Give your full attention
- Find common ground
- Try to remember faces
- Be empathetic and remember everyone's different
- Share what you know
- Notice how you're coming across
- Build up relationships
- Have fun

The 'Thou Shalt Not' list is shorter but asks staff not to:

- Fob people off
- Force the fun
- Act unnaturally, or talk like it's scripted

- Interrupt
- Be elitist
- Be too busy
- Take it personally if people don't want to chat

So rather than hitting new employees up with an ill-conceived blah mission statement like *'Virgin Active is committed to providing the greatest health and fitness club experience to every member every day',* The Guide is a smorgasbord of bite-sized, easy to digest and very pragmatic mini-mission statements that also act as calls to action. It also manages to keep it very real by saying things like, *'As much as we like to think we're a pretty great company, and we want you to love coming to work every day, we can't expect you and our members to love us unconditionally. We've got to earn it.'*

The simple fact is that as important as a good business plan and a clearly defined corporate mission might be, both are worthless unless they are woven into the fabric of your people's daily lives. For this to happen it takes strong leaders at every level of the organisation who recognise that one of their key roles is to continually reinforce the importance of remaining faithful to the corporate creed. To put it differently, a well-written 'mission statement' can be a helpful management tool but only if it can be used to lock in a high level of 'mission commitment' from the staff and is reinforced by senior management at every opportunity.

A MAN, A PLAN, A MANIFESTO

Along with Hemingway's six-word story, the other piece of clever writing that stuck with me from school was the longest palindrome (something that reads the same backwards as forwards) I have ever seen. It reads, 'A man, a plan, a canal – Panama.' But I am getting off track. As memorable as they might be, I am not suggesting palindromes would make good mission statements but when I first read Active's Guide document it struck me that it was neither a mission statement nor an employee handbook; if anything it could probably be best described as a 'manifesto'.

Hopefully that word hasn't been too tarnished by the way it is used by a lot of politicians running for office where the definition of a manifesto would frequently be 'a series of empty promises'. I have to say, though, that given the paucity of good mission statements out there, the time may be ripe for a change, and so 'manifestos' may be the way to go. Certainly in popular usage at least, a manifesto does seem to imply much more of a call to action than any mission statement, however well written.

So consider if you will the manifesto produced by Ron Faris who was formerly head of marketing for Virgin Media and has just started Virgin Mega, one of our newest businesses. Its purpose is to sell – oops, Ron wouldn't approve of that word. Its purpose is to 'enhance the discovery of all things around music'. It features a mobile app where fans can get in-line online to acquire limited edition goods, play all kinds of fun games and enter contests to jump the queue. It also features real-life bricks-and-mortar pop-up stores with all kind of limited edition clothing, art, concert tickets etc. around specific popular artists and upcoming shows where waiting in line is an important part of the mission – a visual demonstration of your fanaticism. There is also a website where fans can get in-line-on-line to acquire the same kind of limited edition goods and play all kinds of fun games and contests to jump the line. But let me have Ron explain it as he does in his 'manifesto', which I found to be an extremely emotive document:

'*These days, too much is for sale. More energy is spent on the convenience of what to buy rather than the passion for what you're buying. Nothing stands for anything any more. Everything is everywhere. Convenience has no soul. It's time to take retail back. Take it all underground. If the world is about ubiquity, then we're about scarcity and intimacy.*

Virgin Mega sells products inspired by bands and pop culture that you can't find anywhere else. We thrive on the "now". Not what's coming in ten minutes or what happened ten minutes ago. It's about what's about to happen. That moment between the line you waited in for hours and its epic payoff. The Hype.

Virgin Mega is not about shopping. It's about hunting and coveting. True fans wait in line. In rain. A lot. Because they care. And sometimes what you go through to get the things that rock is just as rewarding as what you get. It's the experience. The friends 'n' things you discover while waiting in that line.

Virgin Mega is for the fanatic. Whatever makes you tick. The more you love music the more we love you. We'll bring you closer to the artists you love by serving up clothes, kicks, art, and tickets. All inspired by the music and pop culture you dig and all of it fuelling the addiction you have to lifestyle. All our products are limited and numbered. Sometimes what we sell won't be easy to find. And sometimes if you're not paying attention, they'll vanish before your eyes. For ever. You'll have to pay attention. You'll have to prove your fanship. You'll have to wait in line. A lot. And you'll love every minute of it. Come hang at Virgin Mega. Unlock what rocks.'

So if that isn't enough to move you over to pithy, engaging manifestos rather than old-fashioned wimpy mission statements, then I suspect you're a lost cause.

I'm kidding, of course, but if you must have a mission statement, above all else I urge you to keep it real, make it unique to your company and keep it concise. And when you've done all that, just for fun, give it what I call the 'escutcheon test' – try to imagine it on the bottom of a heraldic coat of arms. Maybe it's a throwback to my old school motto or something, but I have always thought that if the Virgin Group were ever to adopt such a motto, then something along the lines of

'Ipsum Sine Timore, Consectetur'

would look incredibly impressive on a scroll right below our familiar red Virgin logo.

Loosely translated from the Latin this means '*Screw It, Let's Do It*' and, as mission statements go, that's about as real as it gets!

PART TWO

BRUSH UP
PREPARE
GAIN
REVIEW
TRAIN IN
DRINK IN
BE TAUGHT
DETERMINE
LEARN
BECOME VERSED
BECOME ABLE
ATTAIN
PORE OVER
GAIN
MEMORISE
LISTEN
STUDY
DETERMINE
GRASP

Chapter 6

DEFINING LEADERSHIP

And its multiple myths

'Leadership is the ability to hide your panic from others.'
Lao Tzu (sixth-century Chinese philosopher)

Based on the above, it seems that some key leadership skills haven't changed much at all in fifteen centuries. I can definitely relate to this one but in the early days of Virgin, at least, I might have been more specific and tweaked it to read, 'Leadership is the ability to hide one's panic from your bank manager!' Something I apparently failed to achieve immediately after the launch of Virgin Atlantic when, fearing we were getting in way over our heads, Coutts Bank pulled the plug on our account. Needless to say we quickly found other sources of more imaginative funding, but Lao Tzu would presumably have been less than impressed with my performance.

'THE ANSWER'S YES. NOW WHAT WAS THE QUESTION?'
In the early days of Virgin, one of our people nicknamed me 'Dr

Yes'. It was a friendly (I hope) dig at my perpetual eagerness to go along with trying new ideas. Only I knew that in part it might also have something to do with my inherent dislike of confrontation. I also mused on whether my new nickname was possibly driven by my strong resemblance to Sean Connery in his portrayal of James Bond in the 1962 movie *Dr. No*, but I fear that was just wishful thinking. Anyway I did have to laugh many years later when I read somewhere that then British prime minister, Tony Blair, had said, *'The art of leadership is saying no. It is always very easy to say yes.'* Hmm, looks like I lost out on that leadership trait as well!

One very positive and rapidly spreading development in the modern definition of leadership is how it is becoming much less about power vested in a single person or role, and more about a collective process in which the authority and power is shared by a group with a shared interest. The way in which the Elders tackle major conflicts and other serious global issues is a perfect example of this mode of operation. The team is comprised of elder statesmen (and women) from all over the world like Kofi Annan, Graça Machel, former US president Jimmy Carter, Mary Robinson and Fernando Cardoso, who have come together with the single-minded goal of working together for peace and human rights. In a world of over-inflated corporate egos and boardroom skirmishes it is truly humbling to see these amazing people's work ethic and dedication to simply getting it done.

This expansive networking of the leadership role means that it is no longer the exclusive domain of just those folks with a 'C' in their titles. It always irks me to hear references to things like 'our leadership team'. Such exclusionary terminology is a big mistake, not only because of its deification of the illustrious chosen few with Cs in their titles, but more importantly the implication that by default everyone else is not a leader! In fact, the only meaningful thing on your business card is your name and your contact information. The title beneath it says nothing about the level of respect you deserve from the person you hand it to – that's all down to what you say and do, or in some cases *don't* say and do from that point on. Just as seniority is usually just a measure of tenure and has specific linkage to contribution, unfortunately titles have no true bearing on anyone's true ability to lead.

The fact is that one way or another and to varying degrees we are all leaders in our own orbits, be it in our families, our communities, among our peer groups or in the office. You can be well below 'C level' and still be a valuable leader. The really good news about the spreading of authority through a more collective approach is that it gives a much bigger stage on which a wider set of cast members get a chance to show how well they can perform.

I'm not at all keen on printed corporate organisation structures. You know, the ones that start with the CEO or president sitting in splendid isolation in the little box on the top row and then fans out line by line in a perceived descending order of importance. I actually once heard a senior executive complain that his position on such a chart was an insult as it had his box positioned a fraction of an inch lower than that of someone he considered to be his peer. My rather curt response to this utterly childish comment is not something I'd want to put in print, but suffice it to say I think he got the point. If you really feel such charts are necessary, I much prefer the orbital variety. That's the type where the CEO sits in a circle in the centre of the page and all of his direct reports are in smaller globes that encircle the CEO – almost as if he or she were the centre of his or her own little solar system. It might sound odd but try it – at least nobody has a beef about their respective levels as they are all in an equidistant orbit from the Sun God in the centre.

In my experience, any culture with an over-emphasis on 'knowing your position' creates problems that get in the way of relationships, causes resentment and, as a direct result of this, can interfere with progress and innovation. The demarcation lines that any form of elitism creates can only serve to harden the walls of departmental silos that need to be softened not reinforced. Also, I've found that hierarchies based upon strictly observed pecking orders are usually denied the multiple layers of leadership that one finds in healthy results-oriented rather than status-conscious structures. Call it the 'Don't ask me, I just work here' syndrome if you will, but when there is an authoritarian ruler at the top of the heap, almost every layer beneath them is much less likely to make timely decisions based on their own instincts, preferring instead to push everything 'upstairs' and thereby reducing the chances of either getting it wrong and/or overstepping their corporate marks.

LUNCH BOXES

To this day some cultures are much more accepting of blind respect (or at least an appearance thereof) for traditional highly tiered pecking orders than others. Japan would be one example of this, and even a few older European companies tend to still have a somewhat 'Upstairs Downstairs' attitude to their employee 'class system'. A few years ago I was invited to lunch in the executive dining room of a long-established London-based company. I was amazed to find that their lordly executive dining room had its own private chefs, more waiters than diners and the food and service were as good as many a top city restaurant – complete with a lengthy wine list. I am sure such things may still exist, even if that particular company is no longer around, but hopefully not for much longer. When the senior management of a company considers itself too precious to share the same food and dining space as the rest of their people, then frankly it would not be a place I'd want to work!

There is a lot of ancient and still valid symbolism involved with breaking bread together. It is something that healthy families will still do, while dysfunctional households seldom sit down to a meal together. In business too there is a lot to be said for encouraging all of your employees to mingle over mealtimes and if you are the head honcho, you too should try and make a point of joining them on a regular basis. When we built our new headquarters building for Virgin Atlantic outside of London – officially named 'The Office' long before the TV show of the same name – I think we spent more time designing the centrally located, ground-floor dining hall than we did any other part of the facility. It was time and effort well spent as it fast became the social centre of the building with every level of employee meeting and eating there on a daily basis – and why not? The food is excellent!

GOOD VERSUS 'EVILUTION'

While a good manager will have the ability to supervise others, keep them within company guidelines, play by the rules and read the maps they're handed, all this tells you nothing about how comfortable they will be going off-road and breaking new ground. Striking out in new unexplored directions takes a whole different mindset and one that often means breaking, or at least massaging, a few of the old rules. Management is much more about maintaining processes, disciplines and systems than about changing them. Strong leaders, on the other hand, while maintaining stability, must have vision, creativity and, perhaps most importantly, the ability to influence others to follow and support them in the challenges of moving an organisation into uncharted and often highly risky territory.

Good leadership is by definition all about taking the venture forward and finding viable new avenues where the business can evolve and prosper. Poor leadership, on the other hand, typically tends to be static, much more about protecting the status quo and, if there are any around, resting on laurels. This 'don't rock the boat' approach may have been a viable business model twenty years ago, but at the frenetic pace of business today it is no longer an option. To stand still today is to go backwards – and quickly!

While I have found that outstanding leadership tends to come in a huge range of very different and often quite quirky and eccentric packages, poor leadership usually displays a lot of common denominators. There are also a lot of contradictions, however. For instance, how would one rate a leader with the reputation for being 'Such a great guy – he never gets in anybody's face and just lets us all get on with our jobs'? Such an individual could either be a highly skilled delegator or just someone who has no stomach for confrontation. While few people – myself included – genuinely enjoy confrontational situations, when they arise, dealing with them in a timely manner is an inescapable and important part of effective leadership. Some leaders are frequently guilty of shying away from anything that might result in an altercation in the mistaken impression that this will make them more likeable to their employees. The reasons for an aversion to facing up to confrontation can be several: either they just don't have a sufficient level of confidence in their own technical understanding of the problem to be able to stand their ground and win, or frequently they'd simply prefer to turn a blind eye in the hope that by ignoring the issue it will over time somehow manage to sort itself out. Unfortunately, failing to confront a problem while it's at the smouldering stage will more often than not only lead to its proliferation into a fully fledged fire that is much harder to extinguish and can do a lot of long-term damage.

Another relatively common confrontation avoidance technique with weak leaders is to always have someone else on hand to take care of the dirty work on their behalf. This will typically involve having a senior management 'hatchet man' to handle anything where they don't want to risk dirtying their own hands or damaging their 'Mr Nice Guy' reputation. Is this an example of skilful delegation? I think not.

There seems to be a lot of confusion around the subtle but critical differences between 'delegation' and its first cousin 'relegation'. Simply stated, 'delegation' is handing on the responsibility for a situation together with the authority to resolve it. Relegation on the other hand is simply pushing a problem away but without including the power to really do anything much about it – except perhaps to shoulder the blame. In short, one of the most common mistakes to be found in poor leaders is an inability to understand the difference between these two ways of working. In the same way that this kind of leader is skilled at relegating blame, they are usually very good at holding their people accountable – everyone, that is, except themselves.

TAKE ME TO YOUR BLEEDER

A classic example of what can go tragically wrong in the absence of smart forward-thinking leadership has to be what happened to Kodak. For over a century Kodak was virtually synonymous with photography all around the world. They invented the automatic camera over a hundred years ago, and 'A Kodak Moment' (a photo opportunity) became part of the English language. When I was about twelve years old, I remember my excitement one Christmas at getting my very first camera. It was *the* coolest camera of the day, a

Kodak Brownie Box Camera, and I was beside myself with delight.

But times change and while Kodak should have been in the driver's seat when digital photography first emerged – in 1975 they had developed a digital camera that was the first of its kind – the product was soon dropped for fear it would threaten their existing photographic film business. Instead of embracing the opportunities that the new technology presented and exploiting their resources to lead the charge, Kodak's senior management instead seemed to bury their heads in the sand. It was almost as if they believed that if, as the industry leader, they were to ignore it then digital might magically go away – but like King Canute who thought he could turn back the tide, they were very much mistaken.

Eventually, seeing the error of their ways, Kodak condescended to try and create contrived synergies such as 'Photo CD' that fell somewhere between their traditional analogue offerings and digital technology, but compromises seldom work. While Kodak tried desperately to hang on to the past and the huge 70 per cent profit margins they had enjoyed from their traditional film business, newcomers to the camera game like Sony swept right on by them and, as they say in the US, 'ate their lunch'. Kodak's share price dropped by 80 per cent in 2011 and they filed for Chapter 11 bankruptcy protection in January of 2012. It took until September 2013 for Kodak to emerge from bankruptcy protection as a greatly pared-down and I suspect, much wiser company. The fact that other major analogue-era imaging companies like Canon, Nikon and Leica all successfully navigated the transition to digital would seem to indicate that the only plausible reason for Kodak's rapid decline was a catastrophic failure in leadership. And as is almost always the case, leaders who spend too much time looking in the rear-view mirror are seldom positioned to navigate the road ahead.

My interest in the Kodak story stems from my own experiences with the winding down of our once-booming pre-digital Virgin Megastore business. Like Kodak, I too was guilty of a very similar reluctance to accept the havoc that digital technology was about to wreak upon one of our core businesses. Virgin Megastores (our music retailing business) was very near and dear to me, I suspect in much the same way as the film business was to Kodak. Virgin had been in the record retailing business since opening our first little shop in London in 1971 – in fact, back then it was our only business! By the early nineties that one shop had expanded to scores of gigantic Virgin Megastores all over the world.

But, just as it was doing in the photography world, digital technology, especially in the shape of Steve Jobs and iTunes, was about to dramatically transform the recorded music business for ever. The industry had seen an ever-evolving parade of different formats over the years, from vinyl record albums and singles, to eight-track tapes (remember those?) to cassette tapes, which heralded the portable era and eventually compact discs that for a while everyone seemed to think were the ultimate solution. But it wasn't to be, and the arrival of online digital downloading rendered CDs, and with them our bricks and mortar retail model, obsolete faster than you can say 'iCry'. We desperately tried to compensate for the nosedive in CD sales by stocking all kinds of other products, like computer peripherals, board games, books, and even pop-culture fashion items. Then in 2005 we made a belated last gasp attempt to squeeze our way into the download business with Virgin Digital and the Virgin Pulse MP3 player, but it was incompatible with the all-conquering iPod and so became a classic case of too little too late.

Mea culpa. As appears to have been the case at Kodak, I was guilty of turning a deaf ear to the dire warnings and as a result I paid the price – literally!

We still have a limited interest in a couple of stores but we could have saved ourselves a lot of money had we – or that should really be 'had I' – been willing to read the writing on the wall a little sooner, cut our losses and bid a fond farewell to a business that had served us well for three decades. As a somewhat quirky friend of mine likes to say, 'If things don't change, they'll be the same tomorrow as they are today.' Well, things do change, and in cases like the digital revolution you have just got to recognise you've come to a watershed and move on.

LEADING FROM THE PERIPHERY

Another myth on leadership is that successful entrepreneurs should be able to take their ideas and run with them when they become the nucleus of a new business. Management guru Peter Drucker deftly defines an entrepreneur as, '*Someone who searches for change, responds to it and exploits opportunities. Innovation is a specific tool of an entrepreneur hence an effective entrepreneur converts a source into a resource.*'

None of that suggests to me that an entrepreneur is expected to stay around to lead a company once he or she has set the ball in motion, but neither does it say that they cannot stay around the periphery as a force for on-going change. I sometimes think that entrepreneurs have a lot in common with scouts for professional sports organisations. They are out there talent-spotting, whether with established stars on other teams or undiscovered, up-and-coming raw young talent that hasn't made it big as yet. They usually understand how the corporate puzzle fits together every bit as well as the team manger but are the unsung heroes who have the insight to recognise something special and recommend bringing in new and better players to improve the team. In fact, they often add more value to the overall picture by *not* trying to manage it – something I didn't cotton on to early enough with Megastores.

It is no small coincidence that I felt such a strong tie to our music business as it was the last one I actually ran before I drifted off into my new career as a serial entrepreneur. That said, over the years I have spent a lot more hands-on time around some Virgin companies than others – the early years at Virgin Atlantic would be one example – but I usually make a conscious effort to try and stay out of the day-to-day decision-making as it really isn't my thing. And besides, when I expect our senior people to take ownership of their decisions then the last thing they need is someone like me continually trying to foist his usually inexpert opinions on them.

What an entrepreneurial eye can bring to an operating business, however, is that same spirit of inquisitiveness that recognises gaps that can be filled with new products and services and, in turn, occasionally new spin-off business opportunities. At the same time, the Virgin way of managing our businesses is all about maintaining and promoting that almost childish curiosity level in our people to ensure they are never accepting of the status quo and always looking for ways to improve upon it. The subject matter experts are often way too willing to take the obvious path (their expertise, after all, is based on what they have seen and done in the past) and so every once in a while a few jabs in the ribs from an annoying entrepreneur is not a bad thing. As David Tait, who was one of the first people at Virgin Atlantic, likes to tell it, in the early stages of the airline I reminded him of his young kids as my favourite question was always 'Why?' And to this day it's probably still my favourite question, especially with a new business segment about which I know very little. It's not that I don't trust the staff, it's simply that I want to understand how things work. The upside to my constant 'why-ing' is often that it makes people start to revalidate a few long-established practices and in the process sometimes stumble on better ways to do them.

Over the years numerous Virgin people have found that telling me something will never work is by no means the best way to convince me we shouldn't try it – quite the opposite, in fact. As trite as it may sound, one of my favourite lines when someone expresses doubts about trying something new for reasons like 'it has never been done before' or 'it's been tried before and no one has ever succeeded' is to say (with a smile), 'Great! Well, why don't we look at how we can do it differently and be the first ones to make it work?' That was pretty much what we did with Virgin Atlantic, and once we got it in the air we have always maintained the same approach. I mean, how many other airlines would have seriously considered a crazy idea like putting massage therapists or stand-up bars on board its airplanes? Sometimes not knowing enough about the 'correct way to do things' and doing them anyway can open up the most amazing new doorways.

While I have never felt either the urge or the need to go back and grab the reins at any of our companies, some entrepreneurs have found that knowing when to step back into a company they founded can be every bit as important as knowing when to exit. The classic example has to be how after a twelve-year exile Steve Jobs returned to Apple and how the company (unfortunately for my beloved Megastores), which was on the brink of failing, really took off when Steve reassumed the full-time CEO role after a spell as what he jokingly called 'iCEO for 'Interim CEO'.

At Google as well, in early 2011, ten years after he had stepped out, co-founder Larry Page returned to the company as full-time CEO. When he left there were barely a thousand employees and when he returned there were 25,000. Needless to say a lot changes in any company that grows twenty-five-fold in just ten years! When Larry returned, his priorities were never officially announced but everyone seemed to agree it had to be stripping away some layers of management to reinvent that start-up energy and buzz that always seems to foster an altogether higher level of creative energy.

Warding off the social media threats of Twitter and Facebook, which were both still in more adolescent corporate stages, was also I am sure a big motivator in Larry's decision to step back in. One way or another the company has continued to flourish since Larry's return to the top job. When he took over as CEO, Google's stock price was hovering around the $500 mark and the last time I checked it had remained in a steady ascent and was pushing $1,200.

So, don't believe anyone that tries to make blanket statements to the effect that entrepreneurs are or are not well suited to the task of running the companies they created. The inescapable fact is that no two people and no two companies are alike and even then circumstances and economic conditions can complicate any given scenario. If they persist in pushing for an opinion, then I would simply respond by saying, 'Do the names Steve Jobs and Larry Page mean anything to you?'

Chapter 7

WHAT CHANCE LUCK?

Fortune favours the bold

I believe that 'luck' is one of the most misunderstood and under-appreciated factors in life. Those people and businesses that are generally considered fortunate or luckier than others are usually also the ones that are prepared to take the greatest risks and, by association, are also prepared to fall flat on their faces every so often. In stark contrast, the 'play it safe for fear of failing' brigade are the ones who just never seem to get as lucky as the risk-takers. Coincidence? I don't think so. Sadly the vast majority of people seem to view their chances of 'getting lucky' in much the same vein as the likelihood of being struck by lightning, as if it is something over which they have zero control. Well, in my humble opinion they couldn't be further from the truth – anyone who wants to make the effort to work on their luck can and will seriously improve it.

I remember watching the final round of the British Open golf championship on TV and seeing one of the leaders chip out of a unker. His shot was high but it just clipped the top nd amazingly the ball dropped right into the hole. One of the British commentary team exclaimed, 'Oh my goodness, what a lucky shot!' Another commentator in the broadcast booth (a retired American champion as I recall) immediately snapped back with a stinging rebuke, 'Lucky! What do you mean "lucky"? Do you know how many thousands of hours we all spend practising shots like that? He was trying to put it in the hole and he succeeded. Let me tell you, he worked long and hard on getting that lucky!' The same sentiment was more eloquently expressed once by Gary Player one of the all-time golf greats, who famously said, '*The harder I practise, the luckier I get.*'

Over the years, like that golfer, I have often been accused of being lucky in business, but I too believe that a lot of very hard work has played a major part in any luck that has come my way. I must admit to sometimes struggling to figure out where coincidence stops and good luck begins, or put differently, how just happening to 'be in the right place at the right time' can so dramatically play into one's path through life.

A LUCKY EXORCISM

One classic example of this phenomenon had a huge bearing on the early success of Virgin Records. To our surprise and delight, our first-ever album release, Mike Oldfield's *Tubular Bells,* had become a huge hit in the UK but we were still trying to get someone to take it in the US. Despite this European success and my persistent efforts,

I just couldn't seem to convince the legendary head of Atlantic Records, Ahmet Ertegun, that an all-instrumental album would sell in North America. Regrettably he just didn't 'get it'. Then one day while Ahmet just happened to be playing the album in his office (presumably still trying to figure out what all the fuss was about) in walked movie director William Friedkin looking for backing music for a movie he had in the works. By an amazing stroke of good fortune, before Ahmet could turn it off, Friedkin heard *Tubular Bells*, instantly loved it and that was that: he had his backing track and we had our US deal with Atlantic. Oh yes, and the movie he was working on just happened to be *The Exorcist*, which was destined to become one of the greatest box-office hits of the day and so it also helped introduce *Tubular Bells* to a global audience. You could call it luck if you want, but there again I'd spent a lot of time yammering away at Ahmet and if he hadn't been intrigued enough to listen to it one more time it would probably never have been playing at that critical moment in time.

THE LUCK OF THE CHILEAN

And then there are those other serendipitous situations that come along perhaps once in a lifetime where being in the right place at the right time can tee up an opportunity with no preparation at all. When that happens it falls to the individual's ability to recognise the situation for what it is and seize the moment.

My friend, let's call him Antonio, was raised in Santiago, Chile and eventually attended California's prestigious Stanford

University where he would earn a post-graduate degree in Business Administration and Behavioral Sciences. One day, while he was attending Stanford, Antonio was standing at the back of a long line outside a movie theatre when he and the stranger next to him were told that the show had sold out and they'd have to come back another day. Equally miffed, the two of them struck up a conversation and, with some unanticipated free time on their hands, ended up going for a cup of coffee together. Over coffee Antonio asked what the stranger, who was also attending Stanford, was up to and was told that he and a fellow student were working on a research project that was something to do with search engines. As they parted company the other student handed over a copy of his research paper and suggested my friend read it over and they could talk some more the next day.

Antonio said he tried reading the highly technical document that night but the bulk of it was all about algorithms and the like and way over his head. He was, however, highly intrigued with the object of the exercise which was to organise the vast amount of information on the web according to the popularity of the pages. In short it struck him as an idea that had a lot of market potential. When Antonio met up with his new friend the next day, therefore, he asked how he could get involved. He was told they were in the early stages of raising capital to launch their business, that it was valued at a million dollars and they'd love to have him as an investor. In what was to become the watershed moment of his life, Antonio responded by saying, 'Well, I have $10,000 that was earmarked for a second-hand car but I might consider putting it into your company instead. What would that get me?' He was told it would give him a one per cent ownership stake and so they agreed that they had a deal.

If you haven't guessed it by now, the student Antonio had been speaking to was one Sergey Brin, and his partner went by the name of Larry Page. Although it was initially nicknamed 'Back Rub', the plan had been to brand their company 'Googol' after the mathematical term, but they opted to change this to the quirkier 'Google'. A wacky word, perhaps, but one that was destined to become part of the vocabulary in just about every language on the planet.

A counterpoint to my friend Antonio's story is that of Ronald Wayne. Wayne had worked alongside Steve Jobs at Atari and became one of the co-founders of Apple with Jobs and Wozniak. At forty years of age, Wayne was almost twice as old as his young co-founders and so he agreed to essentially act as the venture's 'adult supervisor' in return for which he was given a ten per cent stake in the nascent company. Among other things Wayne drew up the partnership agreement between the three, drafted the first company logo and wrote the Apple 1 manual. For a variety of reasons, however, Wayne just didn't feel comfortable that things were going to work out – he also didn't particularly enjoy working with Jobs – and so after only a couple of months Wayne called it quits and relinquished his stock in the company for a one-time pay-out of $800. Had he toughed it out and hung in there, that stock would today have been worth close to fifty billion dollars! So was it bad luck or bad judgement? Maybe a bit of both, but I'll let you make up your own mind on this one.

My Chilean friend was no Ronald Wayne and has been astute enough never to sell a single Google share and has reinvested all his dividends. He never got the used car but that $10,000 is now worth billions of dollars. Suffice it to say that the luckiest thing that ever happened to Antonio was going to see a popular movie in a small theatre. Had there been just two more seats left, his life would have been very different! But in terms of making the luck work for him he had to have the smarts to recognise an opportunity when it came along and greater still the guts to risk his $10,000 – about all he had at the time – on a couple of young fellow students with a dream. This one I'd certainly put down to a combination of good luck and good judgement: two elements that the sum of which will always be greater than the whole.

LUCK DOWN UNDER

Over the years, we have had quite a few events around the Virgin companies that have been described as lucky but perhaps none bigger than in 2000 when we set up shop in Australia with the fledgling Virgin Blue. We started in anticipation of having at least two major competitors in Qantas Airlines and Ansett Australia. Qantas was the flag carrier and Ansett had been around since 1935. We knew that Ansett had been experiencing financial difficulties but they had just been acquired by Air New Zealand and Singapore Airlines so we thought they were probably going to work things out. That was not to be the case, however, and over the Christmas period of 2000 we got a major traffic boost for our then tiny operation when the Australian aviation authorities partially grounded Ansett's fleet for maintenance infractions. They bounced back, however, and in April of 2001 actually made an abortive attempt to buy us out – I was having none of it – which was a clear indication that as small as we were, they probably saw us as a major future threat to their survival.

By September the writing was on the wall for Ansett when, having funded their loss of almost $200 million in the previous year, Air New Zealand and Singapore Airlines cut them adrift. Then on 14 September 2001 Ansett grounded its entire fleet of 100-plus airplanes and ceased operations, stranding thousands of passengers and pitching upwards of 16,000 staff out of their jobs. Ansett's demise not only suddenly thrust us into the limelight as the country's second largest carrier but it also opened up terminal space at a number of airports around Australia where we had been struggling to get decent facilities.

So was it luck or was it more a matter of just happening to be in the right place at the right time? I think as with my friend Antonio it was a bit of both. We went into Australia to start the airline anticipating that Ansett would be part of the scenery for a long time to come. We were comfortable that we could give them a run for their money and our plans were not based on them going out of business. Did Ansett's demise help us to expand and flourish in Australia at a faster rate than we might otherwise have done? Absolutely! But like Alberto having the courage to hand over his

$10,000, we too had taken the step of putting ourselves in the right place when someone else's misfortune became our good fortune.

This wasn't the first time we had experienced such good fortune with our airlines. What happened in Australia was almost a carbon copy of what Virgin Atlantic had experienced in the UK fourteen years earlier. In late 1987, just two and a half years after we took to the skies, British Caledonian (popularly known as 'B-Cal'), then Britain's second largest airline, which had been struggling for several years, was acquired by British Airways. At first we opposed the takeover, thinking it would make for an even more powerful BA, but we quickly realised that this particular cloud had a very silver, if not positively golden, lining. As soon as B-Cal ceased operations it opened up some very exciting new routes authorities for us – we were able to pick up London to New York's main international gateway JFK (we had previously been limited to operating into Newark, New Jersey), as well as Tokyo and Los Angeles, to which we started service to in 1988, 1989 and 1990 respectively. Boston, San Francisco and Hong Kong would follow later. Had B-Cal stayed around, we might never have gained access to these very profitable routes, or at the very least it would certainly have taken much longer for us to get operating approvals. Once again, some called it luck but I prefer to see it as a direct consequence of having the courage to put yourself in the right place at the right time – despite all the so-called aviation experts who, as one, had averred that Virgin Atlantic was the wrong idea in the wrong place at the wrong time!

It has always intrigued me how people are so quick to say, 'Wow, they got really lucky with that one', thereby totally dismissing any possible contribution the lucky one may have made to the positive turn of events. The same people are seldom as swift to say 'Oh that was just bad luck' when someone experiences a problem, even if through no real fault of their own. I firmly believe that smart leaders and clever entrepreneurs have the knack of engineering their luck – it's also known as risk-taking – just as Brett Godfrey rolled the dice and they came up sixes by having us in Australia at exactly the right time. So work hard at improving your luck: remember not to stand under a tree during a thunderstorm and never be afraid to talk to strangers – you never know, your Sergey might be out there!

You can call it what you like, luck, good fortune, coincidence, serendipity, right place at the right time, or even 'hard work', but I think no one has defined this mysterious element any better than the Roman philosopher Seneca who some two thousand years ago said, *'Luck is what happens when preparation meets opportunity.'*

Amen to that.

Chapter 8

TYPICALLY ATYPICAL

An aversion to the average

Several years ago I remember being given a Virgin baseball cap to wear at some promotional event in the US. When I tried to put it on it was way too tight for me, so risking the inevitable jibe about my head getting too big, I politely asked if I could please have a larger one. The response I got was so utterly nonsensical that it has stuck with me to this day – 'Sorry, Richard, but these are "one size fits all" caps, so it should fit you.' Wrong!

Unfortunately for consumers – and luckily for entrepreneurs looking for opportunities – it's not just baseball cap manufacturers who take such an incredibly blinkered approach to their consumers' real needs. Unless you are talking to a roomful of automatons, one size will never fit all of anything or anyone! I may not have been very good at mathematics at school, but I did learn enough to know that catering strictly to the average anything means that, to varying degrees, everyone else on either end of the scale is being seriously compromised.

DO THE NUMBERS ADD UP?

At the time of our two biggest ventures into transportation –Virgin Atlantic and Virgin Trains – both industries had countless similarities. Commercial aviation was in pretty dire straits and in desperate need of a fresh and creative makeover, and the crumbling segment of British Rail that we inherited with the West Coast Line was in a state of utter decay and on the point of collapse. The only saving grace with rail was that with the old nationalised British Rail system, the travelling public had become so completely inured to dreadful service being an inescapable fact that any changes we made could only make things better. In the sky, commercial aviation was not quite as bad as on the tracks but service was generally lacklustre and overpriced.

As a complete neophyte to both businesses (other than as a disgruntled passenger), I was the one continually asking our employees the seemingly silliest of questions. On the one hand I genuinely wanted to learn how things worked, but on the other I also wanted to be sure that we were seizing every opportunity, big and small, to do things better. The response to my questions would often be a resigned, 'Okay, Richard, if you really want to know, getting to XYZ is a simple matter of two plus two making four.' When I saw for myself that the numbers did add up then I was happy; I'd learned something and occasionally we'd even agree that perhaps 3+1 might be a more interesting way than the standard 2+2 to arrive at the same number. Other times, however, the response would be one of, 'Two plus two makes... er, uhmm, sorry, that's strange – it always used to add up to four but I keep getting five as an answer now. I'll take another look at that one and get back to you.'

One such example was in the early days of Virgin Atlantic when I found out we were planning to use the 'typical' crude old rubber tube headsets for listening to on-board movies that were the standard at the time. With the music industry just getting into Walkmen and electronic headsets, it struck me we could be the first to take a giant leap in inflight entertainment sound quality if we went electronic. When I suggested we look into it I was immediately told that it would be too expensive and wasn't something our budgets would allow. Undaunted, I asked our on-board product person (at that stage it wasn't yet 'people') to take a look at it and then, on a whim, said, 'And while you're at it, see what it would cost to give the electronic headsets away at the end of every flight.' With our logo on them it struck me that they could be a great way to spread brand awareness if we got people using Virgin Atlantic headsets on their personal Walkmen. I think they all thought I was absolutely nuts but agreed to humour me and take a look at it.

What came out in the end was quite remarkable. We discovered that giving away the electronic headsets after every flight was actually marginally less expensive than recycling the old-style rubber ones. The time, effort and cost involved in collecting them back, repairing, cleaning and repackaging them was substantial and after all that the passengers still had to live with uncomfortable spaghetti-like tubes that had terrible sound quality to boot. Before long you would see our headsets popping up all over the place and I even recall an American business traveller telling me that his teenage kids encouraged him to fly Virgin because they loved the headsets he brought home after every trip. A good example of finding better solutions for the same or less cost simply by always asking how it can be done differently. I don't think I admitted it at the time, but frankly I was expecting to be told that the new headsets would be way too expensive!

So the moral here is that while curiosity may not be good for cats, for business leaders it is a very healthy and often a very productive trait. And when two and two does make four I have always found that it makes your people feel pretty good about themselves when they get an opportunity to show off their know-how to 'the boss' with a discreet 'I told you so!'

When we started Virgin Atlantic in 1984 I remember a hard-bitten *New York Times* aviation correspondent almost sneeringly asking, 'Why on earth, Mr Branson, could you possibly believe that the world needs another airline at a time when the typical carrier is struggling to survive?' I think he was more than a little surprised when I started out by agreeing that, 'You're absolutely correct. So you can take it from me that this is precisely why there will be nothing "typical" about Virgin Atlantic.' The man's thinly veiled smirk indicated that he clearly didn't believe a word of it, but for thirty years now, what someone once dubbed 'The Little Airline That Could' has surprised a lot of sceptics by refusing to become just another airline.

HORSES FOR McCOURSES

It is pretty well known around Virgin that as a matter of principle, even with things that are better than average, I have always refused to rank anything as a perfect ten. The irrefutable fact is that no matter how good something might be, there is always room for improvement – and furthermore, as my father used to love to say, there are also 'horses for courses'. By this I mean that no matter how well something may work in one marketplace, there are very few products or services that will be as well received in New York as they are in New Guinea.

There are, of course, notable exceptions to this with Coca-Cola and Apple probably topping a very short list. But even such iconic staples as a McDonald's 'Big Mac' doesn't always stand up to a global taste test. In India, for example, a predominantly Hindu nation where beef is not eaten, they were forced to rethink their benchmark burger. I discovered this for myself when on a business trip to Delhi I once made the mistake of asking for a Big Mac and was very politely told that I could have a 'Chicken Maharaja Mac' or a 'McAloo Tikki Mac', which I was informed featured 'a meatless patty of potato and peas'. As I recall, I ended up doing what I should really have done in the first place and went somewhere else for a curry. It did stick with me, however, that to take their show on the road, even a megabrand like McDonald's can, on occasion, be forced to 'think outside the bun'.

APPLE SEEDS SALES

Another brand that is anything but typical in its approach to every element of doing business is Apple. Steve Jobs' fanaticism for product design and detail was (and still is) seamlessly visible all the way from technical form and function to packaging to the Apple Stores. And boy, has it ever paid off – there is nothing remotely 'average' about an Apple Store. I find the shopping experience there to be a disarming cross between visiting an art gallery and some form of an electronics exhibition that has been stripped of everything but the coolest and best the business has to offer. But as is always the case in every field of endeavour, it is not just the store design or the 'stuff' that makes for an exceptional service experience, it is the people providing the service.

In 2012 the research firm 'RetailSails' reported that in the US the annual average sales per square foot in mall-based retail stores was $341. Not surprisingly, perhaps, Tiffany, the iconic jeweller's, was second highest in the country with $3,017 per square foot – nine times the national average. But the runaway leader was Apple with an astounding $6,050 in sales per square foot of store space. According to another retail analyst Asymco, that sales number broke down to a quite remarkable $57.60 *per visitor,* of which around $12 was profit. Simply incredible numbers indeed but why, you might ask, am I so intrigued by them? Well, because even with a great product line like Apple's, fantastic results like this don't just happen – they are a direct consequence of something behind the numbers the techy analysts tend to overlook: excellent and plentiful customer service supplied by real people!

Walk into any Apple Store in the world, as I did on a recent visit to New York City, and you will usually find the place is swarming with people. Look a little bit more closely at the make-up of the crowd, however, and you can't help but notice that almost every other person is wearing the distinctive blue or red polo shirt of an Apple 'sales associate'. They're everywhere! On walking in, there's usually at least one of them there to smilingly welcome you and *discreetly* (which is a vital part of the process) ask if they can help in any way. But it's not just the sheer number of assistants that's so outstanding – it's the people themselves. I have never failed to be impressed by the fact that Apple seems to have truly nailed the vital skill of picking great people to work for them: something that I can unashamedly claim is also the number one secret behind Virgin's success. And as cool (and hot) as Apple's iPads, iPhones and the rest of their product line most certainly is, unlike a lot of boutique hotels I've experienced, Apple doesn't exclusively have a bunch of skinny 'twenty-something' dudes working there. In recognition of the fact that their customer demographic spans every age group from pre-teens to pre-octogenarians, their staffing is equally diversified. In the New York Apple Store I was helped out by a bearded sales associate who must have been almost as young as I am – really!

Contrast the Apple customer service experience with that of the 'typical' retail store – that's the genre that takes in an average of just five per cent of Apple's sales – and one has to wonder if their needle-in-a-haystack approach to staffing levels might have something to do with their comparatively miserable sales statistics. I am no retail sales analyst, but according to Asymco, Apple tripled its average sales associate-per-store count from thirty-seven in 2007 to 117 in the first quarter of 2012. And if that seems excessive, just consider that in 2012 at their more than 300 stores around the world, those Apple employees brought in a phenomenal average of $473,000 per person! That seems to me like almost half a million reasons to make sure that you always have enough, or even more than enough, well-trained, personable sales people on your shop floor, phone lines or wherever you have a customer interface, to ensure that your clients experience great customer service every time they come into contact with your people. Having a great product like Apple's certainly helps, but the icing on the cake is having great people in the front line. Get that part of the equation wrong and 'typically' poor customer service can undermine even the best of atypical products.

We saw an example of precisely this phenomenon at Virgin Atlantic some years ago when Continental Airlines launched a new business-class cabin that bore a, how shall we say, 'striking resemblance' to our Upper Class cabin and service. If imitation is the sincerest form of flattery then we should have been extremely flattered. Not only were all the cabin features virtually identical but they had even copied our on-board catering right down to things like a cheese tray and scones with clotted cream and strawberry jam! While they'd done a pretty good job of copying the hardware, what they'd failed to learn was the importance of the software, as in our cabin crew's ability to breathe something extra into the whole experience. We lost a few of our regular passengers to the new Continental service for a short while but after one or two trips they were mostly back with us telling us, how much they had missed our people.

LOYALTY IS HARD WON

If there is one thing I have learned from our range of businesses over the years it's that *true* customer loyalty is not something that can be bought and retained with bribes like frequent flier miles or occasional discount coupons. If you want to differentiate your products and services from the typical fare served up by your competition and earn the loyalty that tends to tag along then you have to recognise that your most important customers are the ones that are motivated by atypical incentives. And I am not just talking about the standard fare that Customer Relationship Management (CRM) systems can predictably facilitate. Generating employee and consumer loyalty are both about the same thing – creating a level of engagement that supersedes what's in the paycheque or the bonus loyalty plan points. The other day, for example, I heard about a young entrepreneur who had arrived one morning at the Virgin America counter in Portland, Oregon – he was in a state of utter panic. He'd been up most of the night preparing his presentation for a big investor and had somehow managed to oversleep. His Virgin flight from Portland to San Francisco had left already and there weren't any other flights to SFO that would get him there in time for his pitch of a lifetime. Rising to the challenge, our team rallied and rushed him on to a Los Angeles flight with what they described as a 'technically impossible' connection to San Francisco. To say it 'would be tight' was an understatement as his flight from Portland was scheduled to arrive in LAX a couple of minutes before the San Francisco airplane was due to leave. But our people knew the two trips were usually on not-too-distant gates and as the passenger had no bags it might just work – certainly sitting in Portland wasn't going to achieve anything! They assigned the passenger a seat at the front of the plane and told the flight crew as well as the ground crew in LAX what was happening. The pilots played their part and managed to get them to Los Angeles seven minutes early. He was met at the door by a Virgin America agent who rushed the anxious young man to his connecting gate with all of two minutes to spare – the pilot and crew on the next flight even congratulated him as he stepped on board! The icing on the cake was when we learned later that he had made it to his pitch with minutes to spare and it seems it all went well.

He wrote on his blog: 'The people at Virgin went above and beyond that day. Each and every one of them had a hand in making my unintended adventure not only successful, but enjoyable – and the best part, I didn't once feel as if I was inconveniencing any one of them.' The 'typical' and probably the expected airline response to the young man's dilemma would have been, 'Sorry, it's your problem. There's nothing we can do about it.' The demonstration of effort and kindness that comes with the alternative approach of

'You've got a problem – but let's see how *we* can try to fix it' can earn you a loyal customer for life.

And the word-of-mouth/social media buzz that frequently goes along with it can do even more for your social standing. The challenge then becomes living up to your reputation as an atypically customer-focused operation. Something that is much more fun than maintaining a typically average level of mediocrity where no one is a perfect fit.

Chapter 9

BIG DOGFIGHTS

Don't always go to the biggest dogs

'What counts is not necessarily the size of the dog in the
fight – it's the size of the fight in the dog.'

I believe it was Mark Twain who actually first wrote those words,
although they are also frequently accredited to US president Dwight
D. Eisenhower. But, no matter who was the original author, it's one
of those brilliant little sayings that makes everyone – well, me at
least – think, 'Darn, I wish I'd said that!' While 'Ike' was probably
using it in the context of some military action, it perfectly sums up
the mental attitude any entrepreneur or leader of a small start-up
has to assume when considering what will be needed to mix it up
in a space that is dominated by 'big dogs' aka big brands with big
pockets – but often little real loyalty.

WHAT'S BIG ABOUT SMALL

In the business world Virgin has always revelled in being the little guy chasing much larger and, as a result, usually cumbersome legacy-laden competitors. From day one at *Student* magazine and later at Virgin Records we were always in the David role and fighting an uphill battle just to survive against a variety of different Goliaths. The irony of the situation that most such young businesses face is that as long as you just kind of muddle along scraping, or for that matter 'scrapping', out a living, then you are far less of an endangered species than when you start to be a success. As soon as the top guy in the big corner office up the road starts hearing from his sales team that 'That little XYZ outfit that we weren't taking seriously is starting to nibble into our market share' then it's time to watch your backs.

FLY ME FROM THE GLOOM

In the history of Virgin we have run into this phenomenon in just about every new market we've plunged into, but it may have been more marked in our airline businesses than anywhere else. When we set up Virgin Atlantic in 1984 and began flying from London to New York with a single airplane it was hardly surprising, I suppose, that none of the incumbent airlines saw us as much of a threat to anyone but ourselves. Also our own people were having such a good time that casual observers might have been excused for thinking that we weren't all that serious about it ourselves. At first this led to the giants of the day, British Airways, Pan Am and TWA, all just allowing us to get on with it assuming we'd implode before we could do them any harm. And mathematically speaking, even if we'd filled the 400 or so seats on our lone 747 every day (which we often did), it still didn't represent as much as a pinprick in their sacred market share numbers. They were almost right, but they'd totally failed to grasp what we were about and that we were not into playing by the rules. If anything we were learning all the time and very much making them up as we went along.

What routinely fools a Goliath is when, instead of going after their market share, someone instead goes out to create a whole new niche market right under their imperious noses. They are well practised in defending their turf against unimaginative interlopers. This is usually achieved with such no-brainers as deep discounting, leveraging their distribution clout or what can best be described as simple bully tactics. But when someone arrives on the scene with a hybrid product that they cannot pigeonhole – as was the case with the biblical David's slingshot – it can cause massive confusion in the enemy's ranks. When all else is equal then the big guys will usually find a way to outmuscle any pesky upstart, so that is why the newcomer has got to make sure that the playing field is anything but level. In fact, you don't even want to step on to their playing field – it confuses them even more when you sprint up and down the sidelines while they get bogged down in the middle. You always know it's working when they cry foul!

So in any business where new entrants have traditionally had to buy their way in with deeply discounted fares, what do you do with someone who is suddenly pitching value for money and great customer service? Undercutting an intruder's prices alone doesn't work when price is just one of many weapons in their innovative arsenal.

Virgin Atlantic really muddied the equation by arriving on the side of the field with a product that was every bit as good if not better than our giant competitors' first-class product and streets ahead of their distinctly mediocre business classes. The real trick was branding it as 'Upper Class', a move that made most fliers assume it to be our first class. In terms of service quality it was, but by designating it as business class and pricing it accordingly, business fliers whose corporate travel policies permitted business but not first class almost saw our Upper Class as cheating the system – which suited us just fine! We drove the spike in even harder by building in complimentary limos in Upper Class, a feature that the competition didn't even offer to their first-class passengers. For that matter, even Concorde fliers who were paying supersonic fares had to fork out for their own ground transport.

It wasn't all about the front of the bus, however. We learned what customers wanted and greatly improved the economy experience as well with a greater choice of meals, electronic headsets when everyone else still had those awful rubber tube things and the biggest innovation of all (next to cabin crew who were nice to our passengers) was seatback TV screens in every seat on the airplane – coach class included. This was something that was not in first class with other airlines. Our big-dog competitors thought we were certifiably insane (and maybe we were!) and with every added feature became even more convinced we couldn't possibly sustain our presence in the market. What the big airlines failed to recognise was that airline passengers at the time – myself included – were sick of paying through the nose for lacklustre service that had been getting worse for years. They were all in that most dangerous of states where they believed that as long as they are no worse than their competition then they were doing just fine.

All it takes for this status quo of mediocrity to be shaken up is for one little outsider to step into the ring and start punching above their weight.

NO CONTRACT, NO PROBLEM

We pulled the same trick fifteen years after Virgin Atlantic when we created Virgin Mobile to jump into the mobile phone market and duke it out with the likes of British Telecom (BT). Once again, as with the airline, it was my own experiences as a dissatisfied consumer that screamed out to me that we just had to get involved – and quickly. At the time – and to this day – many of the big telecom companies were ripping off their consumers with outrageously high-priced and punitive long-term contracts that stopped just short of you signing away your firstborn. As with our entry into aviation, we really knew next to nothing about the business other than that there had to be a better, more user-friendly and affordable way to provide mobile phone service in a business that was about to take the planet by storm.

There were huge parallels to the challenges we'd faced at Virgin Atlantic. There we didn't own any airplanes or have our own maintenance capabilities or airport counters, so we simply leased everything in or contracted it out and learned along the way. At a glance the barriers to entry for something like a Virgin Mobile seemed almost more daunting than with the airline. We had no phone masts, exchanges, cables, networks and all the other super expensive paraphernalia it takes to start a phone company – at least if we were to do it the traditional way, which of course we had no intention of doing.

At my urging, Gordon McCallum (who had joined us from McKinsey & Co.) and team had been looking into the emerging mobile sector for some time and finally seemed to have identified what looked like the launch vehicle we needed – we'd become an MVNO – a *mobile virtual network operator*. After its privatisation, British Telecom was obliged by EU regulations to allow other operators to piggyback on their excess network capacity by leasing out time to them. While we'd be competing with them on the one hand, we would also be helping them to earn some substantial incremental revenues to set against their huge sunk costs. At this stage we met a couple of impressive young BT executives, Tom Alexander and Joe Steel, who not only recognised the MVNO opportunity but instantly grasped the immensity of what Virgin could bring to the party. At the time the big legacy phone companies were right up there with airline food as material for stand-up comedians, so we were convinced that a fresh new player like Virgin, particularly with our strong appeal to the youth market and an even stronger customer service ethos, would be a natural for this lacklustre sector.

We all sensed we were on to something big here and with my excitement for the opportunity growing daily, I suggested to Tom Alexander that it was time for us to meet and discuss how a 'Virgin Mobile' might function as an MVNO. And what a meeting it was! After a couple of electric hours, it didn't take a lot of arm twisting for Gordon and me to convince Tom to split with BT and come and make it happen for us, bringing mobile phone whizz Joe Steel along with him. So we had our angle of attack and we had our senior team in place, now we needed to decide on a stand-alone product. Given the hideously complex, impossibly confusing three-year contracts that were the mainstay of the industry at the time, it wasn't terribly difficult to define the strategy: small-print-free, affordable, straightforward, simple contracts – with bills that were super easy to read – because, well, there wouldn't be any! With our prepaid format, there would be no end-of-the-month surprises that required subscribers to take out second mortgages to pay their phone bill.

We took Mobile public in 2004 and after a couple of successful years were approached by NTL:Telewest in 2006 and we agreed to sell the company in exchange for £123 million and a ten per cent stake in the enlarged group. A year later the company was rebranded Virgin Media, becoming the first 'quadruple play' media company in the UK offering television, internet, mobile phone and fixed line services. By 2012 Virgin Media had over four million customers and the little dog that was Virgin Mobile took a $6 billion revenue bite out of the previously big-dog-only media market.

In 2013 the giant US cable group Liberty Global acquired Virgin Media in a deal that meant our investment of around £50 million generated more than £1 billion for us – and we are still involved via a brand licensing agreement with Liberty. All in all, not a bad result for something that had its genesis because I wasn't happy with the level of mobile phone service that was available fifteen years earlier. Sometimes, rather than sitting back and complaining about lousy service, it really pays to get out there and find a way to improve upon it by reinventing it yourself.

DIFFERENT THINK, DIFFERENT DO

Twenty years after we started Virgin, the critically acclaimed if grammatically controversial 'Think Different' campaign from Apple defined the spirit of entrepreneurship like never before. It also encapsulated in just two words exactly what Virgin had been doing for two decades and is still at the core of everything we do today.

Thinking differently doesn't necessarily cost any more – it just takes a commitment to not doing more of the same. While no company would ever buy into a marketing campaign of 'We Are Every Bit as Good as Everyone Else in Our Field', that is effectively the way many of the world's biggest corporations have conducted their business for generations. In my experience this bizarre 'stay inside our little comfortable box at all costs' mentality is frequently a by-product of the malaise that goes by the name of 'shareholder accountability'. When the leaders of a public company's primary focus is their stock price – and with it their performance-linked bonuses – it makes it very difficult for them to take in the big picture.

When the going gets tough the standard big corporation approach is to try and slash and burn their way back to profitability, and with labour generally constituting the greatest single cost, cutting heads and/or pay freezes are invariably the first thing to happen. Now maybe I'm oversimplifying things, but if one of the primary reasons a company's profits are suffering is poor customer service, then following a round of morale-destroying lay-offs by asking the diminished workforce that remains to do more for less strikes me as a somewhat foolish expectation. Rather than digging their way out of a hole, such slash and burn tactics will typically only dig it deeper. Smaller companies that have the freedom to turn the traditional corporate pyramid of stockholders first, employees last, on its head and put their employees and customers ahead of shareholder interests are usually doing the latter a far greater service. Learn to look after your staff first and the rest will follow.

CHERISH YOUR PRIVACY

I had a fascinating dinner conversation not so long ago with a good friend who confided in me about a 'problem' he's wrestling with – a problem that just about anyone else would die to have. The company he founded a decade ago has been phenomenally successful and dominates a market segment that he pretty much invented. He loves what he does, is still very much hands-on and involved on a day-to-day basis, owns the company outright, has no debt and has been turning in steadily growing and very healthy profits almost every year for the last decade, so much so that the company has been valued at close to a billion dollars. So you might well ask, 'So what exactly seems to be the problem here?'

Well, for several years now his bankers and financial advisors have been pushing him to float the company but he really isn't sure that it would make sense for him. He could certainly use the funds to speed up his long-term expansion plans, but as he succinctly put it, 'Why sell the farm to force-feed evolution when the business is growing organically at a steady clip?' He is, however, being steadily nudged in the direction of an initial public offering (IPO) to, as they put it, 'unlock the value' in his company. Needless to say the ones who are doing the nudging are his kind-hearted bankers who would make a very tidy killing from the fees and commissions that an IPO spins off – but I'm sure that has nothing to do with their enthusiasm for the project! In any case, my pal knew that I had been down a very similar road once before and was keen to get my take on his delightful dilemma.

I am no banker – or actually I suppose I am now with Virgin Money – but it didn't take me very long to come up with my thoughts on the situation. I first asked the question, 'By the sound of it you're still having a great time running your own independent company and have no urgent need for the cash, correct?' He nodded affirmatively. 'Well,' I said, 'there are really no right and wrong answers here, but in my opinion you have two options: either you sell the whole thing to the highest bidder and create something new with the proceeds, or you keep doing what you're doing until such time as you don't enjoy it any more or you just lose the passion you clearly still have. By that stage the company will have further increased in value and you also won't be left wishing you'd stuck with it for a few more years – which, knowing you, is probably what's going to happen if you sell it now.'

His reaction was a deep sigh and a predictable, 'Sure, Richard. I'm not saying I want to do it, but if I were to go the IPO route I'd only sell a minority stake so I'd have the best of both worlds – we'd raise some cash and I'd still be running the company – right?' My response was a simple, 'Wrong! Trust me, I've been there. While on paper you may still be running the company, I can assure you from personal experience that the company you're running and your freedom to run it the way you're accustomed to doing, are never going to be the same after you've gone public. Let's face it: countries go to war to protect their freedom and independence.'

I then took him through a short history of my experiences when we took the Virgin group public in 1986 – Virgin Atlantic was not included in the flotation. I won't take you through all the details, but in essence the entity that people invested in when they bought Virgin plc shares at 140 pence was a successful, vibrant company run by a group of fun-loving, slightly batty young people with some wonderfully off-the-wall (aka highly innovative) ideas on how to run a business. The ironic fact was, however, that the moment we became a public company we could no longer operate in the same way that had made us such a success to that point in time. Everything changed overnight. Our customary laid-back impromptu meetings where we'd bash around a few crazy ideas and make impromptu decisions were a thing of the past. They were replaced by hideously formal board meetings, which now had to include outside non-executive directors, who through no fault of their own had no idea as to how we or the business worked. All the results reporting and compliance stuff in general was an enormous distraction from the freedom we'd always enjoyed to focus on the business rather than the books.

We suddenly seemed to be spending half our time explaining what we were doing and why to all nature of fund managers, analysts and other assorted 'suits'. 'Screw it, let's do it' became a distant memory! Half the time our most successful ventures had been based entirely on our contrarian intuition or *carpe diem* moments, not on tortuous feasibility studies, business plans and financial projections. It crossed my mind more than once that if we'd had to explain to one of these people why I thought we should put out an entirely instrumental record, *Tubular Bells* would never have seen the light of day! And as for Virgin Atlantic? Forget it – that one would never have made it on to the drawing board let alone off the ground.

As a public company it suddenly felt like the Virgin genie, something that had always thrived as a free spirit, had suddenly been forced into a bottle and was in serious danger of suffocating there. I realised there and then that, if working to improve shareholder value was now our *raison d'être*, as opposed to doing the things we wanted to do in the way that we had to do them, then we could never function successfully as a listed company. I've always seen a business as a group of people trying to improve other people's lives – how do you monetise that in a quarterly report? So, having learned an important lesson we finally cried 'uncle' and in 1988 we went out and raised the money to take the company private again. The stock market had crashed so we could have paid less by going with the diminished value at which our stock was trading, but I was adamant that we 'do the right thing' and every investor got back the 140 pence per share that we'd started out at so nobody lost money on the deal – well, at least none of the outside investors.

Having listened politely to all this my friend didn't say much other than, 'Oh well, we'll see what happens.' I do know, however, that a year after our conversation he still has a private company, is working harder than ever and (based on a recent phone conversation) his revenues and profits are still on the ascent. A clear case, it would seem, of 'he who hesitates' *not* being lost.

One positive lesson I took away from the whole public company experience, however, was that there are quite a few public company-like disciplines that start-ups should voluntarily adopt from day one. The reporting requirements of listed companies leave no room for the levels of creative 'we'll worry about that later' accounting that a lot of start-ups practise for years. While the disciplines are mostly on the financial side, better tracking of your forward progress in all kinds of ways gives your people a better metric by which to measure their own contributions and development. And a big secondary benefit will be, if the day ever comes when you do decide to go for an IPO then the staggering amount of catch-up accounting work will be nowhere near as painful as it was for us.

Don't get me wrong, there are lots of occasions when the IPO route makes total sense and depending on how you have funded your start-up the 'exit strategy' may already have been baked in by your investors. Since our flirtation with operating as a public company in 1986 we have become involved in all nature of joint ventures and licensing deals where we have partnered with listed entities. For all the reasons I've described, however, back then it was not the right way for us to go. There's only one thing that is an absolute certainty in business and that is that we all make mistakes and as one should, we learned a lot of valuable lessons from our attempt to go from the rock market to the stock market! Had we given it a while longer we may have learned to adjust to living in a listed environment, but at the time I just felt that such a major deviation from the Virgin way would have required too many compromises – and I had no desire to run a genetically compromised company. So I trusted my instincts and have had absolutely no regrets ever since.

ANYONE FOR COFFEE?

In the early seventies when we were opening our first record store in London – actually a second-floor shop, to be honest – coffee bars were all the rage. Like every cool kid of my generation I used to hang out for hours over a single espresso (or none at all if I could get away with it) in a little Greek-owned coffee bar right around the corner from our shop. In fact, in some ways these espresso parlours may have been part of our inspiration for the 'just hang out and chill' ambiance we dreamt up to help us sell more records. At the exact same time that we were giving coffee away for free to customers sitting on bean bags, three young friends in Seattle were just setting up in business to sell bags of beans. Originally the three were only going to sell bags of freshly roasted coffee beans but they soon moved into grinding it and selling it by the cup which led to the opening of their first coffee house. Looking at the success they have enjoyed with what was to become Starbucks, particularly in light of what happened to the record-selling business, I sometimes wonder if we had it the wrong way around in our first shop. Maybe we should have been selling the coffee and giving the records away for free!

While we never did get into selling coffee, Starbucks did eventually overlap into the music business by entering into a partnership with Apple to collaborate on selling music as part of the 'coffeehouse experience' and in 2006, Apple added a Starbucks Entertainment area to the iTunes Store, selling music similar to that which is played in Starbucks stores.

The rise of Starbucks as an international phenomenon is actually a great example of an IPO working to the greater good with the funds raised being used to turn a small dog from Seattle into the proverbial 800-pound global gorilla. They may have been able to achieve the same results as a private company with greater control but it would have taken them a lot longer. At the time of their IPO in 1992 Starbucks was almost twenty years old but still had only 140 stores

– all in the US and Canada – and their annual revenues were around $73 million. The twelve per cent of the company that was sold raised around $25 million, which was immediately used as a springboard to doubling the number of Starbucks coffee shops over the next two years, increasing the share price by twofold in the process. By the end of 2012 Starbucks had almost 20,000 stores in sixty-two countries and over $13 billion in revenues! That's a lot of beans!

My favourite, although little known, Starbucks story involves the origin of the company's brand name, which rather like Virgin almost started out as something quite different. In our case the final contenders were Slipped Disc Records and Virgin. I have to admit to having quite liked 'Slipped Disc' but, fortunately for all, it was Virgin that carried the day. I say 'fortunately' because while it would have been an amusing name for a record label, 'Slipped Disc Airlines', 'Slipped Disc Health and Fitness Clubs' and 'Slipped Disc Hotels' would probably have presented some rather steep marketing challenges! Anyway, when Starbucks started out in Seattle, the original owners were planning to call it Pequod after the whaling ship in Herman Melville's classic tale of the great white whale *Moby Dick*. At the last minute, however, for unspecified reasons, they suddenly changed course in favour of another name from the same novel, that of the Pequod's chief mate who went by the name of Starbuck. It's strange to imagine the almost one million people a day who visit a Starbucks somewhere in the world saying, 'Hey, let's get together at Pequod's for a latte.' On the other hand, 'I'm going to grab a Vente Vanilla at Virgin – want to join me?' does have a certain ring to it.

LITTLE DOGS, BUT SHARP TEETH

When Ron Faris was the chief marketing officer at Virgin Mobile USA he once told me how it was a standing joke with the Virgin Mobile marketing team that AT&T would spend more on advertising during one episode of *American Idol* than we would spend in a whole year. This is, in fact, something that, with the occasional exception (like Virgin Media's ads with sprinter Usain Bolt), has been a long-standing tradition in almost every Virgin company. We have always relied on smart, cutting-edge creativity and scads of often quite self-deprecating humour to get ourselves noticed – it's called getting a much bigger bang for a much smaller buck. The social-media revolution has been a game changer in giving smaller dogs a medium in which they can bark a lot more loudly than they could ever have afforded to do with traditional measured media like TV and print. Even so, the level of creativity involved in tweeting a relevant, engaging product conversation into the hearts, minds and ultimately wallets of your target audience is still what sets a winning brand apart from the also-rans. And that degree of creativity has got nothing to do with the size of the dog but is much more about a combination of the sharpness of its teeth and how hungry it is.

Creating strong brand affinity – or 'brand lust' as Ron Faris likes to call it – in today's social media world may be less expensive but is essentially no different to what we've always done – learn to cut through the clutter with a message that grabs them by the throat. When, for instance, Virgin Atlantic added shiatsu massages to its on-board Upper Class services, much to our delight British Airways was openly scornful about it. This gave us the perfect reason to put them in their place with a couple of well-placed billboards around Heathrow Airport sporting a double-edged message that was hard to misinterpret: *'British Airways Doesn't Give a Shiatsu.'*

Another time, in early 1995, British Airways ran a rather odd two-page spread in all the major US newspapers including the *New York Times* that boasted: *'More people choose British Airways to London than any other airline. Duh!'*

If they'd stopped short of the juvenile 'duh' we probably wouldn't have thought anything about it, but that strange little word and the tone of voice it projected sent our US marketing team and the creative people at our US agency, CMG Communications, into a frenzy of activity: within a matter of hours they'd managed to purchase the same double-page spread in the *New York Times* and come up with a response ad to ride the coat-tails BA had so kindly offered up to us. The following morning New Yorkers opened their papers to read: *'More people switch to Virgin Atlantic from British Airways than from any other airline. Hah!'*

We'd pillaged our marketing piggy bank to run the ad one time only in New York but the effect was seismic. Clearly refusing to believe that anyone could have come up with such a response in just a couple of hours, British Airways threatened to sue the *New York Times*, accusing them of leaking their ad – they never did follow through on the threat but they also never ran their bizarre ad again. Some readers even suggested that we had actually run the first ad as well in order to tee up the second! Our one-off ad placement, however, had an unprecedented tail as it was written up and quoted in scores of marketing articles and columns for months to come, with headlines such as, 'Virgin Goes Jugular'. Almost a precursor to 'going viral', wouldn't you say?

PINK SLIP VIPS

As that last story demonstrates, one of the greatest advantages to being the little dog in a big dog pound is the ability to react quickly and ride every competitive coat-tail that comes your way. Ron Faris and his Mobile US team were always masters at this art and it was never better demonstrated than in 2009, a time when the economy had gone to hell in a proverbial hand-basket. With swine flu and job lay-offs dominating the news, Virgin Mobile was faced with a tough decision on its annual music festival. Other organisers had already cancelled their events fearing that fans could ill afford such outings so the easy thing to do would have been to follow suit. Ron and his team, however, were never very good at being trend followers and rather than cancelling they decided to buck the gloom and lighten things up. With a goal of putting out a new energy that would focus on optimism, the upcoming festival in Columbia, Maryland was given the go-ahead. Not only would it take place but the tickets would be free, as would a whole lot more.

When I got wind of what was happening I volunteered to join in and greet concertgoers as they entered the park: my brief from Ron was to 'act like Willie Wonka at the chocolate factory gate.' Inside the grounds we'd created a VIP lounge like no other anyone had ever seen. Rather than being the usual exclusive sanctuary for 'A-Listers', this one was still exclusive but the only people allowed in were those who could prove they'd been laid off. It wasn't quite a Caligulan orgy but it came close! 'Pink Slip Pinatas' were hung from trees and for a short while, young fans could celebrate a day of free music instead of stressing about getting a job. Happily, times have improved and we no longer have to pay homage to those pink slips, but 'Virgin Mobile FreeFest' was born, and to this day (as the name suggests) the festival is still free. The best part is that our festivals aren't just enjoyed by the attendees, they also raise hundreds of thousands of dollars a year for homeless youth.

Doing the right thing and learning to respond quickly to events can also be infectious – that same year, while most of the big car manufacturers were complaining about their free-falling sales, instead of whining, the Hyundai Motor Company came up with its legendary programme to buy back cars from anyone who'd lost their job and couldn't afford to keep up the payments. They may be running with the big dogs now but that kind of 'pay it forward' initiative is just one reason Hyundai (together with its subsidiary Kia) has come out of nowhere to be the world's fifth-largest automaker, producing over seven million vehicles in 2012. What makes this an even more remarkable achievement is that they have done it in exactly the same time that I have been in business – Hyundai produced its first car in 1968, the same year that I published the first issue of *Student* magazine. More proof that scrappy little dogs can take a huge bite out of the biggest and often the most established businesses: in 2012 Chrysler produced one third of the number of vehicles that Hyundai/Kia turned out.

While the likes of Starbucks, Hyundai and Virgin may no longer qualify as bona fide small dogs, all three of us still live by the same principles that we did when we were just cutting our business teeth. Starbucks is perennially voted as one of the best places to work and its people are as important to their brand as anything they put in a cup. Hyundai not only builds great cars but it stands behind them like no other automaker by offering standard warranties of ten years or 100,000 miles, whichever comes first – more than double the duration offered by most of their competitors.

And Virgin, well, I think you know how we feel about customer service and people and although we have been around for forty-odd years now, we're still as scrappy as we ever were and enjoy nothing better than a good dogfight.

So bring it on, big dog, we're ready when you are.

Chapter 10

INNOVATION IS NOTHING NEW

Ask any passing bumblebee

Did you know that according to all the laws of aerodynamics, the humble bumblebee should not be capable of flight? All kinds of scientists have spent time and money on wind tunnel and lab testing to prove their thesis that says because of its body shape and weight in relation to its wingspan the bumblebee cannot possibly fly. The only problem with all this is that no one has ever been able to convince a single bumblebee that they should cease and desist in proving the experts wrong on a daily basis. The inescapable – if frustrating for scientists – fact is that whatever innovative technique it is that the bumblebee is employing, it works: and with no apologies to aeronautical engineers the little buggers just keep buzzing around.

I'm certain that at one time or another, just about everyone has been subjected to the asinine put-down on anything extraordinary that goes, 'Well, it may look good in theory, but I doubt very much that it will work in practice'. Someone who must have heard this lame sentiment expressed more than most was Leonardo da Vinci, truly one of history's most remarkable entrepreneurs. One has to chuckle when thinking what this amazing man's business card might have looked like if it listed all his areas of expertise: 'Painter, Sculptor, Architect, Musician, Engineer, Mathematician, Anatomist, Inventor, Geologist, Botanist and Writer'. Maybe 'Beekeeper' could also have been on that list as he reportedly studied bees closely when he drew up the first ever design for a helicopter. In Leonardo's case, however, I am sure he would have studied all the reasons bumblebees and hummingbirds are able to defy the scientific claptrap and achieve what they do, rather than wasting time trying to discredit their airworthiness. In fact, had da Vinci ever had a personal mantra it might well have been 'This works in practice but not in theory'.

A BRIDGE TOO FAR

Brett Godfrey who founded Virgin Blue has long loved telling a tale about da Vinci that perfectly illustrates the age-old bias that still blocks the path to true innovation in a lot of overly conservative businesses. It would seem that in the early 1500s the Sultan of the Ottoman Empire, one Bayazid II, had a problem. He desperately wanted to build a bridge from Asia to Europe. While not quite as daunting a task as it sounds, at the time crossing the River Bosphorus in Istanbul (or Constantinople as it was then) with a single-span 240-metre-long bridge would have been an unprecedented feat of engineering. The commercial pay-off from linking the east–west trade routes would have been huge, however, and so the challenging project demanded some radical thinking.

A number of the leading bridge-building experts of the time were struggling without much success to adapt the classic and simple keystone arch design to the span and height that the Bosphorus project necessitated. Frustrated with the lack of progress and unwilling to take no for an answer – something I most decidedly relate to – the Sultan turned to a highly unlikely source, an upcoming young Italian painter and designer by the name of Leonardo da Vinci. Excited by the challenge, da Vinci set to work and the dramatic result was an incredibly futuristic bridge design that with the use of unheard of geometric concepts produced a soaring single-span that was, well, not surprisingly perhaps, truly a work of art. The engineering and architectural experts of the day were appalled and condemned it as an abomination and a work of fantasy that could never possibly work.

As anyone who has ever constructed anything in a city knows, obtaining planning approvals can be a long and frustrating task, but in da Vinci's case 500 years is pushing the envelope! Setting new standards in 'better late than never', Leonardo's sixteenth-century bridge design (with a few updates based on twenty-first-century building materials) was finally given the go-ahead in 2012 by the city of Istanbul. Just imagine how bridge-building design could have been catapulted into the future in the sixteenth century had Constantinople's Luddite engineers had the ability to see beyond their comfort zone and envisage just how much one man's genius could have recalibrated the world as they knew it. But history is littered with da Vinci-like tales of how the greatest innovators of their times have had to struggle to get their ideas past the power of incumbents who can only accept those things that fit into their existing pigeonholes and established theory.

VIRGINNOVATION = RE-INNOVATION

The longer I am in business, and it has been almost fifty years now, the more valid I find the famous French saying, '*Plus ça change, plus c'est la même chose*', which simply means, 'The more things change, the more they remain the same'. Maybe it's being around longer than most that has let me figure this out but I've been noticing that some of our most recent innovations are essentially learning the lessons of similar initiatives we introduced in earlier businesses – they are what I suppose you might call 're-innovations'.

Perhaps, as I often find to be the case, Mark Twain explained this phenomenon perfectly when, in a letter to Helen Keller on the subject of plagiarism (of which she had earlier been charged and acquitted) he wrote, '*All ideas are second-hand, consciously or unconsciously drawn from a million outside sources, and daily used by the garnerer with a pride and satisfaction born of the superstition that he originated them.*'

Clearly this doesn't apply to the technology world where things are happening at a rate that even Mark Twain could never have imagined possible, but outside of tech-driven innovations I think he was absolutely spot on. We are just witnessing a perfect example of the old becoming new again at Virgin Money where we have started doing the same thing for our banking customers that we did in our first record shop in the 1970s and later with our Virgin Atlantic Upper Class Clubhouses (airport lounges): going the extra mile for our customers by giving them something well outside the realm of their realistic expectations.

We set the trend with our very first record shop in London, which became an instant blueprint for the rest of the business. Unlike our much bigger competitors like HMV, who ran a chain of soulless, inhospitable music supermarkets, we came along with a Monty Python approach of, '*And now for something completely different...*' We turned our cosy little store into a destination where our customers could lounge around on large pillows, relax, use our headsets to listen to good music over a complimentary cup of coffee and eventually (we hoped) buy an album or a single to take home with them. Our competition thought we were a bunch of whackos but the formula of 'make it a place people want to visit' worked, and eventually, when the model grew up into Megastores, several of them would actually become recognised as official tourist destinations in their own right. The Paris store, which we had once been told was 'at the wrong end of the Champs-Élysées' was listed in most guidebooks as one of the 'must visit' sites in the city and always packed with tourists and locals alike – on an average weekend the Paris Megastore would have around 40,000 visitors.

As in Paris, our choice of location in New York City was more than a little controversial. In 1996 when we announced our intention to open a 60,000 square foot megastore in the then distinctly seedy Times Square, we were warned by the locals that this was 'a place so unsafe that even New Yorkers wouldn't go there'. Thanks, however, to the courage and intuition of Ian Duffell, who had joined us from Thorn EMI to develop our worldwide retail portfolio, we pushed ahead and when we finally opened the store it quickly established itself as the cornerstone to the rebirth of the entire Times Square neighbourhood. Happily it also soon became one of the highest-grossing retail locations in the city with sales of over a million dollars per week.

But that was then. Sadly, as outmoded victims of the iTunes downloadable era, both are now gone, although the Paris store did manage to defy gravity and hang in there until the middle of 2013 with a mixture of live concerts and other events. But like our very first store, it remained a destination as opposed to just a place to shop right up until the very end. *Vive la différence!*

THE WIDE-ANGLE LENS APPROACH

Until Virgin Atlantic came along thirty years ago, airport lounges were pretty dismal places where first-class passengers and airline club members could maybe get a comfy chair, watch a single channel on TV and enjoy a free cup of not very good tea or coffee. When we started our Upper Class service we realised from the get-go that we would have to offer more of everything, not just in the air but on the ground as well. The ground portion of a long-haul flight – getting to and from the airport and negotiating the rigors of the terminal building on departure and arrival – can account for as much as forty per cent of the door-to-door travel experience. Amazingly, most airlines only care what happens to their passengers from the time they board the aircraft until the time they get off. We decided therefore that this called for us to take more of a wide-angle lens view on the passenger experience and expand our vision to include the entire trip. This holistic approach meant we took responsibility for providing transportation and comfortable accommodation for the whole trip: we included limo service to and from the airport and then set about developing lounges (without beanbags) that would actually be a feature for our customers to look forward to as opposed to just a place to mitigate the airport misery.

Over the next decade what evolved was our Clubhouse Lounges, which today offer everything from a full bar, haircut and shoeshine to a light snack or a full meal with table service, full body massages, hot tubs, pool rooms, business centres and lots more – all fully complimentary, of course. At first our competitors all scoffed saying we were insane and that it was unnecessary overkill, the cost of which would be unsustainable. Our passengers on the other hand lapped it up – as did a lot of former loyalists from those other airlines! Today you will find that the naysayers are all playing catch-up as they try to emulate the success of our lounges, which are a testament to our philosophy of seeing how much we can incorporate into our product and customer service to build genuine loyalty and – lest you think we are in the philanthropy business – by driving new business in our direction.

We also never had the advertising and promotion dollars to go toe-to-toe with our larger competitors with their huge route systems and equally big budgets, so rather than spending millions of dollars a month to tell the world how good we were, we decided instead to sink the bulk of our limited resources into tangible product benefits for our customers to enjoy and let them spread the word on our behalf. A million dollars of advertising buys you very little these days – in 2013 in the US a single thirty-second ad during the Super Bowl cost advertisers a cool $4 million! Blink and you missed it. Putting a couple of million into innovative product upgrades, on the other hand, goes a long way and the payback keeps coming for a very long time.

My favourite story on how a business can lose focus and squander big bucks on advertising instead of product is a tale I heard from a former employee of an American airline who came to work for us. It seems that her former employers had been getting a lot of feedback (and a lot of food back too) from their cabin crews to the effect that their passengers were increasingly unhappy with the standard of the economy class catering on their transatlantic services. Rather than trust the word of their front-line staff, however (mistake number one), they spent a couple of months setting up, conducting and analysing an on-board passenger survey to establish whether or not they really had a problem and if so what it was all about. The results ultimately seemed to point to a combination of two things:

first that the passengers were indeed very unhappy with the airline's food – exactly as their crews had been telling them for months – and secondly expectations about how good the food would be had been set too high by a recent ad campaign that the airline had run at great expense.

Eventually the airline decided they had all the evidence that was needed to address the problem. So they changed the food, right? No, that would have been way too obvious! Instead they told their ad agency to tone down any references to catering in future campaigns. The net outcome, therefore, was that the food stayed bad, the passengers kept complaining and the crew, who felt demeaned by the whole process, just stopped passing the information up the ladder as they knew it would achieve nothing. Truly a lose-lose-lose outcome for company, passengers and crew alike when all that time, expense and energy could simply have been directed on fixing the food based on their cabin crew's wealth of knowledge as to what their passengers did like.

'I'M JUST GOING TO HANG OUT AT THE BANK FOR A WHILE'

So enough airline talk, let's circle back to Virgin Money. When we acquired Northern Rock and their high street branches, just like with Virgin Megastores, Trains and Atlantic we saw it as another exciting opportunity to go in and disrupt the status quo in a business that was in desperate need of a serious shake-up. In all these industries the accepted norm had settled in at a pretty low common denominator and the world of retail banking was no different. No matter how much the emergence of ATMs and online banking have served to automate the way most people do a lot of their banking, there is still an important role for the bricks and mortar walk-in branch and with it the all-important people component and, in the UK at least, that part of the banking world had changed little since I was a boy – until now!

We are lucky to have Jayne-Anne Gadhia as our CEO at Virgin Money. In 2001 when we sold 'Virgin One' to Royal Bank of Scotland, I remember calling Jayne-Anne to say I felt very badly about her going and that it looked like she'd been lumped into the deal along with the rest of the furniture. We were sorry to see her go but RBS had clearly seen her as a huge part of the assets they were acquiring. Anyway, I did say at the time that if she ever wanted to come back all she had to do was give me a call, for which she seemed very grateful. It also seems that she remembered this conversation: I was delighted when six years later she called and said she was ready to 'come home'. Jayne-Anne came to see us a couple of days later and within a week the deal was done – she even brought eighty-two staff with her to help recreate Virgin One at the place where it had started many years earlier.

In retrospect I was also glad she just happened to be watching TV at home one Sunday evening and saw a discussion about the struggles facing Northern Rock, an iconic bank in the north of England that had run afoul of the 2007 financial crisis. Apparently some TV banking expert on the show said something to the effect that, 'What this bank needs is someone like Richard Branson to sort it out and run it.' She sent me an email right away saying, 'Maybe it's not a bad idea so let's talk about it.' We did – and following a call to Alistair Darling, the Chancellor of the Exchequer, the next day, we were on our way for what would be a highly frustrating but finally successful four-year pursuit: in January of 2012 Northern Rock officially became a part of Virgin Money when we acquired it from the UK government.

It was agreed that all of the Northern Rock branches would be rebranded as Virgin Money as quickly as possible and just like that we found ourselves with a high-street banking presence for the first time. Northern Rock had a lot of wonderful people working for them but understandably they'd been feeling pretty beaten up as their bank was dragged through bankruptcy and was then run by the government for four years. Talk about one extreme to the other! An overnight leap from being a government employee to working for Virgin is about as dramatic (hopefully not traumatic) a change as I can imagine. The effect was wonderful to see, though, as everyone seemed completely re-energised and thrilled with their chance to be part of a whole new beginning.

We quickly set about giving each branch a fresh new ultra-modern look in addition to new banking products and the same kind of great people service that is an expectation with the Virgin brand. But it wasn't enough. Looking through that wide-angle lens again, the idea of doing something radically different came along. Our inspiration came, in large part, from an interesting but defunct idea that Jayne-Anne remembered from the Royal Bank of Scotland in Edinburgh. It seems that in 1964 they'd opened something they dubbed their 'Ladies Branch'. It was essentially a women-only, tearoom-cum-bank designed to make female customers feel less intimidated by the banking experience. Staffed exclusively by women, it offered complimentary tea and coffee, soft music, and even free paracetamol! By the seventies, however, it was already drawing accusations of being discriminatory against the male of the species and it finally closed its doors in 1997. Flash forward ten years to Virgin Money – Jayne-Anne's ultra-creative mind had recalled the Ladies Branch idea the moment she saw some beautiful oak-panelled rooms we inherited (by coincidence) in Edinburgh that were in excess of our banking needs and bingo – just like that the Virgin Money Lounge concept was born. The big difference of course being that this time it was for everyone, men, women and children – and I'm not sure about the paracetamol.

We have a credo at Virgin Money that goes by the name of 'EBO', which stands for 'Everybody Better Off', and what we had here was a perfect example of what that quest is all about. Just like our Clubhouse Lounges at Virgin Atlantic are perhaps a little 'over the top' by traditional standards, the new Virgin Money Lounges would quite deliberately be more of the same. 'EBO' depends very much on giving people the benefit of the doubt. Too many companies and individuals will shy away from what might be the greatest of initiatives for fear that some customers or employees will 'game the system' and abuse any freedoms or trust you place in them. In other words, because two or three per cent of users may exploit something, the other ninety-seven per cent will be denied access to a benefit they would have enjoyed and respected.

With a lot of crossover thinking from the airline's award-winning Clubhouses, we spent many months with specialist design consultants Allen International developing the Money Lounge concept and working through every detail. A lot of time and effort also went into finding the perfect locations to bring the lounge idea to life. We wanted to avoid a cookie-cutter look so went to great pains to develop custom designs to complement each building. The first two lounges opened in Edinburgh and Norwich with Manchester following a few months later and all three became instant successes.

Our lounges do not sit inside a bank branch but (so far at least) are self-contained havens where Virgin Money customers can come to unwind. They can drop in for a hot drink and a snack, use our free Wi-Fi or one of our iPads, read a newspaper or magazine, or just sit and do nothing. Children are welcomed with a dedicated kids' area in every lounge, complete with toys, books and games consoles. And our Virgin Money Lounge hosts are always on hand to make customers feel welcome. While you have to be a customer or guest of a customer to use the lounges, we've always seen them as a great place for local charity and community groups to meet as well for after-hours community events like exhibitions, talks and book signings. And the *coup de grâce* has to be the fact that every lounge features a grand piano! A little over the top? Probably, but hey, why not? The pianos are frequently and grandly played by some very talented customers (and occasionally by the not so talented, but we all have to start somewhere) and during the Edinburgh Festival we even had some world-class performers drop by to give impromptu mini concerts. And what is the cost of membership for this veritable private club? No more than being a Virgin Money customer.

I perhaps shouldn't be releasing the following statistic for fear that every bank is going to attempt to follow suit, but our branches with lounges last year averaged almost 300 per cent higher sales than those without. Yet another tribute to the philosophy of 'Everybody Better Off'!

Driving meaningful innovation with EBO in mind has always been at the core of every Virgin enterprise and over the almost half century we have been at it, I have had the privilege of working alongside and learning from some of the world's most inspiring and inspired young people. I often get given way too much credit for what we have achieved at Virgin, which is maybe inevitable to a degree when your name and your brand become so closely inter- twined. Or as it has been written by a number of commentators over the decades, 'it's sometimes hard to figure out where the brand stops and the Branson begins'. My role particularly in recent years has more often than not been that of a facilitator or an enabler. I set the table for entrepreneurs and our growing band of home-grown 'intrapreneurs' to do what they do best by giving them the backing in every sense of the word and the supportive environment to incubate their ideas and get them up and going.

Among the many pieces of feedback we got from the Virgin

leadership research I mentioned earlier was this quote from a staffer at Limited Edition (the division that markets our exclusive resort destinations such as Necker Island). Talking about a senior person there it read:

> 'He gives me rope and just says look I'm there to help. I'm there to pick you up if you fall down... he lets me run with it and that for me is fantastic you know. It gives me a sense of purpose, it gives me a sense of drive, it allows me to make decisions.'

This is the kind of leadership that enables and drives the constant level of innovation that every company has to foster in order to keep moving forward. The rapidly moving, ever-evolving business world is one in which, to survive, companies have to behave rather like sharks – if they don't keep moving forward they will drown. And sharks are a pretty appropriate metaphor to use: they may have changed very little over the millennia, but by staying constantly on the move, they have survived for over 450 million years.

The word innovation tends to set most people thinking about places like Silicon Valley – which has its own fair share of sharks – about huge technological advances and companies with even huger research and development budgets. But my favourite stories are always those about people who have come up with a simple idea and with little or no money made a big success of it. Obviously the likes of Sergey Brin and Larry Page, Steve Jobs, Mark Zuckerberg and others qualify for inclusion in such a category but there are also a lot of lesser known but every bit as impressive stories out there – like Sara Blakely's, for instance – a lady whose career track has an amazing number of parallels to mine.

SPANX A MILLION

I first met Sara when she became a contestant on my 2004–05 one-season wonder of a US TV show *The Rebel Billionaire*. When she joined us for the ten weeks it took to film the entire series, I was surprised to learn that she was already four years into building her what sounded like a one-woman business. When I asked who was minding the store while she was away she just said, 'Oh, don't worry about that – I have Laurie-Ann there and I trust her implicitly to keep things going just fine.' I remember wondering if I would ever have had the courage to walk away from Virgin for a couple of months when it was in its fourth year. To be honest, and with no disrespect to my colleagues at the time, the answer was a resounding 'No way!'

Although Sara was the runner-up in the final of *Rebel Billionaire*, she took her ten weeks out and then went back to business where she quietly continued on her track to becoming, at forty-one, one of the youngest ever self-made female billionaires in the US. Oh, did I forget to mention that Sara (if you didn't know already) is the founder and CEO of Spanx, the 'shapewear' company she started in her apartment with only $5,000 in the bank? Sara had failed to pass the law-school admission test and so became a door-to-door photocopier salesperson in Florida – a job she did for five years, which says a lot about her persistence.

The birth of Spanx was a classic entrepreneurial case study where if you can't find something you want then go out and create it. Sara had been wearing tights with the legs cut off but always had problems with them riding up her leg. So she started looking into how she could make a shaper that worked. It took her months of phone calls and visits to different mills before she found one in North Carolina that was prepared to make her product. In the meantime she'd perfected her prototypes – which for the longest time was a weird-looking mingling of underwear, elastic bands and paperclips.

Next came the branding decision. Sara had heard somewhere that names with a K in them sold well, so she came up with the name Spanks, a name that a lot of people in the Bible belt found too offensive. So she put the garments in a red box and changed the spelling to Spanx with an X – people were still offended, but she thought it was more fun. As Sara tells it, 'I was inventing something in one of the most boring categories ever. If you're wearing a shaper you didn't tell a soul.' But that was before Spanx changed all the rules!

Sara the inventor became Sara the sales lady. She didn't have the funds to go to trade shows so she decided to go on the offensive. She started trying to get hold of the buyer at Neiman Marcus, one of the swankiest stores in New York City, but could never get her to take a call. Then one day the buyer accidentally picked up the phone herself and Sara quickly recited her well-rehearsed pitch, wrapping it up with, 'And if you give me an appointment I will fly to New York to see only you.' Impressed by Sara's energy and enthusiasm for her product, she got the appointment and then subsequently the sale. Sara the PR person and the face of the company also got a gigantic break when Oprah Winfrey named Spanx as one of her 'favourite things in 2000'. Incredibly, at the time Spanx didn't even have a website; nevertheless in their first year sales totalled an astounding $4 million! The following year QVC, the TV home shopping channel, took the product and revenues doubled. Sara was on her way, and there's been no stopping her ever since. By 2012 sales were pushing $700 million and Sara owned a brand name that, rather like Google is to search engines, has become generic to the market segment she created.

Okay, so you are probably going to ask what exactly are those parallels between Sara's career and mine? Well, like me she didn't go to university. She had an idea for a product that didn't exist and set about learning how to fill the gap. She was a 'Jack of all trades' (or is that 'Jill'?) during the early years. She picked a brand name that was slightly risqué and controversial. Red is her corporate packaging colour and she has a couple of girls depicted on there just as the original Virgin record label did. More importantly, however, by putting ourselves out front along with a lot of innovative, smart, low-cost sales and marketing, we have both built highly successful companies from the ground up with the help of a lot of wonderfully loyal and engaged employees.

We both love what we do but we both learned the art of delegation at an early stage and we both believe in paying it back. Sara became one of the first (individual as opposed to part of a couple) women to sign up to Bill Gates and Warren Buffett's 'Giving Pledge' whereby she (as I have done) agrees to pledge over half her wealth to charity.

After her wonderful performance on *The Rebel Billionaire*, Sara didn't end up as the winner mostly because I saw she was already well on her way to becoming a huge success with Spanx. In gratitude for her efforts on the show, however, I sent her home with a personal cheque for $750,000 to help her establish The Sara Blakely Foundation which is dedicated to giving (pun intended I am sure) *'a leg up'* to women globally and locally through education and entrepreneurship.

Sara's amazing story should certainly be a huge source of inspiration for everyone, but especially young female entrepreneurs who might feel the weight of the world is upon them. What Sara achieved with no outside funding and nothing except a great idea and grim determination and perseverance to getting it done is truly textbook entrepreneurship!

Chapter 11

HIRING 'EM AND KEEPING 'EM

Engagement in a digital world

Shakespeare's Richard lll proclaimed 'off with his head' with casual abandon and Donald Trump expanded his brand awareness via his TV show *The Apprentice* with his almost joyful proclamations of 'You're fired.' For my own part, letting people go has never made me anything but extremely sad. I almost always feel that firings are much more of an indictment on the company's failure than that of the employee – no matter what the circumstances behind it might be.

On the other hand I always derive great pleasure from telling someone, 'You're hired!'

WHY HIRING SHOULD BE YOUR #1 PRIORITY

Whether you're planning a start-up, preparing to re-launch or expanding your business, it's often hard to know which tasks to delegate, which to delay, and which to tackle right away. In my experience, if there is one area in which you should definitely become immersed and do a lot of the work yourself, it is the hiring process. As much as I believe in delegation, putting your imprimatur on the key management is something you have to do: remember that these are the people to whom you are going to be delegating a lot of important decisions, and quickly, so they'd better be people with whom you feel a hundred per cent comfortable!

And if you're reading this and thinking that your company is just too big already and you are way too important and busy to involve yourself with something as mundane as the hiring of staff ('That's what we have a "people department" for, isn't it?'), then maybe you should think again. I have always insisted on being involved with senior-level hiring decisions in all of our companies, even if it sometimes means flying the applicants all the way to Necker Island to spend time with me, something about which I have received very few complaints! Even at Google – a $400 billion company which is still hiring at a rate of over 4,000 people a year – founder and CEO Larry Page still insists on being the final arbiter on whether or not to make a job offer to anyone being considered for a leadership role within the company. I know first-hand how this critical approach has paid off around the Virgin Group and I know from personal conversations with Larry that he sees his involvement in the hiring process not as some symbolic role that he has to make time for but rather as one of the most important parts of his job.

As I am sure Larry Page and his partner Sergey Brin will vividly recall (given that Google was incorporated as recently as 1998), the founders of a company inevitably must wear many very different hats during the first few crazy years. In Virgin's case – a mere thirty years or so before Google – I handled everything from the secretarial work to (scarily) the company accounts at our first businesses. Like all young entrepreneurs, however, my first big business lesson was that you have simply got to delegate your duties if you want your venture to survive and (ideally) grow. It is almost impossibly hard to acknowledge this in the early going, but you should also be hiring with a weather eye on the day when you're going to delegate even your CEO position and step back from the business's day-to-day operations and focus on ensuring that your company is prepared for what's next. Sara Blakely once told me, 'The smartest thing I ever did in the early going was to hire my weaknesses.' That unusually early level of self-awareness and smarts may be one of the biggest contributing factors to how Sara has managed to build a billion-dollar business from the ground up in just a dozen or so years.

In my case, I think it was in large part down to my dyslexia that I learned very early on in my career that I needed to become comfortable with the art of delegation. As I had already realised in my aborted school career, there were just some tasks with which I really struggled – for example whether it's called 'mathematics' or 'accounting', numbers were just not my forte. We hired an accountant early on. As we grew and I delegated further I still felt I had the knowledge base to be comfortable getting involved in almost all the major decision-making processes. As soon as we stepped outside of the entertainment field, however, that was most decidedly no longer the case, something I quickly discovered when I unilaterally decided it was time for us to take the hugely tangential leap into commercial aviation.

PLANE SAILING

When we were getting ready to launch Virgin Atlantic, and with zero experience whatsoever in the airline industry, I realised how important the ability to delegate was going to be. With a helping hand from Sir Freddie Laker and others, we were soon able to assemble a team of very smart and highly qualified aviation experts to blend with our experienced Virgin business managers. Roy Gardner, who became our first managing director, and David Tait, who ran the US side of the business, were two of the first people we grabbed, both having formerly worked closely with Sir Freddie at Laker Airways. I soon got the feeling that Roy and David were used to having a boss who knew the airline business inside out so I think they quite enjoyed working with someone new to aviation who was prepared to delegate most of the decision-making to them.

For a new company it was almost like managing a merger. And the blending of our existing Virgin Group music industry people with the newly hired career airline people certainly made for an extremely interesting chemistry experiment. A lot of the time we never quite knew how the laid-back Virgin attitude of 'Hey, don't sweat it – rules are made to be broken' was going to react when mixed with the more 'by-the-book' and rigid disciplines of the airline industry. We obviously couldn't tell an engineer to try plugging his gizmos in somewhere else just to see what happened, but we could suggest that maybe we should try using the famous French restaurateur Maxim's of Paris with butlers in tailcoats to serve our Upper Class section. Sadly it didn't last more than a few weeks! The fancy French sauces that worked in a kitchen at sea level just didn't hold together at 35,000 feet and worse still those tails kept tripping the butlers up as they climbed the circular staircase to our Boeing 747's upper deck. But it certainly got us lots of press and – as with all attempts to effect real change – if we'd never tried it we'd never have known.

It was a tribute to the people on both sides of the equation that – surprisingly, perhaps – we never had any violent eruptions and the two groups quickly came together with a healthy balance and understanding as to which elements the other needed to function and where there were grounds for serious further experimentation. Together, in an unprecedented period of just five months, the team not only got a brand-new transatlantic airline off the ground (literally) but in the process they succeeded in creating and delivering the level of service that I had hoped for and that a lot of newly acquired passengers would appreciate for many years to come. Had I not been willing and able to step back and let them get on with it, the outcome could have been very different.

Hiring the right people is a skill, and like most things you get better at it with practice, but there are some good shortcuts that can help you learn quickly. Here are my tips for identifying great people and building your team.

CHARACTERS AND CULTURES

Although almost certainly not involved in hiring people, the nineteenth-century American essayist Ralph Waldo Emerson once wrote that, *'Character is higher than intellect.'* I am sure it will come as no surprise that I wholeheartedly endorse this line of thought, although the task of uncovering the true character of a job candidate can be a challenge. Essentially an interview is a game of figuring out whether or not the character of a candidate will be a good fit with the culture of the company. One great way to test this may be to ask two or three of the employees who will work with this person to join you at some point in the interview, and to come prepared with a few of their own questions.

When your employees start talking to the candidate, it's time for you to listen and observe not just what is said but any tell-tale body language signs that might indicate that what they're saying and what they're thinking might not be the same thing. How is everyone getting along? While a little awkwardness and nervousness has to be expected, look for someone with a sense of humour, who is fun, friendly and caring, because that is a person who likely understands teamwork and will help others. If they are clearly suffering from an extreme case of the interview jitters, I have often broken the ice by asking them to tell me a joke. It's amazing how telling a joke, even if doing it really badly, can make someone laugh at themselves and come out of their shell. In fact, as one of the world's worst tellers of jokes, I relate really well to the ones who get stuck after, 'Did you hear the one about...'

In the US, our hotel team has been doing some innovative things on the hiring front as we gear up for the late 2014 opening of the first property in Chicago. Rather than just wading through hundreds if not thousands of job-seeker applications, we have been creating a local buzz via social media and conducting hiring roadshows. The plan is to touch audiences that aren't necessarily looking to change jobs and grab their attention with what looks like an interesting new career path in a really cool work environment. At our group interviews applicants may find themselves playing Twister with potential co-workers, or role-playing things like taking an eighty-five-year old guest to her room. The idea being to let applicants' personalities shine through in simulated real-life situations – we want people who can laugh and have fun with our guests, which is not something you can easily discover by reading a CV and asking questions over an interview desk.

A CV IS JUST A PIECE OF PAPER

Obviously a good CV is important but if you were going to hire by what they say about themselves on paper you wouldn't need to waste time on an interview. One good question to ask a candidate is what he or she didn't include. I have always valued capability over expertise. While you may need to hire specialists for some positions, take a close look at people who have thrived in different industries and jobs – they are usually more versatile, have transferable skills, and can potentially tackle problems creatively. The would-be 'expert' who has been stuck in a groove somewhere else for years is much more likely to simply replicate their past, almost muscle memory-like, approach to the job. Obviously a healthy mix of experience and novel thinking is the ideal, but on balance I would anticipate more fresh and objective solutions to flow from the smart and curious inexpert outsider than the 'been there done that' experts.

Also don't jump to the conclusion that someone who has worked for five different companies in the last five years 'cannot hold down a job' – it could just be that the job couldn't hold them! Be forth-right and ask pointed questions like what it is they are seeking and why you should hire them if they're only going to be around for a year. Rather than being just another stepping stone along their way, can you perhaps give them what they are looking for in a mutually appealing destination?

Above all, don't get hung up on qualifications alone. A person who has multiple degrees in your field isn't always better than someone who has broad experience and a great personality. By the same token, the expression that someone is 'overqualified for the job' is utterly nonsensical; if they feel they want a change of pace or a new direction then more power to them.

TAKE CHANCES ON PEOPLE

I have always been a great believer in trusting your instincts when interviewing people. First impressions shouldn't rule the day but remember that the initial reaction you have when meeting an interviewee is presumably based on the best impression they can create. So if at first sight your gut screams 'You've got to be joking!' then think how they will come across when they're not trying so hard, and would you want this person walking into a room as your representative.

On the other hand I have also found that some people can seem like oddballs at first sight but then turn out to be indispensable: a maverick who sees off-the-wall opportunities where others see nothing but problems can energise your entire group. So even if their CV may not be quite right, he or she may be a little different than everyone else on your team, this might be a good time to take a risk and hire them anyway.

Whenever possible, promote from within. If you've been hiring great people all along, when an executive or manager does leave you should look long and hard at filling that job from within if at all possible. If, however, as can sometimes be the case with the most senior jobs, you do not have a candidate who is quite ready or a perfect fit then don't make the mistake of moving someone into the role just because it's 'their turn'. And even when you do seem to have a prime candidate in-house, it never hurts to advertise the job and see what is available on the open market. Your inside candidate can suddenly look very different when seen in the context of someone else whom you never thought would be available or interested in working for you.

When you can promote from within, however, it certainly sends a great message to everyone in the company that when someone demonstrates a passion for the job and leadership skills at every step along the way then the sky's the limit. We have countless great success stories all across the group of people starting in entry-level jobs making it into senior management. For example, Chris Rossi who is now Virgin Atlantic's senior vice-president in the USA started out working behind the check-in counter when we first began flying to Boston in 1991. Chris next moved into the local sales team, eventually making it to VP sales before becoming our senior person in the US.

At Virgin Active in South Africa, Xiki Baloyi began her career in 2003 as a receptionist – she had trained in sports management but couldn't find a position in that field. As the first team member that Active members met on entering the club, Xiki's people skills shone through and quickly earned her a promotion to fitness instructor, where she demonstrated her commitment to not just improving members' fitness but also to building their motivation levels. In the last seven years Xiki has been promoted several times and in 2013 was named the assistant general manager of our new Alice Lane Health Club.

Recognising the potential Chris and Xikis at the interview stage takes time and a healthy dose of curiosity. You need to meet a lot of people, ask them about themselves and their careers, and tell them about yourself and your company in turn. So relax and be yourself – the people you eventually choose are, after all, going to play big parts in your shared adventure of building a business.

As important as it is to look at what a candidate has achieved elsewhere, I have always believed that the single most important thing to consider is 'personality fit'. By that I mean, is this someone whose way of being, sense of humour and general demeanour will dovetail easily with your company's culture? Ramming a square peg into a round hole may work well for carpenters but it seldom works with people. While the majority of skills can be learned, when it comes to personality what you see tends to be what you get – with the caveat, of course, that what you'll see on a 'best behaviour' interview showing is not always what you'll get when they're installed on the payroll.

YOU CAN NEVER TELL

Just as it takes many different types of CEOs and top managers to lead Virgin's 50,000-plus employees and keep our businesses purposeful and profitable, you never can tell where your next leaders are going to come from. We find great leaders everywhere: some working hard inside our companies, others working for large competitors, or sometimes they just walk in on us right out of the blue.

Such was the case when Matthew Bucknall and Frank Reed arrived in my Holland Park office in 1997. The two of them had just sold their own fitness club, Living Well, and were looking to do it all over again – but better – and this time with the Virgin brand as a key part of their plan. I talk elsewhere about the value of short presentations: well, their business plan for Virgin Active was about the most concise I have ever seen. It simply read: 'We want to create the first global comprehensive consumer-led branded health and fitness facility – readily accessible to a wide socio-demographic group at a price consumers are willing and able to pay.' I liked the idea right off the bat. Health clubs that would be fun, innovative and inclusive – rather than exclusive – and represent true value for money while enriching the lives of members. What was not to like about such a vision? When they then added the promise that they would turn Virgin Active into our ninth billion-dollar business, what could I say other than, 'Screw it, let's get active and do it'?

I dispatched the two of them with the simple brief to go out and take a year to look at what was happening in the sector all around the world and then come back and make their dream a reality. In 1998 the first club opened in the perhaps unlikely location of Preston, Lancashire and we were on our way. By 2012 they had not only fulfilled their ambition of producing the world's finest health and fitness clubs, but had also reached the promised billion dollars in revenue. As of last count, Virgin Active had almost 300 global clubs, around 1.25 million members and is still 'actively' expanding into new markets.

As an example of 'home-grown' leaders, there's the (now) husband and wife team of Leesa and Kenton (Keny) Jones. Leesa started out as an in-flight beauty therapist on Virgin Atlantic before coming to Necker Island to work as a spa therapist, while Keny began as a junior water-sports instructor on the island. While working together the two of them managed to find the time to fall in love and as a couple became an even stronger team with Keny moving up to activities director and Leesa to front-of-house manager where both became hugely popular with all of the island's (sometimes quite demanding) guests. Their next stop was to spend two years in the Kasbah – as general managers of Necker's sister property Kasbah Kamadot in Morocco – where their continued success set them up for a return to the Virgin Islands – this time running the whole show as Necker's general managers. They also now have two beautiful island children running around – Theo and Zara.

Leesa and Keny live and breathe the Virgin way. They both possess a seemingly never-ending supply of the magical ingredients that has always worked so well for Virgin: a youthful joie de vivre and great people skills, combined with a relentless focus on great service and succeeding at each and every task they take on. Oh yes, and lest I forget, their never-failing sense of humour is especially important when you have a nit-picky 'boss' (that would be me) who not only works but also lives on your patch!

While Keny and Leesa grew up in-house with Virgin Limited Edition, by contrast, some of our leaders have come to us from some pretty huge competitors.

David Cush was an executive at American Airlines for more than twenty-two years before joining Virgin America, where he really took to heart the opportunity to work in a smaller company where every voice could be heard. David pioneered the airline's 'Refresh' training programme which brings employees back to the San Francisco headquarters for an annual two-day session to share their experiences in maintaining the best customer service in the skies, and if my last visit to one was anything to go by – to party up a storm! Attended by every employee, senior management included, the refresher course emphasises communication, recognition and teamwork. David joins in as often as he can and recently sat in on a session where teammates brainstormed improvements to the (always a sensitive area) staff travel policy. He then made sure that the group's best suggestion was implemented, delighting all who'd contributed. David's leadership has turned the first US domestic airline to start up after 9/11 into a critically acclaimed, award-winning and profitable business.

LET MY PEOPLE GO

As I said right up front, we all tend to be products of our upbringing, our home and, for many, our work environments. So when you're interviewing someone who might have been working for years in a straightjacketed, by-the-book, authoritative environment (IBM used to be the favourite example for such regimes), it is important to remember that it can have its pros and cons. Let me explain what I mean. I have always liked to compare the workplace environment at each of the Virgin companies to being like open zoos. This is not meant to conjure up an image of wild animals scaring the visitors but more a place that, though still with perimeters, is totally devoid of cages. Most tradition-bound large corporate environments feature a lot of cage dwellers. The higher up the pecking order you go, the bigger the cage and vice versa. Unlike zoo cages, however, which are to lock the occupant in, the corporate versions tend much more to be used to keep people out – where a perpetually closed door sends a clear 'do not disturb' message and an open door means 'out to lunch'.

At the interview stage, candidates coming out of caged environments will predictably find the prospect of moving into a free-ranging open zoo tremendously appealing. They will usually be quick to point out how their entrepreneurial zeal and creativity was never able to truly take flight within their current (or previous) employer's tight parameters. And while they probably mean every word of it, there is one inherent danger that you must really dig into before you get swept away by their overtures of 'Set me free and watch me soar'. This not insignificant issue is, 'You can take the person out of the cage, but can you take the cage out of the person?' As much as long-time caged executives can crave their freedom, when suddenly stripped of the security that the cage also afforded, some simply cannot handle it. And when that happens the first thing they will start to do is to quietly begin building cages in their new workplace, at first as maybe just a place to run and hide from the unfamiliar and threatening wide-open spaces, but over time there is a clear danger of proliferation.

So, how does one go about the task of separating those who can adjust to and thrive in your culture from those who may never be able to shrug off their old hierarchical habits? In my experience the key is focusing on personality rather than anything that you might see in their CV. It is not something that always comes out in interview – people can be shy. But you have to trust your own judgement. If you're confronted with a slightly introverted person but you detect a great underlying personality, use your own personality and experience to pull it out of them. For a few moments try and find some non-business common ground to discuss, which may be kids or sports – anything that's going to loosen them up. It is easier with an extrovert, but be wary of people becoming overexcited in the pressure cooker of an interview. It's very much the same thing as in school, where certain kids that perform really well in class can be utterly incapable of doing the same thing in a written test. So too some people just don't interview well because of a hugely complex mix of emotions, anxiety and often just trying too hard in a way that masks the real them.

Once you are comfortable with the personality fit, then delve into their experience and expertise and ask them to take you through some of the highlights. If it's a marketing job and they say they headed up a hugely successful campaign at their last job, don't just nod approvingly – ask them to tell you about the strategy behind it and why it worked. Then ask them about some of the ones that never made it off the drawing board or that didn't work out as well as planned and why.

If you hire the wrong person at the top of a company, they can destroy it in no time at all – the same applies equally to external and internal appointments. So if the company is flourishing and the outgoing CEO has it firing on all cylinders, then maintaining that kind of status quo with an internal hire may be the smartest move – assuming there is a natural successor. If on the other hand the company is just plodding along and has done nothing particularly special for some time you might want to make a point of looking outside to see what fresh thinking you may be able to find. Letting your internal candidates get an early sneak peek at the official head-hunter job spec doesn't do any harm either. Their input on any requirements and qualities the spec is missing or that are under-stated will tell you a lot about their readiness to assume the role. Questions like 'So do you think we got it right? Is this really the kind of person we need in this job?' can lead to some very inter-esting places.

Quantity often conflicts with quality and it's no different when it comes to hiring standards. When companies go through growth spurts, they often hire in bulk and such massive influxes can put a real strain on the company's culture. While it may seem necessary to get new bodies through the door as quickly as possible to help share the expansion-generated load, it is always worth being patient. A hasty hiring is seldom a good one and the wrong person being thrust into your team can be very damaging. And if it means you have to operate shorthanded for a spell, so be it.

SO WHEN YOU'VE GOT THEM HOW DO YOU KEEP THEM?

I am sure there have been thousands of books written on the subject of employee retention, so I am not going to bore you with what I suspect you know already. It is perhaps worth mentioning, however, the reasons why people typically quit their jobs. In a huge leadership study dubbed 'Project Oxygen', Google recently found that the three principle reasons were:

1 They didn't feel enough of a connection to the company's mission, and/or their individual contribution was not considered important.
2 They didn't get along with or respect their co-workers.
3 They thought they had a terrible boss.

Conspicuous by its absence is 'not being paid enough' – so often considered the biggest reason people move on. All three of these issues are very tightly interwoven: for instance, bosses have bosses too, so the 'terrible boss' in item 3 might also be suffering from a terrible boss who doesn't appreciate their contributions. Similarly, the failure to get along with colleagues can also be a symptom of a non-inclusive culture, or what I'd call a lack of engagement.

BUSY DOESN'T MEAN ENGAGED

A lot of companies make the mistake of failing to understand the difference between keeping their people busy and keeping them engaged. I was always a fan of the *I Love Lucy* shows with Lucille Ball. There was one hilarious episode in which Lucy and her friend Ethel were making a futile attempt to wrap chocolates on a fast-moving production line – the resulting hilarious chaos was assuredly 'busy' but certainly had nothing to do with engagement. In real life, many an employee has mastered the art of appearing to be perpetually busy, but it is no metric to judge either their productivity or their true engagement level, if any.

Similarly, employees who consistently work twelve-hour days – often to mimic the behaviour and hours of their bosses – don't necessarily demonstrate any real level of engagement. It's more a sign that the boss is not managing his/her own time terribly well and is also blind to how it is affecting the lives of their staff. Such patterns if sustained for any length of time will usually become not only counter-productive but will also result in burned-out, disaffected and unhappy employees. As my father used to say, 'It's not the hours you put in that matter, it's what you put into the hours.' And when engagement levels drop it's not only productivity that goes south, customer service will inevitably also decline: the only things that increase are absenteeism and, off the back of it, turnover.

So what does it take to generate a healthy level of engagement? In my opinion it comes down to strong leadership and developing a culture in which your employees feel valued, empowered and trusted. All three of these things take time and work and require a lot of listening and dialogue. Leaders who have the ability to demonstrate genuine interest in their employees' interests, goals and objectives and let them air their opinions will build the kind of levels of trust and confidence that, over time, translate to real engagement.

And engagement is very much a two-way street in terms of both personal and corporate upsides. One study done by Towers Watson, the international professional services firm, showed that companies with the highest levels of employee engagement averaged operating margins of around twenty-seven per cent. Meanwhile those at the bottom end of the engagement scale were producing margins below ten per cent. As an integral part of the same equation, the study concluded that at the 'disengaged' companies almost forty per cent of employees were likely to quit their jobs in the next twenty-four months, while at those companies with the highest engagement levels that number dropped by more than half to around eighteen per cent. If those numbers don't get you engaged, they should do!

CHANGE THE POLICY – TO NO POLICY

I wrote in Chapter 3 about how one very ill-advised marketing decision seriously damaged video rental firm Netflix and decimated their stock almost overnight. Happily they recovered from it, got back on track, vanquished their one-time giant rival Blockbuster and are now once again flying high as the runaway market leader in the streaming video sector. One clue as to how they intend to remain there this time comes from a very well-advised and downright courageous initiative they adopted that rewrote the book – or to be more precise, threw it away – on something very near and dear to the hearts of most workers around the world: their annual vacation day entitlement.

I first learned of what Netflix was up to when my daughter Holly read a *Daily Telegraph* article and immediately forwarded the piece to me with a clearly excited email saying, '*Dad, check this out. It's something I have been talking about for a while and I believe it would* be a very Virgin thing to do to not track people's holidays.' She then went on to say, 'I have a friend whose company has done the same thing and they've apparently experienced a marked upward spike in everything – morale, creativity and productivity have all gone through the roof.' Needless to say I was instantly intrigued and wanted to learn more.

The *Telegraph* article talked about the new vacation policy that has been adopted by Netflix, which might actually be more accurately described as being, well, no policy! It's a little bit like when you read that someone is offering a 'zero per cent interest rate'. If there's no interest can it really be called an interest rate? Anyway, simply stated, the policy-that-isn't permits all salaried staff to take off whenever they want for as long as they want. There is no need to ask for prior approval and neither the employees themselves nor their managers are asked or expected to keep track of their days away from the office. It is left to the employee alone to decide if and when he or she feels like taking a few hours, a day, a week or a month off, the assumption being that they are only going to do it when they feel a hundred per cent comfortable that they and their team are up to date on every project and that their absence will not in any way damage the business – or, for that matter, their careers!

The Netflix initiative had been driven by a growing groundswell of employees asking about how their new technology-controlled time on the job (working at all kinds of hours at home and/or every-where they receive a business text or email) could be reconciled with the company's old-fashioned time-off policy. That is to say, if Netflix was no longer able to accurately track employees' total time *on* the job, why should it apply a different and outmoded standard to their time *away* from it? The company agreed, and as its 'Reference Guide on our Freedom and Responsibility Culture' explains, 'We should focus on what people get done, not on how many hours or days worked. Just as we don't have a nine-to-five policy, we don't need a vacation policy.'

It is always interesting to note how often the adjectives 'smart' and 'simple' describe the cleverest of innovations – well, this is surely one of the simplest and smartest initiatives I have heard of in a long time and I'm delighted to say that we have introduced this same (non) policy at our parent company in both the UK and the US, where vacation policies can be particularly draconian. Assuming it goes as well as expected, we will encourage all our subsidiaries to follow suit, which will be incredibly exciting to watch.

LIVING IN A MOBILE CELL

While the freedom to leave the office behind whenever and for as long as you want sounds incredibly appealing, this of course assumes that the office isn't going to simply follow you wherever you go on a 24/7 basis. For most modern-day salaried staff there has never really been an eight-hour day or a forty-hour work week, but the advent of emails, texting and smart phones has truly rendered them extinct and made the job of striking a healthy balance between home, family and work even more challenging.

Achieving that delicate balance was always something of a Chinese plate trick, but in recent years it has gone from a trick to a complex science. With almost everyone carrying their own personal telecommunications device every waking minute, the boundaries between work and private lives have all but disintegrated. By that I mean that once upon a time – before BlackBerrys, iPhones and their kin changed all the rules – when people left the office they would physically and mentally disengage from their colleagues, their desktop computer, their in-tray and their office phones and intercoms. Not so any more! The arrival of the smartphone, tablets and laptop computers has meant that almost everyone these days simply puts the office in their pockets or purses and takes it along with them: to lunch, to dinner, home for the night, the weekend, to the kids' football games and yes, even to the beach, the ski slopes or wherever they choose to holiday. Not only that but the typical sender of a business-related email or text is usually blind to the time of day or day of the week – they expect, and usually will get, a response within a matter of hours if not minutes.

I have one very successful friend who is a senior partner in a big financial services firm as well as being the mother of two young children. She became so perplexed by the never-ending volume of spurious weekend emails that she put a weekend auto response message on her business email that says, '*I am away from the office until Monday attending to my other full-time business – my family. If this message is about something that cannot wait, then I suggest you call or text me, otherwise I will get to it on Monday.*' If like me you have ever been on the receiving end of her message, you'll know who she is, but it seems the reaction has been terrific and she hasn't had a single negative comment or any significant incidence of weekend business calls.

In what could well be brewing as a second industrial revolution of sorts, the so-called 'BlackBerry suits' have already started hitting the courts. In Chicago a police sergeant filed a class action under the Fair Labor Standards Act against the city claiming retroactive overtime compensation for all the hours he maintains he and his fellow officers are obliged to stay connected to their jobs via their police department-issued BlackBerrys. As a lawyer representing the plaintiffs put it, 'They are hourly wage earners. If you're going to make people work when they're not on duty, you've got to pay them.' At the time of writing the case is on-going, but it begs an intriguing question: why shouldn't the same criteria apply to all workers, hourly or salaried, whose lives have become subjected to the 'new digital reality'? The Chicago court's ruling is certainly going to be precedent-setting and could have a dramatic effect on the way all 'digitally enabled' employees are compensated – or it could possibly lead to a sudden fall-off in the number of company mandated 'electronic communications devices'.

In the absence of widespread Netflix-like changes to the old workplace norms, it would seem only a matter of time before salaried employees also start to revolt. After all, their hours on the job have steadily increased from what may have averaged fifty hours a week in the traditional context of the workplace to the current ill-defined 'on e-call 24/7' paradigm. Not withstanding creative intercepts like my friend's auto response, there's no turning back the clock. We all live in the world we live in, so the only way to mitigate the transition pain is to focus on quickly dumping outmoded policies that no longer fit our employees' business needs and private lifestyles. When they actually worked 'only' forty to fifty hours a week, then four weeks of paid vacation plus public holidays maybe made sense. Today when our people are expected to work an immeasurable number of hours in their expanded virtual offices by being at the perpetual beck and call of their e-bosses, shouldn't the same approach apply to their time away from the bricks and mortar office? So bravo Netflix and every other company that is taking bold steps to recalibrate the system – just don't email me about it on the weekend and expect a response before Monday!

THERE'S NO PLACE LIKE HOME

Another change to the old norms that has been driven by technology is the number of people who (like me) are now working from their homes. According to the US Census Bureau, that number has risen by forty-one per cent in the last decade with almost fifteen million Americans working out of their homes. In the UK the rise is less dramatic but according to a Labour Force survey is still up by thirteen per cent in the last five years. I am not sure if I was counted in this survey or not but I am certainly the world's greatest advocate of 'doing it from the couch' – or, more recently, from my hammock.

I have not as yet been privy to any statistics on how home working plays into employee retention, but I can only imagine that it has to improve the ability to keep some employee groups happy (like telephone sales or service agents) but will have no relevance to more creative roles that require a lot of interaction with peers. This was certainly the reason Marissa Mayer, the CEO of Yahoo, gave when she caused a major kerfuffle by banning work from home. In defence of her decision, however, when speaking to a group of human resource professionals, she said, 'While people are more productive when they're alone, they're more collaborative and innovative when they're together. Some of the best ideas come from pulling two different ideas together.'

As companies strive to cut costs, I foresee more and more administrative-type jobs being pushed out of expensive offices. One of the earlier adopters of work at home was the US airline jetBlue which, when it started service in 2000, set up all of its telephone reservations agents as home-based employees in the Salt Lake City Utah region. At the time I remember founder David Neeleman proudly telling me that this initiative created several hundred new job openings for stay-at-home mothers who would be unable to work from a call centre but could do a great job while the kids were at school or the baby was sleeping. Apparently the turnover with this group has been negligible.

I know a lot of 'I'd go crazy if I had to stay around the house all week' types who find the very idea of working from home to be quite abhorrent. In my own case I have always found working from home – as I have done all my life – reduces the stress levels I know I'd suffer if I were working from an office and bringing work home in the evenings and weekends. My family life and my work life have never had clear demarcation lines, but have always managed to co-exist peacefully. Okay, I'll concede there have been a couple of times when the sheer volume of people that the business side of my life brought into the house became too much for my wife, but we've always managed to find a compromise and neutral ground. By being around the house (or houseboat as it was in the early days) so much, I got to see Holly and Sam as they grew up in a way that I could never have done leaving for an office every morning and returning after they were in bed. And, by osmosis, they too got an indirect education of sorts in how the business works.

Now, when I am not continent-hopping as I do for almost six months a year, living on and working from Necker Island has taken the blending of home and business lives to new heights. We have the most incredible team of young people running the island and looking after our guests. Our philosophy at Virgin has always been to train our people well enough so they can leave, and treat them well enough so they don't want to. Needless to say, on a little piece of paradise like Necker, our retention levels are quite extraordinary.

PART THREE

SHRIEK
GIGGLE HOWL SNICKER SNIGGER
TITTER WHOOP
CHUCKLE
LAUGH
TITTER
SPLIT YOUR SIDES BE IN STITCHES ROLL ABOUT CHORTLE
GUFFAW CRACK UP ROAR
GRIN
SNORT

Chapter 12

CULTURING THE CULTURE

It takes time and work

To a lot of people the only 'culture' they experience on a daily basis is to be found in their yoghurt at breakfast time. Perhaps this same thought is what inspired Peter Drucker, the internationally acclaimed management consultant and author, when he came up with the brilliantly insightful line, *'Culture eats strategy for breakfast.'* In so doing he nailed what to my mind is one of the most under-appreciated essentials of modern leadership: no matter how visionary, brilliant and far-reaching a leader's strategy might be, it can, and frequently does, all go for naught if it is not fully supported by a healthy and spirited corporate culture.

When people ask me what 'secret sauce' has made Virgin a success over the last forty-plus years, the easy answer is, 'My brilliant, visionary leadership' – I *am* kidding, of course! The honest answer is one hundred per cent down to the people-first culture that we started way back in the last century. We inadvertently created it while lolling around on beanbags in the first-ever Virgin Records' shop in London – the 'megastores' came much later. At the time, the last thing we had on our minds was developing any kind of a corporation, let alone a culture. We were just having a good time, chasing women (and the women were chasing men – we were truly an equal harassment opportunity employer!) and figuring out each week if we'd made enough money to pay the rent and the staff. We enjoyed what we were doing, we liked working with each other and we treated our record-buying customers like they were, well, part of the family. They liked the experience so they came back for more and before we knew it we were on our way – the rest, as they say, is history.

I am sure that most people reading that last paragraph are thinking, 'Yeah, if only it were that easy!' So I'm sorry if it sounds like an over-simplification but that is genuinely how we set the Virgin ball in motion.

There was also a lot of hard work and plenty of sleepless nights worrying about all kinds of issues, but overall we stuck with it because we were enjoying what we did on any given day; and 'tomorrow', as Annie would have said, was always a day away.

HERBAL REMEDIES

Great corporate cultures don't always just come about by chance – they are often an outgrowth of sustained and exemplary leadership such as at low-cost US carrier Southwest Airlines with the legendary

Herb Kelleher at the helm for the best part of forty years. Like me, Herb was not a career 'airline guy', he was a Texas lawyer who saw an opportunity to start an innovative low-fare airline in his home state that would (he thought) be able to exploit some legal loopholes.

He formed Southwest in 1967 (as Air Southwest) to provide affordable air service within the state of Texas and immediately flew into a firestorm of opposition from the three existing Texas airlines. It took three years of legal battling before the Texas Supreme Court upheld Herb's little airline's right to fly and he was off to the races. From the beginning Herb recognised that to survive, let alone succeed, Southwest would have to have more than just low fares and so – truly a man after my own heart – he unabashedly chose sex appeal as the key. Southwest's happy-go-lucky, fun and above all else disarmingly attractive and friendly cabin crews became the talk of the industry – rather like a certain British airline would do a dozen years later by employing exactly the same kind of 'personalities'!

But it wasn't just about good looks. With a company motto of 'Hire for attitude; train for skill', Herb always preached a gospel of if we hire and empower the right people who are committed to 'do as you would be done by' levels of consistently excellent customer service, then everything else will naturally follow. Of all the memorable quotes attributed to Herb, there is one that really should be the mantra for any organisation – it certainly is for Virgin – he once said, 'We tell our people, "Don't worry about profit. Think about customer service. Profit is a by-product of good customer service. It's not an end in and of itself."' And if the proof of the pudding is in the eating, it is no small coincidence that in January 2012 Southwest became the only airline in the history of a notoriously cyclical business to report an incredible fortieth consecutive year of profitability!

I have only flown Southwest once, on a short flight to Dallas, from where I can't recall, but what I do remember is being struck by how much fun their cabin crew seemed to be having doing their jobs. Other than with the mandatory safety messages, this group was clearly anything but scripted, very much into being themselves and having a lot of fun with their captive audience. A lot of cabin crew attempts at humour come across like they're trying too hard and so tend to fall flat as a result. Not so here. But they weren't finished yet – when we touched down it was a bit of a bumpy landing and over the PA the lead flight attendant welcomed us with a breezy, 'Well, ladies and gentlemen, as you probably felt just there, we just touched down in Dallas – twice!'

Stories abound about such things like the time passengers boarding a Southwest flight were surprised to find the airplane appeared to have no cabin crew on board to greet them. Then, on some cue, the overhead bin doors suddenly sprung open and in unison the three flight attendants hiding in there all screamed 'Surprise!' This genuinely fun-loving culture has established Southwest as one of the best places to work and in the process built a powerful bond between employees and customers alike. As in everything about a successful business, establishing a framework in which employees feel truly comfortable expressing themselves requires a leader who is prepared to set the standard and lead by example and Herb Kelleher, for one, could always be relied upon to speak his mind and be almost crazier than his staff.

An example of Herb's ability to exploit every opportunity to sustain the airline's fun culture and generate favourable PR in the process came when Southwest was threatened with a trademark lawsuit in 1992. When Southwest started to use the slogan 'Just Plane Smart', another smaller company, Stevens Aviation, which had been using the very same tagline for some time, threatened to sue. In a classic Kelleher move, however, rather than going to court to settle the squabble, Herb challenged Stevens' CEO Kurt Herwald to a three-round arm-wrestling match. The winner would get to keep the slogan and the loser of each round would give $5,000 to the charity of his choice. The younger Herwald readily took up the challenge and the much-publicised build-up began. Among other things, Herb put out a video showing his 'rigorous' daily training routine for the upcoming bout, one scene of which involved a single painful-to-watch 'assisted sit-up' followed by a cigarette and a glass of bourbon! To nobody's surprise Herb lost all three rounds of the bout, but $15,000 went to charity and the two CEOs agreed that both companies could use the slogan – so not only was a courtroom confrontation avoided but everyone ended up a winner.

'ANYONE FOR WILD TURKEY?'

My first face-to-face meeting with Herb took place in his hotel suite one afternoon in New York City while we were both attending an airline investment conference there. I was excited to meet the man as it had always seemed we were kindred spirits when it came to fun being at the core of running a successful airline – and making sure our customers shared in the experience. Herb was scheduled to be the speaker that evening prior to dinner and I was to address the group the following morning. The conference organisers, however, had suddenly come up with the idea that it would be fun if I were to give the introduction for Herb that night. As we'd never met they'd hastily arranged for us to get together that afternoon and so around three o'clock I duly arrived at Herb's suite with a couple of our people.

Herb welcomed me at the door with a hug as if we were old pals and set about introducing me to his entourage of senior people. We'd barely settled in when there was a knock on the door and room service wheeled in a cart that normally, at least in the UK, might have been expected to have tea and biscuits on it. Not here! All that was on the cart was a bucket of ice, a dozen shot glasses and a large bottle of Herb's favourite tipple, Wild Turkey bourbon. Without missing a beat, one of Herb's VPs jumped up and proceeded to pour large shots of Kentucky's famous whisky for everyone in the room— the only question he asked was, 'Y'all want ice?' Certainly a much warmer way to get the party started than 'Anyone for tea – how do you take it?'

Over the next hour, as per his reputation, I found Herb to be an amiable bear of a man with a laugh that rattled the windows. With such an obvious thirst for life (and bourbon), he reminded me very much of an American Freddie Laker – although Freddie preferred rum and orange juice! We talked about how Herb's earliest vision for Southwest had stayed true to its course while all kinds of other start-up and legacy airlines had come and gone. Avoiding any and all unnecessary complexity is the cornerstone to Herb's business philosophy. For example, whereas in its fleet of over 900 aircraft, American Airlines has thirteen different types of airplane (even more now with the US Airways merger), Southwest's fleet of around 600 airplanes consists of just a single aircraft type – the workhorse Boeing 737. This makes every employee's job simpler: every pilot can fly every aircraft in the fleet and every engineer knows where every part goes and that just about every part will fit every airplane. An intimate familiarity with the aircraft means airport ground crews can keep turn around times to an absolute minimum, which drives higher productivity, and the list continues. They have also avoided getting into relationships (known as 'interline' agreements) with other airlines, which means they control one hundred per cent of their own scheduling decisions and don't get blamed for losing other airlines' baggage. If ever there were a business case for the benefits of going it alone, Southwest has to be it.

But as important as hardware like airplanes might be, what shone through when listening to Herb that afternoon was how acutely aware he was that it's your people that have the greatest influence on the success or failure of the business and, as at Virgin, how creating and maintaining a fun, family culture is critical to achieving your targets. Another similarity between Southwest and Virgin is how intensely proud our respective workforces are to be associated with their companies. Or as a twenty-something staff member once said to me, 'Hey, Richard, it's really cool to work at a place where it's really cool to work.' I must say I found that to be... really cool!

Anyway, in New York that evening, only slightly buzzed on bourbon, I climbed up to the podium to introduce my new best friend Herb to the assembled senior airline executives, bankers and press. I started out by saying a few highly complimentary things about the man and his airline, and then assuming a more serious tone said, 'Herb and I met this afternoon and I was so impressed that I have instructed Virgin's bankers to make a major stock acquisition.' As expected I saw the reporters in the audience suddenly sit up in rapt attention. This was news – Virgin was about to acquire a stake in Southwest! Barely managing to keep my face straight, I continued, 'Yes, I told them I wanted to buy 50,000 shares of Wild Turkey stock.'

WEAR LAURELS – DON'T REST ON THEM

The flipside of the kind of corporate culture enjoyed at Southwest and Virgin can be found at those dreadful cultural catastrophes where 'we' is supplanted by an entrenched 'us against them' standoff. Environments where management and labour are on two different sides of a great divide separated by long-festering quagmires of distrust, bitterness and malcontent. Such situations can almost always be laid at the door of senior management's prolonged failure to provide strong leadership and/or willingness to change with the times. While the true meaning of the word 'legacy' is quite simply something good, bad or indifferent that is 'handed down by a predecessor', when applied to corporate entities it seems to have become almost exclusively a pejorative. And the sad fact is that a lot of older, set in their ways, laurel-resting businesses tend to share the common denominator of failed or failing cultures which, like barnacles on the bottom of a boat, impede forward progress to the point of eventually sinking the whole ship.

Back in the early retailing days of Virgin, as we began to grow with more stores, a record label, recording studios and the rest, we never lost sight of 'serious fun' as a driving force behind the business. We carried that same culture – which was and is really just a passion for having fun with what we do while doing it better than the others – into banks, trains, telecoms and planes plus a multitude of other very diverse businesses all around the world.

As I often say (okay, I say it a lot!) – a company is nothing more than a group of people and people are like plants. I'm not sure that I buy into the benefits of talking to plants but if you water them and tend to them – more listening than talking, in other words – they will grow and flourish.

'THEY SAY...'

I have always found that one of the simplest ways to monitor the health of your culture is to constantly subject it to the 'we/they' test. In a healthy corporate culture you will hear employees embracing the first person plural – as in 'Certainly, sir, *we* can do that for you right away' – to describe everything the company does. In an unhealthy culture, the third person plural 'they' and its cellmate 'them' take centre stage, and usually in an arm's-length, accusatory fashion as in, 'Sorry, *they* don't do that even though I've been telling *them* for ages that the customers would love it.' Brett Godfrey summed it up perfectly when describing the difference in (then) Virgin Blue's work environment and that of Qantas, our major competitor in Australia, by saying, 'Our people are always in "volunteer mode", while over there, certainly if industrial unrest is any indicator, they seem to be in perpetual "prisoner mode".'

One of the many things that makes the Virgin group of companies unusual, dare I say unique, in the corporate world is the hugely disparate range of products and services that carry our brand. We have never been into vertical integration as the primary reason for starting something, albeit that a lot of our ventures have over time started to connect at the edges – like airlines and hotels. A lot of companies make it an overarching policy to 'stick to their knitting', that is to say, stick with what you know best and don't stray too far from the comfort zone. Not so at Virgin! In many ways we could in fact be accused of 'vertical disintegration', given our inability to stick to any particular knitting pattern for too long. Unlike Unilever, General Mills or Procter and Gamble, we are not a 'house of brands' but we are a truly 'branded house'. With the exception of our brief foray into the condom business, we paint the Virgin brand on to everything we do. When we start a new venture we are proud to add our brand to it in the same way that we do when we rebrand and reinvent a bank or a rail service.

The only reason we can do this is because even the most disparate of businesses are not just about bricks and mortar, rolling stock or airplanes – sure, those things are important pieces of infrastructure – but it's the people that breathe the life into them. All of our seeming hodge-podge of businesses has one critical element in common: the service culture that comes with our people – call it the 'we' factor if you like – is the pulse that drives everything we do.

As a result of my work with the OceanElders and their on-going efforts to save the fragile ecosystem of the world's oceans, I have become quite the expert on coral reefs, and it didn't take a lot of dot connecting to draw an analogy between corporate cultures and coral reefs. They both take a long time to grow and, as many a company has found at their cost, they are a fragile living entity that if abused can be destroyed very easily and very quickly. Most established coral reefs are between 5,000 and 10,000 years old and yet we have managed to kill off ten per cent of them in our lifetimes. While a corporate culture can be developed a whole lot faster than coral, when either one is destroyed the chances are that they're gone for ever.

CULTURAL DESTRUCTION

David Hoare, the co-founder of Talisman Management, has been a friend and associate of mine for many years during which time he has worked as a chairman, CEO and advisor to a wide range of underperforming companies. Sorry, I take that back – what I intended to say is that he has taken on the challenge of *fixing* a wide range of underperforming companies which is Talisman's specialty. David comes from an intriguing engineering/private equity background but he is also a genuine disciple of the invaluable 'people equity' that a healthy culture brings into play. David explained to me one day his concerns on the way the standard private equity model is supposed to work. This is the one where you take a leading company in a growth market with a strong management team, add some financial leverage and a generous dollop of management incentives, which are of course tied to ambitious financial targets and 'hey presto' – value creation! But what happens when the results fall short of expectations? That's when the new owners stamp their feet, change the CEO and set even more ambitious targets, the assumption being that the next one will do a better job. Sadly this often doesn't work either and the company's value continues to be destroyed.

David can reel off a long list of companies where he has seen this storyline playing itself out. Starting in 2006, parcel delivery service CityLink had four CEOs in five years who jointly erased £1 billion of value; at the DX Group, an express mail service, it was five CEOs in four years and £450 million; and waste management company Biffa lost a staggering £1.2 billion under six different CEOs in just five years.

The obvious question is how such disastrous collapses in value can possibly happen in companies that had been leaders in their market areas. As David sees it, in every one of these cases the senior teams were incentivised into marching the company to the drumbeat of totally unrealistic financial targets. Doing the 'right thing' in the long-term interests of the business was pushed to one side and as a result a lot more than value was destroyed. One of the key components that had made the business successful in the first place, the corporate culture, was another more tragic victim of the destruction! And while changing CEOs may be easy, restoring a badly damaged culture is never a simple task. As with any trust-based relationship, 'making up is hard to do'.

For start-ups too, the ability to develop the kind of healthy, people-focused culture that is so critical to a company's sustainability is seriously impeded if from day one the primary focus is on short-term gains and rapid force-fed growth. I am always alarmed when I hear start-up leaders talking more about fulfilling their investors' 'exit strategy' than about creating a great product around great and happy people. In many such cases the exit may well arrive involuntarily and much sooner than the strategy ever foresaw! Had we failed to recognise in time that Virgin's short-lived experience as a public company was going to extinguish the culture that had made us what we were, we might not have been around today to talk about it. Thankfully we'll never know.

I must apologise if I am starting to sound like the proverbial broken record (jamming iPod?) on this but let me quote Herb Kelleher's successor at Southwest, who could easily have been channelling Herb or myself when he said, '*Everything begins and ends with our people. If we keep our employees happy and engaged, they will keep our customers happy who will then reward us with their loyalty. That repeat business helps our bottom line and creates value for our shareholders.'*

So too at every Virgin company, none of which could survive without the dedication, energy, wit and wisdom of our incredible family of people. In simple terms, in their blind stampede to deliver superior economic results, too many business owners and leaders fail to understand enough about the importance of carefully developing a company's culture.

When Peter Drucker said, *'Culture eats strategy for breakfast'*, he might have added that when there's too much focus on profits and growth and too little attention to nurturing your people and culturing the culture, there's a very serious risk that somebody else might soon be eating your lunch.

Chapter 13

THE FRUITS OF PASSION

Beyond definition

I often think how terribly sad it is that so many people – the 'Thank God it's Friday' brigade – are not in the least bit passionate about what they are doing with their lives. I'm talking about the ones for whom life is all about 'making a living' as opposed to making every living moment count.

My wife tells people it is my fetish. I have heard that Tony Collins who runs Virgin Trains has often said I am a 'nutcase' about it. Maybe. But whatever I have contributed to the success of the Virgin companies, I believe that, above all else, my hard-wired passion – some call it obsession – for consistently giving our customers, both internal and external, a better work environment or service experience than they can find anywhere else is what's at the very heart of everything that I, and by extension the Virgin brand, stands for. I genuinely believe that if you care passionately enough you can take just about any facet of the human experience and improve upon it. Now while the words passion and virgin (note the small v) may not be something you are accustomed to seeing in the same sentence, Passion (capital P) is unquestionably the secret sauce, aka the brand essence, of every one of Virgin's scores of highly diverse businesses.

In the same way that you cannot be 'almost unique' or 'partly pregnant', true passion isn't something that comes in half measures. You are either a hundred per cent behind the quest for excellence a hundred per cent of the time or you aren't really a player. As a leader you cannot possibly expect your core brand values to be understood, embraced and become ingrained in the psyche of your people if you yourself are not passionately and uncompromisingly committed to them. I am sorry if this might come across as overly trite or preachy, but if you fail to understand the significance of having and sharing such a palpable passion for what you do, then the chances are that you really do not belong in a leadership role.

PASSION IS INNATE

The first thing that has to be recognised is that one cannot train someone to be passionate – it's either in their DNA or it's not. Believe me, I have tried and failed on more than one occasion and it cannot be done so don't waste your time and energy trying to light a fire under flame-resistant people. If that basic, smouldering fire is not innate then no amount of stoking is ever going to ignite it. The exact same principle applies to positive attitudes in people – you don't train attitudes, you have to hire them. It always amuses me when I hear people declaring that someone 'has an attitude' as this is always said with a negative connotation. The fact is that having an attitude is absolutely fine, just as long as it is consistently positive and upbeat, or put in another way – 'passionate'.

One of the key elements of what has become known as 'the Virgin way' is giving our people the autonomy, freedom, support and a highly flexible (in everything except quality) brand image that gives them the tools to go out and make amazing things happen. It is this passion-fed formula that has allowed the Virgin Group to launch hundreds of new Virgin companies in scores of very diverse businesses and I have no doubt that it will continue to do so for many years to come.

Over the years the Virgin group of companies has been very fortunate in identifying a steady stream of passionate business leaders. Many come from outside the Virgin family but some are 'homegrown', like Brett Godfrey who started Virgin Blue in Australia. Brett is an Australian who after about five years with Virgin Atlantic moved over to the finance area at Brussels-based Virgin Express, a relatively short-lived European airline we operated in the mid-nineties. I'd never met Brett but started hearing nothing but good reports of his steadying influence on Virgin Express's multiple problems. For a 'numbers guy' he had the reputation of being a really good people person, which was something we desperately needed to unite the staff, having gone through three CEOs in a little over twelve months. With all the uncertainty and constant changes of direction at Virgin Express, inevitably the spectre of unions had raised its ugly head; something that at the time had never before happened in Virgin. And it was in fact the union leadership that came to me to suggest that 'the Australian' was by far and away the best candidate for the vacant CEO job. I was a little concerned as to their motives – did they perhaps want Brett because they thought he'd be a pushover? – but we decided to give him a shot and initially slotted him in as acting CEO.

We knew quickly we had made the right choice. Brett soon managed to get the unions onside and in so doing sidestepped a total meltdown and stabilised the situation. Apart from the fact that I have never been a fan of 'acting' roles, it seemed a no-brainer to ask Brett to accept the CEO position on a permanent basis. Normally offering a CEO role is something that generates an excited response but in this instance Brett looked very awkward and almost embarrassed as he responded with, 'Erm, well, sorry, Richard, but I am going to have to say no as my wife and I have decided it's time for us to take our two boys back home to Australia.'

Nobody had anticipated this response so I was shocked and more than a little disappointed, but admired him for putting his young family in front of his career. It was then that, according to Brett, I uttered the words that were to change his life for ever. All I said was, 'Okay and if there's anything you would like to do in Australia be sure and let me know.' To which with a big smile Brett responded, 'Well, actually, Richard, I am glad that you asked as there is one thing I'd very much love to discuss with you!'

It was only then that I learned that Brett had been working diligently for five years on a business plan to start an innovative new domestic airline down under. It seemed he'd been seeking investors for several years and without my knowledge had already pitched it to the Virgin executive team who had rejected it. As I would learn, their rejection of the project was based on a mixture of conventional wisdom and standard accounting and, at a glance, seemed like a very rational decision. Of course, my personal brand of 'wisdom' has seldom been known for its rationality. So much so that one of many things I've been called over the years is 'The ultimate don't-confuse-me-with-the-facts man' – something perhaps spurred by my legendary inability to read complex balance sheets. So when Brett gushed out an excited overview of his Australian airline's business plan, my immediate take on it was more instinctive than by the book – a book that I have never really read.

More importantly, however, what I detected in Brett that day was something that the executive team had clearly overlooked: a passionate belief in the need for and viability of what he was proposing. It was also outrageously reminiscent of the opportunity we'd seized upon fifteen years earlier with Virgin Atlantic – a plan that my colleagues at Virgin Records had unanimously condemned as utterly outlandish! Brett saw a crying need for a new disruptive airline model in the stagnant Australian market and the passion I saw in his eyes when talking about his vision sold me on taking a serious second look at it. Given the nod, it didn't take Brett long to successfully reaffirm some of his business plan's bold projections and we were off to a flyer. Our initial $10 million investment to start what would become Virgin Blue – now rebranded Virgin Australia

– turned out to be one of the smartest we have ever made. Putting it differently, I suppose, with tongue firmly in cheek I could say it was a classic case of, 'Screw It, Let's Blue It.' Sorry!

ENVISAGING VISIONARIES

Brett is just one of many true visionaries I have been lucky to know with the passion, drive, focus and skills to turn their often seemingly impossible dreams into game-changing realities. Like a lot of people before him, Elon Musk had a vision to build a commercially viable electric car. This is a space in which all the early movers have focused their attention on the mass market by developing affordable, compact fuel-saving vehicles almost completely devoid of anything in the way of sex appeal. Musk decided instead to come at it from the premium sports car end of the market and over time move into more mainstream vehicles. The luxury/sports sedan market is much smaller in unit sales opportunities but hugely effective in switching the mindset of influential car owners to finally wanting to own an electric car for looks, performance and cool, first adopter cachet, as opposed to just fuel efficiency. And let's be honest, if you can afford to fork out the price of a luxury vehicle, the cost of fuel is usually the last thing on your mind!

The $70,000 Tesla Model S not only looks like a very cool sports car but behaves like one: it reportedly accelerates from 0 to 60 mph in an incredible 3.7 seconds *and* for those like me who have a conscience about such things, it is almost twice as energy efficient as the homely sector-leading Toyota Prius. And as if all that were not enough, the influential 'Consumer Reports' magazine ranked the Tesla as 'the best we have ever tested' with a ninety-nine per cent overall rating. Rate this one an A on all counts.

Of course Tesla is not Elon Musk's first big success at breaking new ground in emerging industries. His vision of creating a new form of payment to accommodate the unique requirements of online retail sales started life as X.com and soon morphed into PayPal. His other current major dream coming true is SpaceX, which, along similar lines to Virgin Galactic, is developing a private sector satellite launch vehicle to take over where NASA left off. There is even talk of Musk merging his PayPal and space ventures with PayPal Galactic to tackle the challenges of 'off-Earth' payments – I will have to give some more thought to that one! In any case Elon Musk's successes at Tesla, PayPal and Space-X only serve to demonstrate the incredible results that can flow from vision and leadership coming together in one inspired individual with the assistance of an army of equally inspired followers.

PASSION KNOWS PASSION

Another great advantage to having truly passionate leaders is their inherent ability to recognise raw passion in others when they see it. If Tony Collins thinks that I am the one who's a nutcase about customer service, then I am happy to report that he is right there with me every step of the way.

Tony joined Virgin Trains in 1999 from the company that was building our rolling stock, and has been head honcho there since

2004. He is a pragmatic, straight-talking, call a spade a 'bloody shovel' kind of a guy, and his impassioned take no prisoners approach to making our rail service the very best in the business has been a joy to behold. He was fast to paraphrase my favourite phrase when he said to me one day, 'This is a case of "screw it, let's undo it then do it again".'

If you will please excuse another punishing pun, Tony is 'the rail deal' – he totally embraces the belief that your front-line people who deliver the service *are* the business. He supports them to the hilt, puts his trust in them, listens to their observations (good and bad) and in return expects them to bleed Virgin red in the same way that he does. Turning around the crumbling ruin of a business that was the British Rail system for generations was no mean feat for anyone.

The kind of a calamity of an organisation we inherited from British Rail is illustrated by the story of how their train drivers once threatened to go on strike over management demands that they improve their abysmal on-time performance – and maybe even have a train leave on time once in a while! The union representing the drivers argued there was nothing in their collective bargaining agreement that specified their members had to own watches and so inferred that as a result they could not be held responsible for on-time departures. I think it was Timex that was the beneficiary of a very large order for 'Property of BR' inscribed watches. Hard to believe, I know, but that was the prevalent kind of employee 'no can do' attitude that we inherited. So with or without a brand like Virgin behind it, the kind of transformation that Tony and his people have achieved with our 'train set' has been nothing short of miraculous.

Tony is one of those people who always has a ready supply of wonderful stories, but the one that really stuck with me was a tale he told me over dinner one night about a cleaner he spotted one day on one of our trains. Tony was doing one of his routine but ad hoc check rides when he spotted a uniformed employee who was doing a quite exceptional job with our passengers. She didn't know Tony was watching as she helped an elderly couple to their seats, passed out newspapers and so forth, all with a wonderfully cheery disposition. What made it so interesting was that she didn't actually work for Virgin Trains – she was an on-board cleaner employed by Alstom, the company we contract to clean our trains. Impressed, Tony introduced himself and complimented the woman on the outstanding 'above and beyond' job she was doing, before asking if she'd ever considered working for us as opposed to cleaning. He was stunned by her answer: she'd tried a couple of times but, as she put it, 'I wasn't good enough to pass the entrance test.'

Stung by this, Tony got on the phone to our HR team and asked that they conduct an immediate review of the hiring criteria as, based on what he'd just been told, they were clearly filtering out exactly the kind of people we desperately wanted to filter in. They did, and within a couple of weeks the lady was hired as an on-board service assistant. She didn't last long in that job, though – over the next four years she steadily made her way up through the ranks and is now one of our regional station managers looking after several of our train stations. Ever since that day's chance observation, Virgin Trains has been very clear in its recruiting priorities – we now hire for attitude and not paper qualifications.

CHEERS

The way Tony identified someone with the prerequisite attitude and passion has probably been repeated a thousand times in different ways around Virgin over the years. After all, when one is in the business of customer service and you stumble upon someone who is a natural at it then you have to do your best to scoop them up.

I remember David Tait telling a very similar tale to Tony's. Around the corner from Virgin Atlantic's first home in New York City's Greenwich Village was a popular local bar that David, various staff members and I (when in town) used to visit on a regular basis. One particular bartender there by the name of Phil never failed to impress David with the way he looked after his patrons. No matter how busy it was, or how rude and demanding some customers became, he always got the correct drinks out quickly, kept multiple conversations going at the same time and settled altercations with a smile. He was clearly an accomplished professional at what he did and, as Tony had done on the train, David recognised the kind of intuitive flair for great customer service that we are always looking for. He thought Phil would be every bit as good at an airport counter as he was behind a bar.

When David finally made the less than compelling pitch to Phil of, 'How'd you like to consider a new job where you'll earn no tips and work highly irregular hours?' he laughed it off as some kind of a joke. A few days later, however, after some coaxing by David, he came around and said he'd do it. As suspected, Phil Cain's people skills were an instant fit for the airport customer service agent role and quickly led to a supervisor's job. Next it was onwards and upwards to duty manager and eventually he became an exemplary airport manager, working for twenty years or so at a number of Virgin Atlantic gateways around the world. I used to see Phil quite often at Newark and one day couldn't resist asking how David had talked him into giving up the bar job and coming to work for us. His response was, 'Well, to be honest, Richard, he didn't.' Then with a wink he confided that as a (then) single guy, it had really been the thought of all those attractive flight attendants getting off our flights every night that had swayed his decision!

Whatever his motivation – and I can't fault him on that one – countless thousands of others like Phil Cain bring their own personal brands of passion to work with them every day all around our companies. They also bring along their knowledge, vitality, enthusiasm and vision (collectively known as 'passion') to either give birth to a dream of their own or more often to contribute to the efforts of a team of like-minded Virgin family members.

Chapter 14

THE PARTY LINE

Fancy dress and April fools

There was once a popular saying that 'everybody loves a good party' and it may still be true but there just don't seem to be nearly as many of them as there used to be. Or perhaps I'm just not getting invited like I used to be!

Everything that's really worthwhile in life usually involves some degree of risk and in all we do at Virgin we have always revelled in taking on the seemingly impossible rather than shying away and playing it safe. This applies as much to having a good time as to business, and we have never had any qualms about kicking back and enjoying a fun party with our people. I have always believed that the benefits of letting your staff have the occasional blast at an after-hours get-together is a hugely important ingredient in the mix that makes for a family atmosphere and a fun-loving, free-spirited corporate culture. It also goes a long way to tearing down any semblance of hierarchy when you've seen the CFO doing the limbo with a bottle of beer in her hand.

From the very beginning the Virgin companies have grown up on the back of some of the biggest and heartiest parties known to (almost) civilised man. For years our annual summer staff parties at the Manor, our former recording studio in the Oxfordshire countryside, were the stuff of local legend. They started out on a fairly controlled basis with a single day's get-together for all the Virgin UK staff and their families. We'd set up big tents in case it rained – which it seldom ever seemed to do – and had loads of food and drink, live bands, face-painters, bouncy castles and pony rides for the kids (and a few adult children) and a great time was always had by all. One of the highlights of the event for everyone, except possibly me, became my annual version of a tightrope walk. This involved me, often with a drink in both hands to help my stability – at least that's my story – gingerly wobbling my way across about the seventy-five-foot ridge atop the biggest marquee, with the assembled crowd loudly cheering me on – or more probably off! I honestly have no recollection as to how this custom got started, which probably explains it, but I think it was either the tent owners, my life insurance company or sobriety that eventually brought the practice to an end.

As the business started to grow by leaps and bounds – when Virgin Atlantic arrived on the scene we probably doubled our group headcount within twelve months – it began to make the big annual bash a logistical and practical challenge. In the final analysis the mega parties were killed by their success, as they simply grew too big to handle. The last one was over a whole weekend and we (and the local police who were charged with handling the traffic jams) estimated something like 60,000 people showed up. This included a lot of spouses and children of employees, which was never the case in the earlier days when most people were single with no inhibitions about having a wild time – something far less likely to happen in front of spouses and kids.

AIR PLAY

If the Manor parties could have made it into the *Guinness Book of World Records* so too could the 1984 inaugural flight of Virgin Atlantic. Not because of any particular aviation achievement but rather for the greatest amount of champagne ever consumed in a single flight between London and New York. Not since Wilbur and Orville kicked the whole thing off can anyone have come close. It was one huge transatlantic party from the moment the seat-belt sign went off until it came on again for landing in Newark. The late TV personality and journalist David Frost, who was one of our celebrity guests on the trip, was renowned for commuting across the Atlantic almost every other day. Just before landing I remember him saying to me, 'You know, Richard, I've probably flown across the pond a thousand times but that's the first trip I've ever made standing up all the way with a drink in my hand!'

The other little-known fact about that inaugural flight into New York is that the very first passenger that Virgin Atlantic landed in the USA was an illegal immigrant. When the aircraft door opened at Newark, we were met by a bevy of local officials at the end of the jetway, all of whom I suspect were more than a little curious to see what this rock-and-roll airline actually looked like. There had been stories all week on New York City radio stations about how Boy George would be flying the airplane, that we would likely be met by drug-sniffing dogs and all sorts of nonsense. While the cabin crew were doing their document handover, I was anxiously looking for David Tait who ran our US operation, hoping that, as planned, he'd managed to beat us across the Atlantic that morning on Concorde. When I finally spied him and caught his eye, I very deliberately mouthed the words, 'I – don't – have – my – passport.' Knowing my penchant for pulling pranks on people, David laughed out loud and shouted back, 'Yeah, right! Of course you don't, Richard. Nice try, though!'

The unfortunate thing was that it was true. In the desperate rush to get to Gatwick Airport that morning I had dashed out leaving my passport on the kitchen counter. When the inflight supervisor laughingly told David it was actually true (he believed her but not me), he managed to quickly square it away with the head of immigration who fortunately happened to be standing right there. I remember thinking how incredibly impressed these senior federal officials must have been when the chairman of the new airline has to beg to be allowed into the country without any documents. Things didn't get much better for me in the next hour when, at the welcome reception the city threw for us at the airport, I mistook the Mayor of Newark for one of the caterers and asked him if there was any chance they could find some more shrimp! Oh well, I suppose we all have our off days!

Our three airlines, Virgin Atlantic, Virgin America and Virgin Australia, still turn almost every new route launch into an excuse for a party (or three) and all of the companies in the group still love to party at every possible opportunity. The days of the mega-parties at the Manor may be a thing of the past but generally we have reverted to the original smaller more intimate roots and settings in which everyone gets a chance to glimpse an 'other side' to the people they work with – including myself, whenever I can work an invitation.

ROCKING THE ROCK

In January 2012, Virgin Money finally acquired Northern Rock, the British high-street bank that had been nationalised four years earlier, and we had a lot to celebrate. After their brief spell of working for the government, Northern Rock's 2,000 or so employees were clearly excited about joining the Virgin family. They didn't have to wait long to get a taste of their new corporate culture when Jayne-Anne Gadhia, CEO of Virgin Money, and I hosted a huge street party inside Northern Rock's headquarters in Newcastle upon Tyne, at which everyone got an opportunity to behave in very 'unbankerlike' ways! It was kind of an initiation by friendly fire for all the former Northern Rock people who I don't think had ever seen their previous bosses loosen their ties, let alone their purse-strings for a bank-sponsored megabash.

By the end of the night I must have shaken a thousand hands and my fingers were literally numb from the process. Jayne-Anne and I posed for scores of group photographs and the bank's staff even got to rub shoulders with some true local heroes in the form of several Newcastle United football stars who we'd invited to join in the festivities. Virgin Money had just agreed to be a kit sponsor for the Magpies, Newcastle's Premiership pride and joy, and it would seem the energy from the party must have rubbed off on the players. A couple of days later, in front of a packed home crowd, while wearing their new Virgin Money logo shirts for the first time, they managed to pull off a spectacular 3–0 upset victory over champions Manchester United – all very much to Jayne-Anne's confusion as she is a life-long Manchester United fan. So you see, there's nothing like a good party to get everyone's juices flowing! Though I must confess that, being conscious of the fact that several of our businesses, Northern Rock (now Virgin Money) included, do a huge amount of business in Manchester as well, I thought it only prudent to tweet, 'Okay, I accept we're jammy bastards!' Anyway, all in all we got off to a memorable start with our new banker friends and it has kept on getting better ever since.

We had another great party not so long ago to celebrate the opening of the Virgin Group's new corporate headquarters in London. We held it on the rooftop of the new building – it was a fancy-dress affair with everyone coming dressed as pirates and buccaneers. We had flaming torches and a Caribbean steel band, plus lots of Red Stripe beer and rum-based cocktails. I showed up with Joan and my two kids, who also brought their new spouses along to make it truly a family affair. At one point in the festivities, surrounded by hundreds of dancing Virgin staff, I looked down from our rooftop perch and realised that behind a clump of trees I could just about see the houseboat that was my home and office when we started the company over forty years earlier. When we had staff parties on the *Duende* (which I still own), we maxed out at only twenty or thirty people, but the bonhomie we generated was no different to the present day with ten times that number on the roof of an office tower. As silly as dressing up as Captain Morgan the pirate or walking along the top of a tent might sound, I have always believed that parties have been an essential part of the Virgin way and, political correctness be damned, I wouldn't have it any other way.

WHAT'S FIRST – A HAPPY CHICKEN OR A HAPPY EGG?

For most people the assumption seems to be that the more money you have in the bank the happier you'll be – that success has some straight-line correlation with happiness. 'If I work harder I'll be more successful and if I'm more successful I'll be happier.' While nobody is likely to argue that being penniless might not detract from one's *joie de vivre*, according to recent research, happiness actually fuels success, not the other way around.

Shawn Achor's fascinating book *The Happiness Advantage* is based on a decade of positive psychology and neuroscience research at Harvard University and Fortune 500 companies. His book reveals that when we are more positive our brains are 'more engaged, more energised, creative, motivated, healthier, resilient and productive' – a pretty compelling list! His conclusion is that ninety per cent of one's happiness is generated from within, not by external factors like fat bank accounts and expensive possessions. The book cites the power of positivity in the present and how we can rewire our brains in as little as twenty-one days by way of things such as starting each day with a 'random act of kindness' like sending at least one email praising someone, or writing down three new things each day for which we are grateful. Such actions get one's dopamine flowing, which, in simple terms, makes you feel better about yourself and, well, the better you feel the better you perform. So, having fun and enjoying the work experience at every turn is not just the Virgin way but it is also scientifically proven to work to everyone's benefit. I just wish I'd read Shawn's book forty years ago, as it would have greatly helped in my annual attempts to vindicate the excessive party bills with a succession of tightwad CFOs around the group!

APRIL – COME SHE WILL

While staff parties are all about having a big get-together and lots of collective fun as often as possible, I have to admit to also taking a somewhat different and more selfish delight in having a devilishly good time just once a year – on April Fool's Day. In fact, anyone who knows me well will usually make their best efforts to stay well clear of me between midnight and noon on 1 April – which in case you weren't aware of the 'official fool rules' are the hours between which any tricks have to be played out. So if anyone ever tries to pull a stunt on you after noon you should call them out for foul play.

When I was a boy I used to pull all the usual April Fool's pranks on my parents and sisters, like tying bedroom doorknobs together across a hallway so neither occupant could open their doors. Unlike a lot of kids who quickly grow out of April Fool's tricks, however, quite the opposite happened with me. Ever the contrarian, in my case the older I got the more demonic and elaborate my tricks became. In time they also became a fun annual vehicle for me to draw attention to the Virgin brand – sometimes with the most amazing results.

For example, in 1986 I decided it would be fun to put one over on the music industry. So we hatched a fiendish plot and on 31 March I gave an exclusive interview to *Music Week*, then the UK's biggest music industry trade publication. I told them that for years Virgin had been secretly developing a giant computer, on which we had stored every music track we could lay our hands on. This revolutionary device would be called Music Box, and music lovers would be able to use it as a source from which, for a small fee, they could download any individual song or album they wanted. Much to my surprise and delight, they swallowed it hook line and sinker and so the following day, in their 1 April edition, the shocking headline blared *'Branson's Bombshell: The End of the Industry.'* Surprisingly oblivious to the 1 April dateline on the article, all kinds of music business senior executives called throughout the morning to beg, threaten and plead with me not to go ahead with such a crazy scheme. With all of them I just kind of muttered half-apologies, saying I would make another statement later in the day – which of course came at lunchtime, when I announced that the whole story had been an April Fool's joke. That afternoon I got a lot more calls from music industry types with comments that I am afraid I will not be able to repeat!

It was many years later when I ran into Steve Jobs at some event or another that he told me that he too had read the bogus Music Box story and been utterly taken in by it. At the time he had just been edged out of Apple and founded NeXT but he said he'd never forgotten my spoof and at the time thought that, joke or no joke, there was definitely something to be said for our Music Box idea. So while we will never know for sure, since that chance conversation I have always been haunted with the thought that my April Fool's idea might well have inadvertently helped trigger the birth of iTunes and the iPod – which ironically were to become the death knell for our Virgin Megastores and a game-changer for the music industry in general.

Clearly the moral behind this story is that if you're going to let others know – even as an April Fool's joke – how you think your industry might look in the future then you had better make sure that your company has a plan already in place to get you there first. If you don't, then the joke could very easily be on you!

ONE BAD TRICK DESERVES ANOTHER

There was another April stunt that most definitely did backfire on me even if a lot more of our people got a big kick out of it. I had decided to pull an April Fool's trick on Ken Berry, one of my early partners in Virgin Records. On 31 March I invited Ken and his girlfriend to a late dinner at the Roof Gardens, the rooftop restaurant and club we own in the Kensington area of London. The plan was all set for some 'hired hands' to go and break into Ken's apartment a few minutes after midnight (I play by the rules) and remove a bunch of things like some furniture, his TV and stereo equipment. We had some actors dressed up as policemen who were going to come in to ask questions and dust for fingerprints and eventually I'd yell 'April Fool', we'd all have a good laugh, bring the stuff back and it would be over. At least that was the plan. But as Robert Burns pointed out, '*The best laid schemes of mice and men gang aft agley*' and this one was about to go as 'agley' as it gets!

The problem started when, after I got tied up talking to someone else, I got back to our table about fifteen minutes after midnight to find that Ken and friend had left for home leaving a note saying, '*Thanks for dinner, see you tomorrow. Ken.*' I panicked because I knew they'd be home already and as such it was already too late for me to get there to stage-manage the prank. Not knowing what to do I headed for home and was greeted by my wife Joan (who wasn't in on the joke because she would have totally disapproved of it) saying, 'Richard, something awful has happened. Kenny's flat's been broken into and the police are there now. He called to ask if his girlfriend could spend the night with us as she's too scared to stay in the flat.' So I had no alternative but to call Ken and come clean, apologise profusely and arrange for all his stuff to be returned straightaway. His reaction was one of, 'Well, Richard, I don't really know if I can do anything because the police have filed the report already. But leave it with me and I'll try to explain it to them.' Feeling more than a little embarrassed at the whole screw-up, I was about to head for bed when the doorbell rang. Sensing this wasn't good, I opened the door to find two very large London bobbies who seemed anything but amused at my antics and gruffly asked if I would accompany them to the station to 'assist them with their enquiries'.

I was dressed for bed but they didn't seem to care and hauled me off still in dressing gown and slippers. In the car they said nothing in response to my repeated whines of 'This is all a terrible mistake' and 'Please, just call Mr Berry, he can explain that there was no robbery here.' They remained inscrutable as they marched me into Harrow Road Police Station, took away my dressing gown cord – presumably so I wouldn't hang myself – shoved me into a cell and departed without saying another word. It only got worse. A half hour later I was awoken from a fitful sleep by screams from the unseen occupant of the cell next to mine. It sounded like a beating was underway as I heard, 'Please don't hit me again. Honest, guv, I didn't do nothing!' It stopped soon after and I lay there the rest of the night feeling more than a little contrite and extremely sorry for myself.

Finally, around midday, the same two policemen arrived at the cell and without saying a word took me upstairs where they charged me with a dozen or more offences including wasting police time. They then handed me my dressing gown cord and told me I was free to leave. I still wasn't too sure what had happened but as soon as I stepped out into the grey morning light the penny dropped with a resounding cheer: the cheer came from the assembled Virgin Records staff led by Kenny and the policemen standing outside the police station as they celebrated my release with my familiar cry of 'April Fool!' I'd been set up – big time!

If ever a joke backfired on me this had to be it. I later found that when Ken had told the police that the burglary was all a joke gone wrong by a friend of his, the officers in charge were not in the least amused. They at first wanted to charge me with either criminal mischief as well as wasting police time, but at Ken's pleading (that's his story at least) instead agreed they'd drop it on one condition: that Ken would support them in teaching his wayward friend 'a lesson that he won't soon forget' by keeping him locked up in a cell until noon when April Fool's Day officially ended. Needless to say Ken had agreed immediately, in all probability thinking it was an absolutely wonderful idea! And as for the whole beating thing in the next cell – that too had been staged by some of our people.

TO INFAMY AND BEYOND

I suppose after such a lesson most, dare I say, 'normal' people would have been traumatised at the mere mention of April Fool's tricks forevermore. Unfortunately that is not how my brain is wired. If anything, I simply became more determined than ever to make a better job of future stunts – like the one we *almost* pulled off on 1 April 1989.

At the time I was thirty-six years old and very much into ballooning, which is what inspired me to come up with the idea for what is arguably my most elaborate April Fool's stunt ever. I commissioned the creation of a custom-designed, hot-air flying saucer from my friend Don Cameron at Cameron Balloons and to my delight he came through with what was really a quite remarkable piece of equipment. Shaped like a classic comic-book flying saucer, our UFO came complete with rotating flashing strobe lights, which by night offset the eerie glow that was produced every time the hot-air burner was fired. The icing on the cake, though, had to be the 'little person' (I am told I'm not allowed to say 'dwarf') we hired to go along on the trip wearing a custom tailored little green Martian costume. Not to be outdone, I joined in the fun with a Captain Kirk-like sparkly silver space suit.

So while I played Captain Kirk, Don Cameron, one of the world's top balloonists, came along to co-pilot his company's brilliant handiwork. We took off from north London at around four in the morning, flew over the city and then found ourselves – with balloons you go where the prevailing winds choose to take you – heading down the M25 in the general direction of Gatwick Airport. For the three of us in the air, it was all plain sailing. What we didn't know about, however, was the havoc we were creating 500 feet below us back on planet Earth!

Apparently we were spotted by some night-shift workers early in our flight and the 'UFO sighting' they called into their local police station had set a *War of the Worlds* repeat performance in motion. As radio stations excitedly speculated on the origins of the low-flying alien craft, with every mile we flew the furore on the ground grew crazier by the minute. Before long there were three police forces tracking us, and the army had been called out too. The busy M25 motorway, already slowed by a heavy morning fog, was now at a standstill as motorists stopped and got out of their cars to marvel at the mysterious UFO as it flew over them in the pre-dawn gloom.

By this stage we were getting a little too close to Gatwick Airport (London's second busiest) for our liking and so decided it was time to call it quits. Despite the fog we managed to spot a level field and with strobe lights flashing and the burners glowing mysteriously in the gloom, Don brought us down without incident – or so we thought. Looking out of my little window in the 'space capsule', I remember thinking that this was like an eerie scene from a Steven Spielberg movie and it was right about then that I spied a line of police vehicles and army trucks surrounding the field. When Don landed us perfectly without a bump, a brave young bobby, truncheon drawn, started walking none too confidently in our direction.

It was ET time! We started our own fog machine before slowly lowering the ramp-like door and dispatching our little green ET to meet him. Without a second thought, the terrified policeman turned on his heels and ran as fast as I've ever seen anyone move. It was at this stage that I decided I'd better intercede before someone got hurt, so jumping onto planet Earth I welcomed its brave defenders with the universal peace declaration of 'April Fool!' The first reaction from the fleeing officer was one of utter relief but according to a report on the website Alien UFO Sightings, the policeman involved would later tell the press, 'I have never been so scared in twenty years on the force.' His senior officers were not at all amused, however, and for the second time in my April Fools career I was threatened with charges of wasting police time but survived to fight again.

Needless to say I am not the only one who has indulged in some pretty wild April Fool's stunts. Two of the better ones I heard about were 'perpetrated' upon Eric Schmidt when he was at Sun Microsystems. One time his friendly staff took apart his office and rebuilt it on a platform in the middle of a pond – complete with working telephone, which I thought a really nice touch. Another time they emptied out his office and replaced the furniture with a Volkswagen Beetle, which they'd taken apart and reassembled in order to get it through the office door. Eric's subsequent employers at Google are also renowned for their own stunts such as 'Google Nose'. On 1 April when pulling up the Google home page, visitors found a new tab that professed it would let them smell various things (strangely these included 'a wet dog') by putting their noses up close to the screen. No one I know would ever admit to being fooled by this prank but one can only imagine the gullible millions who must have sniffed their screens that morning!

One of the all-time April classics, however, has to be 'Google TiSP' ('Toilet Internet Service Provider') which on 1 April 2007 was featured on the Google search home page as, '*A fully functional end-to-end system that provides free in-home wireless access by connecting your commode-based TiSP wireless router to one of thousands of TiSP Access Nodes via fiber-optic cable strung through your local municipal sewage lines.*' Google boasted that TiSP used 'GFlush' technology and it came with an eight-step installation kit for the '*quick, easy and largely sanitary process*'. Item #8 read, '*Congratulations, you're online! (Please wash your hands before surfing).*' Considering that in 2007 Google averaged 1.2 billion searches per day (in 2013 that number was up to 5.9) there's little doubt that TiSP qualifies as the most viewed April Fool's stunt in history. Absolutely brilliant stuff! And then there was the joint Virgin and Google (or 'Virgle' as we dubbed it) April Fool's stunt that Larry Page and I dreamed up at the bar on Necker – but let's save that for another day!

FUN IS INFECTIOUS

As you may have started to appreciate, like Google, Virgin takes the business of fun very seriously. I know that many unhappy souls will inevitably condemn stunts like these as being needless distractions and a waste of company time and effort with no tangible commercial benefits. How sad! If the workplace, where most adults spend almost half their waking weeks, cannot be an environment in which to enjoy some spontaneous good times, then what's the point of it all? I have always believed that a sense of humour and the ability not to take oneself too seriously are critically important attributes for any healthy corporate culture. One highly tangible upside is seeing how much of a buzz our staff get from talking about 'the crazy stuff we do at Virgin' with friends. When those friends work at stuffed-shirt companies that would never in a million years consider such nutty antics, you just know that they're thinking, 'Wow, how do I get a job there?' I don't think it any coincidence that, like Google, we are snowed under with thousands of applications every time we have job openings or start a new company. Fun is infectious and, as Shawn Achor's research can testify, it's also good for the general well-being of the individual and their businesses – it has certainly worked for Virgin and Google!

Oh, and just in case you are wondering, as many did at the time we first broke the news, I should make it absolutely clear that Virgin Galactic is very much for real – if you care to check you will see the first announcement in 2004 was *not* made on 1 April. If you want to see one great company party, however, then you should watch out for the celebration we have in mind when SpaceShipTwo completes its first commercial flight. It has been a long time coming but I can assure you it will be one heck of a bash that will have been well worth the wait!

And for those of us on board that first Galactic flight, rather like the first transatlantic Virgin Atlantic flight some thirty years earlier, I am sure we will have to run some serious experiments on how well champagne sprays in a weightless environment – strictly for scientific purposes, of course. Cheers!

PART FOUR

LEAD

DIRECTION
EXAMPLE
EDGE
MODEL
ADVANTAGE
HEAD
GUIDANCE
PRIORITY
LEADERSHIP
PILOT
AHEAD
FRONT RANK
SPARK
POINT
VANGUARD
MODEL
ADVANCE

Chapter 15

LEADERS OF
THE FUTURE

New skills for a new world

When I started out with what was to become Virgin more than four decades ago, I wanted to make people's lives better. I know this can very easily sound like a load of unmitigated self-serving twaddle, but it's true.

I felt then, and still do today, that business, every business, has enormous potential to be a force for good in the world. Companies can realise this potential by looking for ways to do things differently, and by putting our people and the planet right up there alongside growth, and profit as our *raison d'être*. And the amazing thing is that, contrary to popular perception, these are not opposing poles but are mutually reinforcing opportunities. Business doesn't have to be a zero-sum game, where some win and others lose. When done properly, everybody stands to gain: companies, communities, and the beautiful planet on which we are privileged to live.

To achieve lasting progress we must identify, nurture and learn from the next generation of business leaders. Some of these rising stars are already ahead of the curve, especially in the way they weave together their social and entrepreneurial passions and I wish all of us in business could wise up to this fact and start doing more to encourage and support them. Businesses have a major role to play in tackling the world's toughest challenges so to my mind it makes perfect sense to tap into the energy of the legions of up and coming young business leaders who are not afraid to start companies, challenge the status quo and see how their products and services can make a difference in the world.

TRAINING FOR SUCCESS

That's what we had in mind when Virgin Unite was instrumental in opening the Branson Centres of Entrepreneurship in Johannesburg, South Africa and Montego Bay, Jamaica a few years back. And thank goodness we did! Now, hundreds of entrepreneurs later, we can point to countless success stories about start-ups that have given hope where there was none, created jobs, stimulated local economic growth, and reduced poverty.

Take, for instance, the story of Claire Reed, one of the budding entrepreneurs supported by the centre in Johannesburg. Her business Reel Gardening produces a patented pre-fertilised biodegradable 'seed strip' that makes growing food in a garden setting simple, easy and extremely productive. By reducing water wastage by eighty per cent in the germination phase, Reel Gardening is forging to the forefront of the fight against food insecurity in Africa. Since attending the Branson Centre, Claire, who lives by the perhaps clichéd but still apt motto of 'Better to teach a man to fish than give a man a fish', has created numerous jobs for previously unemployed single mothers in the production of the seed tape. She has also provided training at some 150 school and community gardens, thus enabling countless others to take control of their food security and employment.

Over in the West Indies, another Jamaican Branson Centre alumna Robyn Fox has developed three distinct, but closely interwoven businesses: the Mount Edge Guest House; the 'Europe in the Summer' (or EITS as in eats!) Café, 'offering European and Jamaican flair using the farm-to-table concept'; and Food Basket Farm, a weekly delivery service for fresh, locally grown, pesticide-free produce. Robyn now has a steady stream of customers throughout the year and has identified opportunities to expand her operations further afield as well as how to educate others in the community about farming methods, hospitality and tourism. As Robyn tells it, 'Among so many other things during my time at the Branson Centre I was introduced to the opportunities that are to be found in harnessing the power of the local community. We hire only locals in the businesses, we grow almost all our food locally and we embrace the community at every turn whether it's fish fries with our guests or local "Rasta" drummers playing for them. It adds so much more satisfaction knowing that we are not just running a healthy business but that its impact on the community has been nothing but positive.'

STUDENT ENTREPRENEURS

Claire and Robyn's stories are all the more encouraging considering the similar socio-economic challenges that South Africa and Jamaica both face – looking at the bigger picture, however, they are merely a drop-in-the-bucket. So, why not work to take entrepreneurship and leadership to a whole new level?

Let's start in our schools. Having dropped out of school at sixteen, I've always felt that the UK's education system never really caught on to the idea that entrepreneurship can and should be nurtured at an early age. This may have improved slightly over the years but it certainly still has a very long way to go. Today's teenagers are tomorrow's leaders and with very few exceptions they are bursting with natural inquisitiveness, drive and spirit that schools need to learn to harness and channel rather than tame. Our educational systems need to give young people the opportunity to plug into curriculums that encourage them to rise to their full potential, take risks, embrace failure, and challenge the established norms wherever and whenever they can. The leaders of tomorrow will be so much more effective if they are taught to retain and refine that childlike curiosity for the unknown, rather than having it 'schooled' out of them, as seems still to be the case today in so many schools and universities.

Secondary education should be encouraged to place greater emphasis on developing emotional intelligence, critical thinking, and real-life problem-solving skills – algebra and calculus don't cut it – all of which are key traits of successful entrepreneurs and indeed successful adults in any walk of life. One of the problems facing any such classroom revolution is that schoolteachers tend to teach the things they themselves were taught in school, and entrepreneurship was almost certainly not one of them. In fact, when I went to school the only 'job' teachers ever talked about was teaching, presumably because that was all they had ever wanted to do – they too, however, were likely victims of the same phenomenon at the hands of their own teachers. Career guidance counselling was not that big back then!

So how exactly can entrepreneurship be wedged into school curriculums? For one, we should encourage schools to bring in entrepreneurs of all ages to talk to pupils about their own personal journeys. There is no greater inspiration than hearing about someone's first-hand experiences – warts and all. Not just the glowing tales of 'How I made it big' but all of the seemingly insurmountable challenges, near-misses and failures, which are every bit as valuable as the success stories. We should also support more small business challenges and competitions in schools and universities. Wonderful models exist for such things in programmes such as 'Young Enterprise' in the UK and 'Junior Achievement' (JA) in the USA.

Young Enterprise and Virgin Money have collaborated on a wonderful competition aimed at primary school children (ages five to eleven) called 'The Fiver Challenge'. Participating children or groups are pledged five pounds to set up a 'mini-business' and have thirty days to make as much profit as they can while engaging with their local communities. At the end of the month each group's earnings are tallied up, pledges repaid and the kids decide how they want to use any profits – maybe a day out, books for school or a donation to their favourite charity – the choice is entirely theirs. The purpose of the challenge, however, is not about the winnings so much as introducing young minds to the concepts of risk taking, team working, problem solving and in short – that money is not just for spending!

In the US, not-for-profit JA distributes a classroom-based teaching module entitled 'Be Entrepreneurial'. The seven-part programme introduces students to the essential elements of such things as writing a practical business plan and then challenges them to start an entrepreneurial venture while still in school. As per their website, JA students learn about *'Advertising, business plans, competitive advantages, customer demographics, entrepreneurial spirit, ethical dilemma, ethics, financing, franchising, long- vs. short-term consequences, market needs, marketing, non-profit businesses, stakeholders, product development, profit, social entrepreneurship, social responsibility'* and of course, roll all these together and they are essentially learning how to become well-rounded leaders!

I don't think any one of those words or phrases ever crossed the lips of one of my teachers when I was in school. Okay, 'that was then', you say – but the real problem is that I don't believe they are terribly common in today's schools either – certainly not before university level. But we shouldn't fall into the trap of blaming everything on the schools. One way or the other we could all do a better job of promoting activities outside of the classroom that support the entrepreneurial experience. It is certainly encouraging to learn that, at last count, 150 countries now celebrate Global Entrepreneurship Week and that more and more business schools are offering courses on how to become an entrepreneur.

Consider my own story. When I was in school, my friends and I saw a need for young people to have their own voice on the bigger issues of the day. So we started a magazine for students, aptly titled *Student*. We were attempting to change the world and run a business all at the same time. As you will have read, we made all kinds of mistakes big and small along the way, and although we didn't always realise it at the time, these inevitably turned into valuable learning experiences. But the factor that most contributed to our early success was the support we got from our families and friends – at the time our schools didn't even pretend to understand what we were up to. *Student* soon led to other, bigger endeavours that benefited greatly from the life lessons that we gleaned from this first entrepreneurial venture and I have often thought how much less daunting the experience might have been had we had the support of the school system and local businesses. Having access to a study course like the above Junior Achievement programme might have made all the difference in the world. I say 'might' rather than 'would' only because, given my teenage disaffection with just about anything taught in a classroom, the chances are I might just have decided that this 'entrepreneurship thing' was not for me. We will never know!

A PIONEERING TALE

Several Virgin companies have been making concerted efforts to support burgeoning entrepreneurs. For example, working closely with Virgin Unite, Virgin Media decided it had all the tools to offer meaningful online assistance and so in 2010 launched VirginMediaPioneers.com. This has spawned an incredible online community of enterprising young people using videos and blogging to help young entrepreneurs share their ideas and experiences. The Pioneers programme also has real (live) people there for participants to talk to, network with, collaborate with and get tips from. The online video channel Pioneers TV brings it all to life with Pioneers' spotlights and behind-the-scenes insights into all kind of industries. In the real world there are also free events for training and face-to-face networking as well as contests and competitions that will help entrepreneurs get experience and build their profiles. I have been thrilled to take part in several events where I've had the opportunity to sit down with some of our Pioneers and let them pitch their projects and discuss their hopes, aspirations and fears.

One of the more amazing tales of success that we use to inspire Virgin Media Pioneers is that of Londoner Jamal Edwards who now frequently attends VMP events to share his experiences. His story began when at age fifteen his mother gave him a digital video camera for Christmas. He started filming clips of his friends rapping and posting them on the newly emergent YouTube. When people started to follow Jamal, he next started poaching interviews with rap artists outside clubs and adding them to his YouTube content. Seeing the niche he was filling, at sixteen he launched his YouTube-hosted SB.TV online music channel. Jamal was on his way. Now, at just twenty-two, his millions of followers have translated to millions in the bank and Jamal has become a youth broadcast sensation. He is accredited with giving several new stars like Ed Sheeran their starts on SB.TV and I have to say that looking at Jamal's emergence on the scene gives me some déjà vu shivers, as in so many ways it's like a digital era remix of my roots with *Student* magazine and Virgin Records. Go get 'em, Jamal, you are an inspiration to millions of young entrepreneurs!

HOW GOVERNMENTS CAN HELP – SERIOUSLY!

Unfortunately Jamal's amazing story is very much the exception to the rule. While support from schools and families is critical, governments need to contribute as well in supporting young entrepreneurs and future job creators who, as I did at age sixteen, decide that academic pursuits aren't really the best path for them. Determined to dig deeper into exactly these issues, in 2011 Virgin Media Pioneers (VMP) conducted an extensive survey of young entrepreneurs and their responses confirmed the usual problems: young people are still held back by a lack of support, a lack of practical training and the often impossible task of sourcing start-up capital.

Drawing on these findings and working with a number of youth issues experts and groups, VMP issued a comprehensive report calling for corporations to find tangible ways to support start-ups, such as freeing up unused office space and providing mentors who would volunteer their time to assist aspiring young entrepreneurs. At the same time I suggested to the government that it should seriously reconsider the way it invests in young people. The argument was really very simple: why should a university-bound student be able to borrow (in the UK) around £30,000 to get a degree in business but then when he or she is ready to take their new-found entrepreneurial skills to market, struggle to raise a measly £5,000 or £10,000 to launch their shoestring start-up? Or, in the event that halfway through their planned time at university a student stumbles on a 'must do, Eureka moment' opportunity and wants to seize the moment – why shouldn't there be a way for them to parlay the balance of their student loan into a start-up loan? I further boldly suggested that the British government could address this scenario and in so doing unlock huge economic benefits. The recommendation was for the existing Student Loans Company, which administers tuition fees, be reinvented as a new 'Youth Investment Company'. Under the new, broader-based business model it would continue to administer student loans, but would also have the remit to make new or crossover loans available to young entrepreneurs on the same favourable terms.

Remembering my own struggles to find funding after I dropped out of school, this ingeniously simple concept certainly resonated with me. As supportive as my parents were during those first years, it was an incredibly challenging hand-to-mouth time and besides, even if your parents have the resources, no one really likes asking their family for hand-outs – but the government? Well, that's a very different thing!

To everyone's delight, in 2012, behind the efforts of Lord Young, the government formed a new non-profit called the 'Start-Up Loans Company', to provide financing to young businesses and appointed James Caan as its chairman. The company has since built up a network of more than fifty delivery partners who are lending money to new businesses all across the UK. To date, more than 15,000 businesses have borrowed over £80 million– an impressive feat by any standard. Through our bank, Virgin Money, we took part in a pilot programme last year, and have now launched our own delivery partner, 'Virgin StartUp', to help provide training and mentorship in addition to funding. Of course, this is not just an issue in Britain, governments all around the world should be working to figure out ways to put more capital in the hands of entrepreneurs in order to drive economic growth, broaden the tax base, and create jobs.

When one considers that in 2013 (according to the UK government's 'Private Sector Employment Indicator') small businesses of ten to forty-nine employees accounted for ninety-nine per cent of all UK private sector companies and fifty-nine per cent of all private sector employment, it certainly is an incredibly fertile field in which to plant some new entrepreneurial seed money.

'FEMTREPRENEURS'

As tough as starting a business is for everyone, special attention should be paid to young female entrepreneurs who, inexplicably, still face many more barriers to credit, markets and social networks than do their male counterparts. I say inexplicably because we know that women reinvest more of their earnings into the health and education of themselves and their families, which has a valuable multiplier effect from which we all stand to gain. Furthermore, according to the Boston Consulting Group, women make seventy per cent of household purchasing decisions and not just on children's clothing and groceries but also the big-ticket items like cars and vacations. So given that almost fifty per cent of the workforce is now female and they are making seventy per cent of the buying decisions, what possible rationale or justification can there be for the comparative dearth of women in senior executive roles and boardrooms?

According to the European Commission, in the largest EU companies the ratio of female board members across member states averages only about fourteen per cent: the Italians are the worst with only six per cent while the French do better with twenty-two per cent. To try and redress (no pun intended) the balance, the EU is considering following Norway's lead. Back in 2003, the Norwegians set a minimum target of forty per cent for women on boards and by 2008 and that number was up to an admirable forty-four per cent. The UK government meanwhile has tamely 'recommended' that British companies should have twenty-five per cent female board participation by 2015. Don't hold your breath on this one – first of all it's way too low a target and secondly it's going to take something a lot stronger than a polite nudge from the government to break the very British 'old boys' club' mentality at board level.

The focus on board gender ratios, though, is putting the cart before the horse. This is a step-by-step process and before anyone can hope to increase the amount of female representation at board level there first has to be a much higher ratio of women in senior executive roles. According to the 2013 *Fortune* 1000 list of CEOs, only 4.6 per cent (that is, forty-six) are women and that number has been virtually stagnant for a decade. I find that quite appalling but hopefully the infamous glass ceiling is about to become a distant memory with the new generation of dynamic women leaders that are now running a lot of formerly very macho organisations like General Motors (Mary Barra took over in January 2014), Pepsico, IBM, Lockheed Martin and General Dynamics. Others like Sheryl Sandberg, the vociferous COO at Facebook and Marissa Mayer at Yahoo are also gaining momentum in the drive to make gender a non-issue in the workplace. At Virgin we have our own powerhouse women leaders such as Jayne-Anne Gadhia at Virgin Money, Jean Oelwang at Virgin Unite and Cecilia Vega who has just joined us as CEO of Virgin Mobile in Mexico: but I'll be honest and admit – we too still have work to do.

CORPORATIONS AND ACTIVE START-UPS

Whatever the gender, one question I get asked frequently is, 'So what can established businesses do to help young entrepreneurs?'

One quick and easy option is to incorporate young entrepreneurs and their businesses into existing supply chains. On Virgin America flights, for example, our passengers are offered healthy snack foods made by passionate entrepreneurs, such as 'Krave Turkey Jerky', 'Holly Baking Company's Chocolate Chip Cookies', and 'Hail Merry Seasoned Nut Blend'. All three of these companies were started independently by young entrepreneurs who, after discovering they couldn't find the food product that they wanted on the market, decided to go out and create it for themselves. A very familiar scenario in the Virgin story and the entrepreneur world in general!

In South Africa, the township of Soweto is one of Johannesburg's poorest suburbs and, perhaps not surprisingly, it didn't have a single health and fitness club. As a result, when Virgin Active announced we were opening one there it drew equal gasps of surprise and admiration from the local community. Better still, this was no cookie cutter club but was uniquely tailored to Soweto's particular needs. It features such things as a DJ booth, and a boxing arena with commercial spaces for local entrepreneurs, including a hairdressing salon and even a car wash: in total the club has created more than a hundred much-needed permanent jobs. It is at the core of Virgin's DNA to support and celebrate innovation and the spirit of entre- preneurship, but in order to reach true scale we need others to do the same. That means getting active and getting creative – nodding in sage approval of other people's efforts or even the occasional donation of cash is fine, but without assertive action it doesn't get it done!

MENTORING – FROM THOSE WHO'VE 'BEEN THERE, DONE THAT'

When talking about the importance of mentoring, the American author and businessman Zig Ziglar couldn't have said it any better – *'A lot of people have gone further than they thought they could because someone else thought they could.'* Ask any successful businessman and, if they are honest about it, they will almost certainly admit to having benefited from the advice of a mentor at some point along the way.

I have always been a huge believer in the inestimable value good mentoring can contribute to any nascent business. As a young man entering the mysterious and somewhat scary world of business for the first time, I was lucky enough to be taken under the wing of David Beevers, a friend of my parents. David was an accountant and out of sheer kindness (and I suspect some desperate pleading by my mum and dad) he used to spend one evening a week trying to guide me through the basics of bookkeeping – it was hugely helpful and he displayed amazing patience with my repeated requests of, 'Erm, can you run that one by me just one more time, please.' I talk elsewhere about how much the late Sir Freddie Laker's mentoring did for me with Virgin Atlantic and how greatly his down-to-earth wisdom accrued to my entire approach to business.

The first step to finding a good mentor, is of course, coming to terms with the fact that you actually can benefit from having one. Understandably there's a lot of ego, nervous energy and parental pride involved, especially with one- or two-person start-ups

– factors that tend to manifest themselves in a cocoon-like state of mind where, 'Only I/we get it and nobody else can possibly help make this thing work'. Trust me: they can and they will. Going it alone is an admirable but foolhardy and highly flawed approach to taking on the world.

Just look at the high-fliers who have sought out mentors. Steve Jobs' variant of my Sir Freddie was former Intel manager Mike Markkula. His investment of $80,000 in equity and $170,000 as a loan earned Markkula a one-third share in Apple but it was his role as what Jobs called the 'adult supervisor' that was by far and away his greatest contribution to keeping the unruly Apple youngsters on track. At Google, Larry Page and Sergey Brin brought in a similar overseer in Eric Schmidt (formerly of Sun Microsystems and Novell) who was appointed CEO when they realised the company's explosive growth was outstripping their ability to manage it. Schmidt's greatest contribution was building the corporate infrastructure needed to maintain Google's frenetic growth.

So please, take it from me: no matter how incredibly smart you think you are, or how brilliant, disruptive or plain off-the-wall your new concept might be, every start-up team needs at least one good mentor. Someone, somewhere, has already been through what you are convinced nobody else has ever confronted! Okay, so their version may have been analogue rather than digital, but trust me, many of the business fundamentals are exactly the same. Building a new business takes more than technological skills and creative genius – it needs people, and if you're going to create a great culture as well as a great product, those people need tending to in a plethora of different ways

RENT A MENTOR

If you are going to be bold enough to go into business for yourself then you should have no qualms about seeking out the dream mentor. If you have someone you admire that you think will understand your objectives, whether it's a friend of your family's, an old university professor, a local businessperson or even a senior executive from a multinational company, then be bold and go for it.

Phil Drolet at Entrepreneur.com suggested that, '*An ideal mentor will have achieved what you want to achieve and be someone who you could see yourself going out for a drink with.*' Just be sure and offer to pick up the tab when you do! But seriously, if they are the right choice, the chances are they are going to be extremely busy too, so Drolet stressed the necessity to respect a mentor's time by following up with well-crafted and concise emails and not expecting them to do all the work.

Most people – as Sir Freddie was with me – are flattered when a young, enthusiastic entrepreneur comes seeking the wisdom of their advice and counsel. The worst that can happen is that they fail to respond or just say no, which falls into the category of 'nothing ventured nothing gained' – one that every good young entrepreneur will quickly become very familiar with!

In many ways starting a company is akin to having your first baby – it's an exciting and slightly terrifying experience. When the first child coughs or cries too long, your natural instinct is that something's terribly wrong and you want to take them to the doctor. With the second child you'll say, 'Don't worry, it's only a cough' and by the third it's already a case of, 'Darling, did you hear something just then?' The right mentor will probably have raised a bunch of infant ventures and be able to smooth your way through the teething troubles that every young company experiences. They will help you and your team members navigate your way through those seemingly overwhelming (and often daily) early-stage crises and later, all being well, still be there to coach you through the equally daunting process of an orderly – as opposed to runaway-train – expansion process.

Later, if you have successfully negotiated the start-up years and perhaps had someone mentor you along the way, are you ready to pay some of it back by assisting local social entrepreneurs? If so, take a look at your own business or the company you work for: do you and your team have the skills and the energy that would be valuable when helping others? If so, could you perhaps find new partners and take on a new sector? Alternatively can you carve out some time to invest in helping a non-profit tackle its tough first few years?

I can assure you, it will be time extremely well spent and whatever time and energy you invest will come back to you in what I have certainly found to always be true win-win experiences. The leaders of the future have got a lot going for them but are always going to need all the help they can get from the elder statesmen who have been there and done that.

When it comes to finding the right mentors I can think of no better example than what we have achieved with all of our mentor/partners at Virgin Unite over the last decade.

Virgin Unite is a foundation that alongside all kinds of amazing partners, brings together the best of entrepreneurial spirit with ideas that help to tackle some of the tougher social and environmental challenges around the world. We've worked with our partners to create leadership collaborations like the Elders, the Carbon War Room and the B Team. We've also had the privilege of working with some inspirational young entrepreneurs through the Branson Centres for Entrepreneurship and a global mentorship platform that helps connect successful entrepreneurs with those just starting out.

We created Virgin Unite based on the principle that business can and must be a force for good – so much of our work has also been leveraging the wonderful people and assets we have in our family of businesses to change business for good. Most importantly, as the name Unite suggests we always seek out the best local or multinational partners: no matter how big you are, going it alone is seldom, if ever, a viable option. And as we have found, particularly with the Elders, a good mentor can be an amazingly telling mirror and can also open a lot of doors that previously looked impenetrable.

Chapter 16

BEING THERE

Driving the chariot

Growing up in England, history was one of my (very few) favourite subjects at school. TV heroes like The Lone Ranger were fine to a point, but the people we learned about in history lessons were for real. Great British explorers like Sir Francis Drake, Sir Walter Raleigh and Scott of the Antarctic filled my head with dreams of far-off conquests, and to this day I still love reading about and learning from past visionaries who were unwilling to accept the established boundaries of their times.

TERMS OF ENGAGEMENT

One area in which all these great leaders past and present behave very differently is their degree of personal involvement when it comes to engaging with the enemy – or, in polite business parlance, that would be 'the competition'. Some prefer to have their 'people' manning the barricades or leading the charge while others, myself included, love nothing better than jumping into the trenches for some good hand-to-hand combat with the opposition. Okay, maybe I am getting a little bit carried away as the commercial world pales somewhat in comparison to the physical risks taken by my history book heroes, but there is a lot of common ground in what leading from the front-line does for the morale of one's troops as well as the message it sends to the other side.

When it comes to leaders being prepared to put themselves out there, my greatest all-time idol has to be Admiral Horatio Nelson and in particular his heroic last stand at the Battle of Trafalgar – which as every good British schoolboy can tell you, took place in 1805. Even in the heat of battle Nelson's way of operating was to fearlessly position himself (in full naval dress uniform – there were no camouflage fatigues back then) on the poop deck and, quite literally, put himself directly in the line of fire. The brave admiral did, of course, pay the price when a musket ball from a French sniper duly dispatched him to a heroic death. Nelson was truly a leader who led by inspired example and who would never ask anything of his men that he was not prepared to do himself.

I have often wondered how differently history might have viewed the story of Trafalgar had the good admiral somehow managed to direct the same great naval victory from the safety of his cabin below decks. How much would the same outcome have lost in the telling were it deprived of the heroics of a leader who laid down his life for the cause? We'll never know for sure, but I seriously doubt I would be writing about Nelson 200 years later had he died quietly in bed instead of by taking that musket-ball for the team!

And having already just addressed the subject of women in the boardroom, I really should also give equal coverage to women on the battlefield. The greatest British female hero that we studied in school was the legendary Queen Boadicea who, between 61 and 63 AD, led an uprising in East Anglia against the occupying Romans. She almost pulled it off but was finally outmanoeuvred by the superior military might of Rome's armies. Her place in history was secured, however, and she is immortalised with a huge bronze statue near London's Westminster Bridge that shows the warrior queen – accompanied by her two daughters – fearlessly driving her two-horse chariot into battle!

History abounds with tales of military leaders who died bravely for their countries although not always wisely, and here there can be few better examples than the infamous Charge of the Light Brigade, immortalised in Alfred Lord Tennyson's poem of the same name. This is something else that most British schoolchildren of my generation had to learn in English class, although, 'Half a league, half a league...' is about all I remember today. The infamous charge took place in 1854 during the Crimean War when a miscommunication from well behind the lines sent 673 lightly armed British cavalrymen thundering to their deaths down the *wrong* valley. As with Nelson at Trafalgar fifty years earlier, their leader, one Lord Cardigan, died there alongside his men. Unlike the glorious victory at Trafalgar, however, this was a misbegotten adventure that sent the doomed sabre-wielding cavalrymen riding into 'the valley of death' where they were confronted by a deeply entrenched Russian heavy artillery battery.

In warfare as in business there is often a very thin dividing line between courageous success and foolhardy failure. While history tells it that the Light Brigade never stood the slightest chance of success, had Cardigan's horse-soldiers miraculously managed to pull off an against-all-odds victory they would surely have been memorialised with something more significant than a poem dedicated to their needless demise.

CORPORATE COURAGE

While it still demands courage aplenty, leading the corporate charge in today's dog-eat-dog business world is thankfully nowhere nearly as hazardous as it was in Cardigan, Nelson and Boadicea's days. Nevertheless, when it comes to morale and team building with one's own troops, few tactics have a more positive impact than a leader who is prepared to drive the corporate chariot and put himself or herself right there in the front lines, fearlessly staring down the enemy.

It was exactly 130 years after Lord Cardigan's misadventure that one Richard Branson, music industry executive, announced that he wanted to get into the commercial aviation business. Based on the stunned reaction of my partners and colleagues at Virgin Records, you would have thought I was about to charge into my very own 'valley of death'. They were convinced I had totally lost my marbles. Not unjustifiably, they were terrified by the immensity of the financial risks involved in such a capital-intensive industry, and believe me they used a lot of choice words to let me know just how they felt about such a lunatic venture. Not least they quite correctly observed that, other than as an (economy-class) paying-passenger, my knowledge of commercial airlines hovered right around the zero mark. So, without backing down, I decided it would be smart to talk to someone who did know the space – and quickly – before I got in way over my head.

WITH A LITTLE HELP FROM MY FRIENDS

Sir Freddie Laker was a British aviation maverick turned guru and an utterly fearless example of an entrepreneur who could also be a great leader. If you were born after 1960, Freddie's name maybe doesn't ring a bell as his ground-breaking Laker Airways was driven out of business in 1982, and even more sadly Freddie died in 2006 at the way-too-early age of eighty-three. A lifelong entrepreneur par excellence, Freddie was one of the greatest innovators of twentieth-century aviation and an utterly inspirational human being.

Freddie invented what today we'd call a 'low-cost carrier' and in the process, made transatlantic air travel an affordable reality for a vast new cross-section of consumers. He was a swashbuckling hero whose larger-than-life personality, street smarts and indomitable good humour made him a standout leader in what at the time was a moribund industry desperately in need of someone to take it in a new direction.

Freddie was a pragmatist; even his basic business plan for 'Laker Skytrain' was pure common sense. The big airlines of the day were all flying the Atlantic with high fares and half-empty airplanes. Freddie calculated that if he were allowed to break the big airline stranglehold he could slash existing fare levels by fifty per cent or more and not only fill his fleet of wide-bodied DC-10s but grow the market in the process – maybe even double it! And despite the best efforts of the establishment to shut him down before he got started, Freddie eventually achieved both.

After five years of competitive and political stonewalling, Freddie's revolutionary Skytrain scheduled air service finally took off in 1977. It heralded a new era in air travel with 'walk-on' service – initially there were no reservations – that meant that just about anyone could afford to fly from London to New York. At around $135, a transatlantic ticket on Laker cost the same as British Airways and Air France were charging for a flight from London to Paris. And when you mixed in the fact that, even at these unheard-of fare levels, with his low operating costs and in-your-face-marketing stunts Freddie could also turn a profit, then it wasn't surprising that the incumbent carriers didn't hail his coming quite as lustily as did the man in the street!

In the stuffy world of 1970s' aviation Freddie was a tour de force, a one-of-a-kind salesman and an utterly unabashed showman. For a time his image was everywhere; his ever-smiling face appeared on the covers of *Newsweek* and *Time* magazine in the same week. With the press, Freddie was always available and ready with an insightful comment or a fun anecdote and so they adored him – as did his rapidly expanding and intensely loyal band of customers who revelled not only in the low fares but also the excellent service doled out by Laker's band of customer-friendly employees, features that in those days were anything but the norm in commercial aviation!

If this is starting to sound at all familiar you may have realised where I am going with this as to just how much Freddie's trail-blazing helped influence my views – not just on how to run an airline (or not!) but on just how far bold, hands-on leadership can propel any business.

Sadly, Laker Airways would eventually be killed by its success. The early eighties were a tough economic time for all airlines and Freddie's upstart Skytrain, which had quickly grown to become one of the largest operators across the Atlantic, was becoming a serious thorn in the sides of the establishment carriers. While Freddie was also now losing money, his airline was actually (to double my negatives) in a much less unhealthy state than UK-taxpayer-funded British Airways.

In February 1982 Laker Airways was driven out of business when BA led a pack of ailing major airlines that threatened retaliatory action against several institutions that had agreed to prop up Laker's sagging finances. Absurdly, rather than supporting the free enterprise they were supposed to champion, Maggie Thatcher and Ronald Reagan jointly turned a blind eye in their blinkered quest to do whatever was necessary to help save their failing flag carriers. As it turned out it would be a case of 'too-little too-late' as British

Caledonian, Pan Am, TWA and others would eventually also fail, albeit of no real consolation for Freddie who had been robbed of his life's work.

So, in late 1983 when I searched out Freddie and confided in him that I wanted to pick up where he had involuntarily left off, I found an ally who was uniquely qualified – and highly motivated – to mentor me with a treasure trove of invaluable advice. Not one known to mince words, he came out swinging with 'Sue the bastards!' as his counsel on how to deal with British Airways should they ever try to sucker-punch Virgin in the same way they'd knocked him out of the skies. Needless to say, I followed this advice to the letter and as a result won the biggest libel action in British legal history against British Airways over their so-called 'dirty tricks' campaign.

As it turned out, however, it would be another piece of guidance from Freddie that would change my approach to business for ever, and with it, the way we set about taking the Virgin brand down hundreds of new and diverse global alleyways. When discussing the challenges a penniless start-up faced in attempting to go up against the colossal advertising and marketing budgets of established competitors like BA, Freddie looked me in the eye and said, 'Listen, Richard, you'll never make even a dent in their armour with traditional marketing methods. I learned early on that you yourself have got to get your arse out there. Be visible, take risks, get creative, make yourself heard and take the fight to them before they bring it to you. If you can't find ways to generate a lot of attention through free ink they'll eat you alive.'

THE BEST FORM OF DEFENCE …

The infamous American bank robber Willie Horton once responded to the question 'Why do you rob banks?' with a tongue-in-cheek, 'Because that's where the money is.' Well, in our case, if we were going to steal passengers away from other airlines then British Airways was where most of them were to be found, and this made them a natural target for some good-natured kidnappings – aka 'diversion of market share'.

As fate would have it, one of our fun assaults on BA was inspired by a throwaway comment made by their chairman Lord King when he publicly referred to me as a 'pirate'. When I read this I was actually more amused than miffed, and it might have been swept under the carpet had I not mentioned the comment to John Caulcutt, whose company Watermark worked closely with Virgin Atlantic on everything from in-flight giveaways to outrageously creative promotions. Hearing Lord King's comment, John laughed and with a mischievous twinkle in his eye said, 'Really! Well, we'll have to do something about that, won't we.' And so John set about hatching a plot whereby we'd make Lord King's 'pirate' comment come true. We huddled on what would be an appropriate counter-attack and in true buccaneering fashion decided plundering BA's flagship, their huge Concorde model at the entrance to Heathrow Airport, would be fair game.

On our first reconnaissance trip to Heathrow, we were taking measurements to make a Virgin logo that would fit over Concorde's tail: John was holding one end of the tape measure and I had the other. What we hadn't realised was that the building just above us was the local police station and those 'spotlights' on the ground were in fact security beams! Within minutes the boys in blue were upon us, demanding to know what exactly we were playing at! The ever quick-witted John blurted out something to the effect that I was so in awe of what BA had built that I'd asked him to build me one. Surprisingly they thought this a plausible story and we were back on our way!

It turned out that this near mishap was valuable as it taught us that for the actual hijack (when we planned to cover the BA tailfin with a Virgin logo) we'd have only minutes to complete the task before we could expect another visit from security. The customised plastic tailfin would have to fit instantly or it could blow the whole thing: likewise the sticker that would cover 'We Fly to Serve' with 'Virgin Territory' had to be an equally rapid fix or we'd risk the Virgin brand being embarrassed.

The big day arrived: the handpicked journalists we'd invited along were sworn to secrecy, I was attired in a Central Casting pirate outfit complete with a stuffed parrot on my shoulder, and the whole hijack was flawlessly executed in under thirty seconds.

As always John had covered all the bases by booking every portable crane within a twenty-five-mile radius for the balance of the day, so despite the reported ranting of an enraged Lord King, the offending Virgin tailfin remained in place until nightfall. And, as you can imagine, the whacky stunt generated immense press coverage for Virgin Atlantic and its real-life pirate.

This kind of attention-getting trick helped set a trend that continues to this day with all the Virgin companies and (having got over my early shyness fairly quickly) often with a little help from yours truly. Anyone who has followed my various highly public attempts at self-destruction in transatlantic speedboats, trans-global hot-air balloons, rappelling off high buildings and all the rest will know how I have heeded the advice Freddie gave me that day in 1983 and have been getting my derriere well and truly out there!

Contrary to what some sceptics might have suggested, this was never an exercise in self-aggrandisement, far from it. From the first transatlantic speedboat attempt at recapturing the Blue Riband for the fastest-ever crossing (that's the one that sank off the coast of Ireland) to the second attempt that succeeded, the same critics should note that there was always a Virgin logo strategically positioned close by and how that logo almost always showed up in TV news stories and on the front page of major newspapers – places where you simply cannot buy advertising at any price. Typically, I was desperately climbing into a life raft and the Virgin logo was on the side of a boat or balloon pictured just before it sank below the Atlantic or Pacific. I have often wondered if we might have inadvertently invented reality TV shows twenty-five years ahead of their time? But one way or the other it worked. We raised the Virgin brand's recognition factor to amazing new heights and while I may have used up my nine lives, I am still here to tell the tale!

Not everyone was a fan of some of these highly dangerous stunts although my wife and family, outwardly at least, always managed to put on a brave and supportive face. Unable to resist the opportunity to feign displeasure with one of my transatlantic ballooning attempts, the US marketing team at Virgin Atlantic ran an ad in the same edition of the *New York Times* that had the news of my failed attempt on its front page. The ad copy chided me with, '*It's not easy convincing people to fly our airline to London when our chairman chooses instead to cross the Atlantic in a hot air balloon! When you're ready we have a seat for you, Richard – just call reservations.*' Apparently we were accused by some of staging the potentially fatal end to the crossing in order to set up the ad. I'm sorry, folks, but even I draw the line at some point!

IT'S THE (ALMOST) REAL THING

As the Concorde story serves to demonstrate, we have never been shy about going head-on with our biggest competitors. While in international airline circles the BA brand is one of the bigger ones, on the global brand awareness chart it's a minnow by comparison to the likes of Coca-Cola – the most recognised and respected brand name on the planet.

Arguably, therefore, it may not have been our smartest-ever business decision, but in 1994 we decided to launch Virgin Cola. We had figured that, by the numbers at least, if we could manage to steal just one measly percentage point of Coke's global market share we would have ourselves a $100-million-plus soft drinks franchise. So with the maximum 'screw it, let's do it' courage we could muster, we went for it. Someone once said that when trying to promote anything in the US one really has to 'Go big or go home' – well, we went big! So when we brought Virgin Cola to the US marketplace we didn't sneak into town via any handy side door, instead we headed straight for the epicentre of Coca-Cola's kingdom, New York's Times Square, and boldly launched ourselves into the abyss.

Once again John Caulcutt was the mastermind of a plot that this time around saw me dressed in military uniform driving a lumbering vintage Sherman tank down Broadway. First we heroically smashed through and crushed a giant wall of Coke and Pepsi cans – a purchase that must have helped their sales quite considerably that day. We then ground to a halt and dramatically swung the turret around, took aim and opened fire (well, sort of) on what is surely the holy grail of outdoor advertising, Times Square's giant Coca-Cola sign. The appearance of a rogue tank making a successful strike was facilitated by John having booked a couple of hotel rooms strategically located right under the Coca-Cola sign and it was from these windows that he set off several smoke bombs on cue from a walkie-talkie from the tank below. Fortunately we had paid in advance for the hotel rooms as the NYPD was already in the hotel lobby as our crew calmly walked out.

We couldn't have pulled such a stunt after 9/11 without serving a long time in jail but back in those gentler times it was another memorable launch event that brought the centre of the world's greatest city to a shocked standstill for several New York minutes, and generated press coverage galore. Of course, what Freddie had never promised was that putting yourself out there in the line of fire and generating buzz, or in this case fizz, would ever guarantee the success of a product no matter how good it might be. We genuinely believed we had a winner with Virgin Cola, which (like the failed New Coke had done) had scored extremely well against Coke in all kinds of blind taste tests. For a short while it was very successful in several markets – the UK in particular – but as had been Freddie Laker's problem with Skytrain, ironically that success was to prove our downfall.

When taking on Coke, I fear that we failed to stick with the playbook that had worked for us before when going up against Goliath competitors. At Virgin Atlantic we had deliberately under-played our ambitions and so stayed under British Airways' radar until it was too late for them to snuff us out. Had we employed the same stealth tactics against Coke we might have pulled it off but when we poked the Coke Goliath in the eye with the Times Square stunt and the UK sales figures made it back to their Atlanta headquarters, they decided enough was enough. There were stories around at the time that Coke dispatched a huge SWAT team to the UK – one version had them filling a 747 – to take us out of play. Whatever the truth, it seems they managed to leverage their distribution clout to the maximum, our stock started mysteriously disappearing from supermarket shelves, Coke was discounted everywhere to unprecedented levels and, well, the rest is history.

As one should, we quickly moved on and put our Cola adventure down to experience. It taught me a huge lesson, though: while in some markets, like aviation, we had managed to sneak up and outsmart some huge and cumbersome competitors, we should never underestimate the might, determination, distribution and sheer marketing clout of a mega brand like Coke! Also, with something such as an airline, differentiating your product with tangibly superior and different customer service benefits is a lot easier than when it's a matter of the consumer's personal taste preferences for a fizzy drink.

Deciding whether or not to climb into that chariot (or tank) to lead the charge can be a tough one for a lot of very good leaders. Quite apart from the fact your efforts will be all over YouTube within a matter of minutes, not everyone is comfortable stepping into the spotlight. I for one was desperately uneasy with it in the early going and I am by no means the exception. In an unauthorised biography by Nicholas Carlson, published by businessinsider.com, Marissa Mayer, now the CEO and very public face of Yahoo, admits to having been 'a socially awkward and painfully shy geek' as late as in high school. Clearly she managed to work her way through it as I did, so no matter what your initial inclination, I would strongly encourage corporate leaders to step up and try driving the chariot into battle.

At Virgin we obviously don't demand that our leaders take physical risks – that seems to have become my prerogative – but getting out there and leading boldly and visibly from the front is very much a part of the Virgin way. As a shy young entrepreneur I could never have imagined myself doing a fraction of the crazy stuff I've done over the years but, as I did, you might really surprise yourself at what you can do when you put your mind (and body) to it. Queen Boadicea has one, so just imagine what your bronze statue will look like some day!

Chapter 17

COLLABORATION IS THE KEY

Getting it together

This may sound like a truism but I'll say it anyway: collaboration, whether external or internal, is a vital component in building a healthy company, as well as an integral constituent of any entrepreneur's life. Many people have this almost ethereal vision of 'the entrepreneur' as someone who operates alone – kind of like an artist in his garret – overcoming challenges and bringing ideas to market through sheer force of personality. Sorry, but this is the stuff of fiction! Going it alone is a wonderfully romantic notion but few if any entrepreneurs ever brought an idea to life without a lot of help. It can come from family, friends, mentors, business partners or all of the above but to be successful in business, collaboration is the key.

If you think about it, most of the important relationships in your life started out with a chance meeting with a friend, a friend of a friend or, as my friend who invested in Google discovered, sometimes it's with a complete stranger. The digital age may have dramatically changed the social scene, but real life (as in face-to-face) networking with real people is still a business essential, especially for an entrepreneur whose instincts have to rely heavily on trust-based relationships – you can't look someone in the eye by text.

This innate gregariousness among entrepreneurs is the primary reason why communes of like-minded geeks are taking the Silicon Valley concept on the road. I'd call them simply 'Silicon Valley clones', but creative hubs aka 'venture hotspots' or 'technology clusters' are springing up all over the world. Whether it's in Tel Aviv, Cambridge, Helsinki, Bangalore or Hsinchu-Taipei, entrepreneurs and techies are clustering up a storm and revelling in the collaborative opportunities that result.

WALKING BRAND IN BRAND

Another form of corporate collaboration that has been 'reimagined' in recent years is the good old-fashioned joint venture. 'Co-branding', the cross-pollination of sometimes seemingly highly disparate brands and individual products, is becoming relatively common, sometimes even between some of the staunchest of competitors.

Among the ranks of the tech giants, for instance, Microsoft Windows runs on Apple computers and Google Maps is featured on Apple – or at least it was until Apple kicked Google Maps off the iPhone. When Google refused to give Apple access to its voice-driven map navigation, Apple, prematurely it seems, launched its own system with some pretty disastrous results. The new Apple map system was plagued with errors – there were thousands of much publicised howlers, like Helsinki's main railway station vanishing and appearing instead as a park! Apple apologised, and when Google maps was allowed back as an app, there were over ten million downloads in forty-eight hours.

A FIVE-RING CIRCUS

One of the unexpected talking points to come out of the Sochi Winter Olympics was all about co-branding – even if it was for all the wrong reasons! The sleek aerodynamic suits that sports clothing manufacture 'Under Armour' and unlikely collaborator aerospace giant Lockheed Martin jointly developed for the US speed-skating team were supposed to ensure a gold rush for the Americans. Instead they turned into a PR disaster for all concerned, as the previously untested suits became the scapegoat for the American team's failure to win any of the early races in which they were highly favoured. Before the end of the games they had reverted to using their old, low-tech suits, albeit with only marginally better results. Perhaps this just serves to demonstrate the importance of picking the right dance partner – after all, the F-35 Lightning jetfighter and speed-skating suits have seldom appeared in the same sentence before!

Other interesting, and more successful, brand marriages I've spotted are: Apple and Nike – who developed a wireless system that allows sneakers to talk to the owner's iPod and record their activities; Audi and Leica – with a camera not a car; JBL and Nokia on matching smartphone and portable speakers; and perhaps most tempting of all the trio of HP, Google and GoGo the leading supplier of inflight WiFi systems to the world's airlines, who hooked up to produce the very cool 'Chromebook 11' laptop, which among other things features complimentary in-flight WiFi on all GoGo-equipped airlines. This last one is a great example of the really smart upsides than can come from partnering with the right people. The free inflight GoGo offer (which usually costs between ten and fifteen dollars per trip) means that if you are a frequent flier you could recoup the entire price of the laptop (around $300) in as few as a dozen or so round-trip flights – clever stuff!

In commercial aviation circles 'alliances' (yet another word for collaborations) have become 'the big thing' and they seem to be working – for the airlines at least. The sixty-plus member carriers in the big three alliances, Oneworld, SkyTeam and the Star Alliance (which was the first of the breed) account for almost 1.5 billion passengers a year, which equates to a staggering 77 per cent of all airline traffic. In each of the alliance groupings, all sorts of direct competitors have found there is more to be gained by teaming up with each other than fighting a lone battle to survive. In some cases, carriers such as American Airlines and British Airways or Air France and Delta have formed even tighter collaborations that stop short of merging their companies but still accrue many of the same advantages. With Delta replacing Singapore Airlines with a forty-nine per cent equity stake in Virgin Atlantic, we are looking forward to collaborating with them by feeding traffic into each other's route networks around the world. At the time of writing we have not thrown any of our own airline caps into any alliances but that could change if we can be convinced that there is sufficient upside. Clearly with sixty other airlines doing it there has to be something positive going on here but we won't do anything that might negatively impact our ability to do things in our own peculiar way – lowest common denominators are not a healthy measurement of any grouping.

SILOS ARE FOR GRAIN

As significant and compelling as outside liaisons may be in expanding a business into new markets or extending the reach of a brand, there is another much more important and often overlooked area in which collaboration is often sadly lacking or even absent – and that's within your own company!

There are lots of arguments for keeping the number of employees in a company below a certain critical mass – one of them is certainly minimising the silo effect that seems to proliferate in bigger companies. This is the phenomenon where rather than working as one on achieving a single corporate objective and maintaining a uniform healthy corporate culture, a workforce separates into its own distinct silos. Senior management will often be off somewhere else in their own ivory silo, while sales, marketing, product development, finance, IT and all the other components will be firmly entrenched in their own hard-shell silos. The bridges connecting them will usually only be on the upper floors so that the heads of each group can have access to each other even if it is not used or a regular enough basis. The lower echelons seldom if ever cross over to 'the other side' for fear of appearing disloyal to their own commune members.

Within each silo there is usually loyalty to their immediate group but nothing except distrust and suspicion as to the motives and/ or capabilities of every other division in the company. Sales will think marketing knows nothing about their real world needs, while marketing thinks product development hasn't got a clue – which in the absence of sufficient feedback from sales and marketing may well be the case. Finance doesn't see the business as anything except a bunch of data that they usually get late and believes that everyone is out to cheat on their expenses. And IT, well, they're just doing their own thing as nobody speaks to them except when they have a problem. In a multinational company the problems are usually only multiplied. The Brits will often treat the Americans with xenophobic disdain – 'The Yanks can't even spell "aluminium", for goodness' sake!' – and so on and so on.

The lack of communication that results from such a stultifying situation makes for a series of self-fulfilling prophecies at every level. Product development is rushing to design a new triangular widget because they heard from someone that the competition was doing the same. Sales is out selling the new round one that has been promised by their boss who failed to read the email from marketing that they'd recommended changing it to a square one. When the triangular widget is finally unveiled everyone is unhappy, especially the customer service group which had put in a request for an octagonal one but never received a response. All overstated caricatures, perhaps, but not that far from the truth at many a dysfunctional, silo-ridden company.

Real life examples of this abound, particularly in the fast-moving technology world: I mentioned one earlier with Apple's rush to get their own flawed version of Google Maps to market. Another was Microsoft's 'me too' attempt in 2006 to produce a competitive product to the iPod which at the time enjoyed a sixty-five per cent market share. The short-lived 'Zune' would never make it out of single digits in market share, lacking the design flair of the iPod, and it wasn't compatible with Apple's iTunes – an oversight that became a major drawback. You can just imagine the Microsoft sales team looking at their new Zunes while wringing their hands and moaning, 'And this is what they give us to unseat the iPod?'

SYMPTOMS OF CHRONIC 'SILOSITIS'

The good news is that signs your company is suffering from the silo effect are pretty easy to spot and two simple questions should give you the answer:

- In a normal week, do you spend at least twenty-five per cent of your time speaking to colleagues from outside of your own division?
- Do you have frequently scheduled briefings with the heads of other divisions?

If your answer is 'no' to both of these questions, then the chances are pretty good that you are operating in 'silo mode' and you need to take steps to dismantle it before it dismantles the company. The good news is that some of the fixes are not that difficult to initiate. But first, where there is an effect there is always a cause. So if things haven't always been like this and 'in the good old days we all used to work so well together' then what, or more likely 'who', has changed? If it has just been a general slide into this state of affairs then it really has to be down to the CEO to step up, be accountable and take responsibility for curing the malaise. If the root of the problem can be traced to when someone new came in or was promoted to lead one of the divisions, then perhaps some corrective surgery is called for. In the meantime there are some simple first steps to be taken:

- The CEO should call a meeting of all the division heads and their deputies to tackle the internal communication problem and hammer home why it has to change. Don't mince words and use any pertinent examples of late delivery of projects or cancelled programmes that might have been avoided with better collaboration between divisions.
- Clear the air and flush out any lingering feuds, finger pointing or negative rumours so that there can be a fresh start and consensus on the way forward.
- Set a weekly senior management meeting schedule

(maximum one hour in length) that will be mandatory for all unless there is a very good reason to be elsewhere. At these meetings the CEO should give a corporate update, followed by each division head's report on their divisions. Division heads should use this as an opportunity to invite input from other departments and seek their assistance if appropriate.

- Take a long hard look at how effectively management communicates with the staff. Use technology and social media to ensure that all of your employees always hear about breaking company news from the company and at all costs before they read about it in the business pages. I am an almost daily blogger and I know a significant percentage of my 'followers' are Virgin employees.

I should perhaps make it clear that I am not a big fan of meetings-for-the-sake-of-meetings-based cultures as, somewhat paradoxically, I have found that a prime reason for poor corporate communications can often be that there are simply too many meetings. I have even seen some cultures in which management appears to spend eighty per cent of its time in meetings discussing what they plan to do with the other twenty per cent of their time – the catastrophic British Rail operation we inherited in 1997, for instance, was certainly one such organisation. BR employees repeatedly told us how happy they were to see Virgin at the helm as previously they could never get hold of anyone in management as 'they were always in meetings'.

These 80/20 rules seldom seem to work out very well, do they? What I am suggesting, however, is that a weekly meeting – where there was none – can be a good start to unclogging the communication arteries. Maybe even the start of a new era – although getting the workforce thinking and acting as one and revitalising the company culture at the same time will take a lot more than just a few meetings. So now we get to the more interesting and even fun parts…

WE DID THAT TOGETHER

The first additional prerequisite of the new silo-free environment is an across-the-board commitment to getting other divisions involved in new products from their genesis. That means from the very first discussions on the concept – not just when it's already half-baked and at a stage where any changes will be costly and difficult to make. One of the saddest phrases you can hear in any company is, 'I wish they'd told us about this sooner', when there is absolutely no valid reason for the communication failure.

At all of the Virgin companies we always make a concerted effort to ensure that everyone who might be able to offer any valid input is involved from the very beginning of a new product development. From something as simple as a new menu for our Upper Class passengers to the floor plan of a new Virgin Active health and fitness club, we will seek the involvement and advice of the people who will be working at 'the sharp end' – namely those staff members who will have to deliver the product on a daily basis. There is no point in developing a new menu if the cabin crew is going to tell us that it's not practicable because of on-board galley oven limitations, or that they have seen in the past it is not something the majority of passengers will want to eat. Or if an architect hasn't got experienced Virgin Active staff giving input on how the gym floor works, we risk opening the new club and having them ask 'Where are we supposed to store the towels?' or some similar seemingly minor but important oversight that could have been avoided with better up-front collaboration. Someone once put it very cleverly when they said, 'There would be no problems with square pegs and round holes if the peg department and the hole department were the whole department.'

Tearing down the silo walls has a multitude of upsides. Not only do the different co-workers learn more about the needs and priorities of other divisions and create relationships there, but it also builds buy-in to innovative ideas and pride of ownership when the final product goes live. When a company embraces the benefits of collaboration, the old cynical silo-dweller's classic moan of 'I wish they'd asked for our opinion on this' will be replaced with, 'We developed that together and we can all be proud of it.' This is truly a win-win-win for the company, the staff and – lest we forget – for the customer as well.

The fun part of a post-silo renaissance is learning how to have a good time together. As I discussed in an earlier chapter, I am still a firm believer in the power of the party. This is not a political statement – I am talking about a good old-fashioned let-your-hair-down-and-have-a-good-time-with-your-colleagues company celebration, and we don't have to wait for Christmas to do it. Getting the troops to have some fun together is the surest way to make sure the silo walls don't get rebuilt. If there are opportunities for company sports teams then that's another great area to explore – and twist your controller's arm to spring some cash to supply the company logoed football shirts or softball jerseys.

PAYING IT BACK PAYS OFF

Another great way to reunite your people is to encourage them to team up and get involved in community or other charitable events. We have seen countless examples of our people doing good together whether it's running as a team (raising money for their favourite charities) in the London or New York Marathons or black-bagging it and clearing up the fields around a local children's playground. Doing good things for our communities is an integral part of working at any Virgin company and we know that it's incredibly important to our staff.

At Virgin Media UK, for example, each employee is given a day off every year to give back to their local communities. The tricky bit about these kind of things is figuring out the best way to assist your people in optimising their precious time and in ways that don't require a financial commitment – an important factor in these tough times. To this end Media came up with five ingenious themes for five different days; three of them – 'Give Time', 'Give Stuff', 'Give Life' – are all ways to use time and existing possessions to make a difference; while 'Give a Shout' and 'Give a Pat on the Back' are ways to recognise what people are already doing and to encourage them to keep up the good work.

'Give Time' is about volunteering and, to plan the most productive use of their day off, we encouraged people to spend ten minutes looking at what they could volunteer for and telling their manager about it. 'Give Stuff' is based on the old saying that 'One man's junk is another man's treasure' and we ask people to do a quick raid of their old clothes, linens, furniture – anything they no longer use – and bring it all in for central collection. 'Give Life' encourages people to go and sign up for blood donations, the organ donor register and (in the UK) the Anthony Nolan stem cell and bone marrow register. Virgin Media also introduced a policy that gives anyone called up for stem cell or bone marrow donations one week's paid leave to recuperate. The internal (tongue in cheek named) 'Give a Shout' programme allows people to recognise the efforts of their peers with a message on their personal homepage – also entering them into a draw to win one of many £50 vouchers each month. 'Give a Pat on the Back' also allows colleagues to recognise each other (even bosses!) for their outstanding contributions to the programme and, as with everything else, serves to build the team spirit in a fun, rewarding and (by way of the funds raised, pints of blood donated etc.) quantifiable way – the Virgin way.

The expression 'The sum of the parts is greater than the whole' encapsulates the critical difference in the upside that accrues from truly collaborating with each other versus simply working with one another.

TEEMING TEAMS

To use the analogy of a marathon, running one as part of a team is a much more exhilarating and rewarding experience than slogging around on your own. The task at hand is essentially the same but having teammates to urge you along and set the pace while enjoying every minute of it together makes for an altogether more uplifting experience and almost certainly improves your time. When I ran the London Marathon in 2010 – in a highly undistinguished tad over five hours – I had my kids to drag me along, which made all the difference in the world.

In the workplace, exactly the same team dynamics apply even if, like running 26.2 miles, the task at hand may still be a rigorous one. Working as a truly collaborative member of a group of like-minded colleagues means everyone – no matter what their job title – has to be prepared to check their ego at the door and be willing to freely share their knowledge and expertise. Above all else, every team member has to trust the people as well as the process – something that has to be carefully choreographed and conducted by a strong leader.

As part of the process, assigning team members with clearly defined roles and objectives would seem to be a natural thing to do, although one interesting idiosyncrasy uncovered by Harvard Business Review research into the subject showed that teams actually work better when group members are clear on their own responsibilities but uncertain on how they can achieve the team's goals. They found that rather than too much spoon-feeding, a healthy degree of uncertainty forces participants to think more creatively about how to accomplish the group's objectives. On the optimum size of teams, the same research concluded that while groups by necessity frequently must run into much larger numbers, the level of effective collaboration starts to tail off quite markedly when the number of team members exceeds twenty. Just as 'small is beautiful' has always been the Virgin way in terms of company scale, so too we tend to favour keeping the size of project teams to a minimum whenever possible.

Mike Rutherford, who with my good friend Peter Gabriel was a founding member of Genesis, one of my all-time favourite bands (on the Virgin label, of course), very succinctly summed up the power of collaboration when he said, '*Being in a band is always a compromise. But provided the balance is good, what you lose in compromise, you gain by collaboration*'. And it goes way beyond the old notion that 'a problem shared is a problem halved'. I prefer to see it from the perspective that a challenge not shared will often equate to a missed opportunity. Everyone knows there's nothing quite like the early days of a start-up when everyone is hyped up and energetically pitching in with their ideas and visions of the future. It falls to management at every level in the pyramid to foster an on-going, openly collaborative culture that sustains and facilitates that same 'early-stage' kind of energy and freedom of expression. This means as few walls as possible – real and imaginary. It also calls for leaders that are out there getting their hands dirty every day. Steve Jobs put it perfectly when he said to his biographer Walter Isaacson, '*Creativity comes from spontaneous meetings, from random discussions. You run into someone, you ask what they're doing, you say "Wow" and soon you're cooking up all sorts of ideas.'*

MEET ME IN THE PIAZZA

Collaboration should have been Steve Jobs' middle name as he was forever going to amazing ends to foster it – and not just at Apple. When he created Pixar, home to *Toy Story*, *Monsters Inc.* and many other animated classics, he went to great lengths to make unplanned collaboration part of the company's foundations – literally! At Jobs' behest the company's Emeryville, California headquarters campus was designed around a large open-space atrium – a kind of latter-day version of the great Roman piazzas, which were and still are the centre of social activity in most Italian cities. For me, Venice's wonderful Piazza San Marco is without equal. According to his authorised biography, Jobs even wanted the only toilet facilities on campus to be around the atrium but modern building codes squashed that idea! Steve explained the concept behind the Pixar piazza saying, '*If a building doesn't encourage collaboration you'll lose a lot of innovation and the magic that's sparked by serendipity. So we designed the building to make people get out of their offices and mingle in the central atrium with people they might not otherwise see.'*

Now I'm not necessarily suggesting that withholding toilet facilities should be used as leverage for driving collaboration but there is no question that any combination of silos, walls and hierarchies makes for serious literal and figurative obstacles to working together. Conversely, their absence greatly facilitates the ability of leaders to work arm-in-arm with their teams and vice versa. The next generation of senior leaders will come from the ranks of the so-called 'millennial generation' (aka 'Generation Y') – those born between 1980 and the early 2000s. As anyone who has parented a teenager in recent years will attest, this is a generation that likes to do things their own way. They are less inclined to take orders and more into problem solving through collaborative interaction – live and online – with their peer groups. So get with the movement – don't try to fence them in and control them with the old, broken, 'divide and conquer' model. Instead we should all work to foster physically and emotionally unfettered corporate cultures and working environments that supports this natural proclivity for collaborative progress – aka entrepreneurialism.

So, if like Apple, Google and others you are one of the more enlightened leaders that have already gone into 'piazza mode', take a step back and enjoy the amazing energy that's being generated there. If, however, you are still living in a world of silos and little boxes, then let me paraphrase President Ronald Reagan's historic Brandenburg Gate speech in 1987 and say it's time to 'tear down these walls' and think outside the silo. You'll never look back.

Chapter 18

DECISIONS, DECISIONS

Putting the pro in procrastination

In manufacturing circles, 'Just in Time' (JIT) inventory control has become an accepted standard with most major companies. This is the supply chain logistics model that eliminates a huge percentage of the capital costs and administrative headaches associated with the traditional approach of stockpiling giant warehouses full of parts to feed into the future production process. In extremely over-simplified terms, the strategy is to let the car headlight maker or whatever bear the cost of inventorying their product and deliver it to the automaker 'just in time' for it to be installed in the vehicle and driven off the assembly line to be shipped off to a dealership.

When I first learned about JIT I remember thinking, 'Wow, wouldn't it be great if the process of executive decision-making could somehow be as well synchronised with the needs of a business as the supply chain.' In other words, neither jumping into something with a knee-jerk decision way before it needs to be made nor procrastinating for so long that the opportunity may have evaporated by the time the nod comes down from on high. Certainly it makes for an appealing dream even if the human factor makes it a lot tougher to put into practice given decision-making's dependence on the personality traits of the would-be decision-maker. In my experience there are essentially three different types of personality that show through when confronted with the need to make a business decision.

'SCREW IT – DO I REALLY HAVE TO DECIDE?'

First and possibly foremost there is the serial procrastinator. I am sure everyone knows several members of this frustrating human subspecies. This is the one with a perennial approach of 'Why make any decision today when I can put it off until tomorrow?' – and as we all know 'tomorrow' never comes! I am not talking here about someone who takes as much time as possible to conduct due diligence on a project, I am referring to those individuals that seem mentally and physically incapable of ever making an on-the-spot decision no matter how obvious or straightforward the matter at hand may be.

So why exactly do people behave like that? One reason is almost certainly the fear that if they are pushed into making a quick decision, there is always a chance that it could turn out to be the wrong one. So it is much safer to delay as long as possible and maybe in the process someone else will step up and put their seal of approval on the initiative. That way if it goes wrong the procrastinator can always say, 'Hey, that wasn't my idea. In fact I always thought it was a very risky play.' Alternatively if the thing turns out to be a raging success, having never gone on record as saying it wouldn't work, the procrastinator will usually be the first one to jump on the bandwagon and grab their share of the glory with phrases like, 'I always said it was a great idea.' Sound familiar?

But it's not just the big decisions that professional procrastinators struggle with, it's often all the little day-to-day ones too. For a business to run smoothly the process can't be held hostage to one person's unwillingness to sign off on a lot of relatively mundane items that, when taken collectively, can suffocate progress.

'SCREW IT – WE'LL DO IT – TODAY'

The second personality type is the one into which, by reputation at least, I am most likely to fall. As lots of Virgin colleagues past and present would likely tell you, my notorious 'Screw it, Let's Do It' approach to decision-making can have its pros and cons. As the antithesis of the procrastinator, I have over the years made snap decisions to jump into some pretty big businesses. For instance, we got into commercial aviation with Virgin Atlantic and Virgin Blue very much on the basis of my gut feeling rather than on any huge files of carefully researched market data and financial projections: on these two I played the odds and won. On other occasions, such as our foray into fizzy drinks with Virgin Cola and a few other less high-profile ones like Virgin Bride, my instincts haven't served us quite as well and we didn't always emerge a winner.

Of course, a company's size and ownership structure has a lot of influence on the ease and spontaneity of expedient executive decision-making. Making quick, instinct-based judgement calls of any importance is a heck of a lot easier when you own the company outright and it's still sufficiently small and nimble enough to facilitate sudden changes in direction. Or as someone once put it, 'It's a lot easier to bet the farm when you own the farm.' The minute you go public or get too big, it becomes much harder to take the 'Screw it' approach. That's not to say that I don't still try my hand at it on a fairly regular basis, but without the impetuousness of youth, aka the wisdom that comes with age as well as from learning by your mistakes, I like to think that I now have at least a couple of toes – not yet a whole foot – in the third category of decision-makers. And that would be...

'SCREW IT – LET'S THINK SOME MORE ABOUT IT'

The third and probably smartest all-round approach is what I like to call 'the art of orchestrated procrastination'. This is an acquired discipline whereby the first thing to be addressed as part of the decision-making function is timing. Is it a 'carpe diem' situation or not? If you don't seize the day might the window of opportunity close or might it be filled by a start-up or existing competitor? If, however, you know that you have the luxury of some time to play with, then make it work for you and use it to understand the deal's full potential – or not – as with a deal we looked at a few years ago with Goldman Sachs.

Some of our Virgin Money people wanted to jump on the deal but, never having previously heard of the commodity in which they wanted us to invest a sizable sum of money, I urged that we drag our feet for a while. Sometimes ignorance can be bliss. The more we looked at the deal the more questions arose, so in the end we decided we'd say 'thanks but no thanks' to the Goldman people who by this stage were becoming quite agitated about our foot dragging. Not long thereafter we felt very glad that we'd passed on the deal. At the time no one outside of financial circles had ever heard of the term 'subprime mortgages' but that all changed with a vengeance in 2007 when everything fell apart. Suddenly 'subprime mortgages' were on the tip of everyone's tongue as one of the alleged primary causes of the disastrous real estate lending crash. As things turned out, Goldman Sachs was left wishing they too had never heard of subprime mortgages. In 2010 the US Securities and Exchange Commission (SEC) fined them $550 million (the second largest penalty ever paid by a Wall Street firm) for 'having misled investors in a subprime mortgage product just as the US housing market was starting to collapse.' Goldman also acknowledged that its marketing materials for their subprime product contained incomplete information. Guess who was one of those misled investors that had been looking at those very materials? On this occasion our orchestrated procrastination had saved us a lot of money – and probably a chunk of our good reputation as well!

THE ART OF THE DECISION

'To do or not to do, that is the decision' – and making smart informed decisions is why leaders get paid the big bucks. There is really no science to getting it right every time which is why (unfortunately) decision-making is not a process that can be programmed to come in 'just in time' across the board. Making a good informed decision is not that different to sitting on a jury – all reasonable doubt has to be removed before you can pass a verdict one way or the other. Thankfully, though, corporate decisions are seldom a matter of life or death!

Here are a few general rules that I have found help me to get to the point of taking the plunge (or not) within the appropriate time frames:

- Like me you may be someone who's big on first impressions when you meet people but you can't let the same thought process influence your decision-making. If on first hearing an idea strikes you as a really good one, you may well be correct, but you mustn't allow that first reaction to influence your ability to objectively weigh the cons as well as all the pros when they are presented.

- Just because no significant cons are presented it doesn't mean they don't exist, so get someone on to digging them up and evaluating them while you still have the time – discovering them after you've launched the deal doesn't do you any favours. Insisting that this kind of archaeology is conducted becomes doubly important if and when everyone is unanimously in favour of going ahead with the project. Nothing is perfect, so work hard at uncovering whatever hidden warts the thing might have and by removing them you'll only make it better still.

- Avoid making decisions in isolation. Every decision has some degree of impact on your ability to adopt other future opportunities in what the experts call 'the decision stream'. This one may be a 'too good to miss' opportunity but how will it affect other projects or priorities and, if now is not the best time to do it, what risks if any are there in putting the thing on hold for an agreed period of time? If you cannot manage this project in addition to another that's waiting in the wings, which one gets the nod and why?

- Do everything you can to protect the downside. All wise investors go to great lengths to do this with their stock portfolios and when setting up a new business you should try to employ the same strategies. For example, when we started Virgin Atlantic, the only way I got my business partners in Virgin Records to begrudgingly accept the risks involved was by getting Boeing to agree to take back our one 747 after a year if things weren't working out as we hoped. To this day, with giant, capital-intensive ventures like Virgin Galactic and our newly announced Virgin Cruises, we always spend a lot of time in finding inventive ways to mitigate the downside.

If you have the time to use the 'orchestrated procrastination' approach then do so. Without getting into the 'paralysis by analysis' mode, doing more rather than less homework on a project is seldom a bad thing. While looking at it more deeply you may find better alternatives or the marketplace may change – think of our Goldman Sachs example where the whole world changed!

'SORRY, BUT THIS IS THE WAY I WANT TO DO IT'

I think it was Plato who said, '*A good decision is based on knowledge and not on numbers.*' Try telling that to your CFO if you dare! If you are confident in your depth of knowledge on a given concept, however, there will most likely come a time (or times) in every major decision-maker's career when you will pull rank and say, 'Sorry, I don't care what the numbers say, but we're going to do it my way.' Think Virgin Atlantic! You will have gone through all the right steps and every litmus test will have come back positively against doing the thing, but your intuition will still be blaring at you not to be confused by the facts and just go with your instincts. Call it 'executive privilege' or just plain pigheadedness (if it fails it will certainly be called 'utter stupidity') but it will happen some day and one way or the other your entire legacy may be hanging on the outcome. What fun!

TRAIN SET TROUBLES

In the summer of 2012 I had just such a situation come out of nowhere when the British government shocked us with the news that Virgin Trains had lost out to a rival bidder, FirstGroup, in our effort to retain the operating rights to the £7 billion West Coast rail franchise.

We had run the franchise for fifteen years and in that time had grown our annual passenger numbers from thirteen million to thirty million, introduced new high-speed tilting trains and been voted the best-loved rail company several times. We had been quietly confident that our excellent bid and track record would carry the day. When we first got the shocking news, I was both stunned and baffled. I did a lot of listening and reading between the lines (no pun intended) as our lawyers and advisors outlined our position, which frankly didn't seem very positive.

The lawyers told us there was no more than a ten per cent chance of winning an appeal, but listening to my own instincts, which have served me pretty well over the decades, I knew we had to fight the decision. It may have looked like sour grapes to many, but as much as I despise being on the losing end of anything, I always know when I've been beaten fairly and squarely by a superior opponent (except perhaps on the tennis court) and this decision qualified on neither count.

With nothing really concrete to back up this feeling, I stayed quiet for quite a while and did a lot more listening than talking while the people whose job it is to know about such things discussed our options. Everyone had a slightly different view on just how our very well formulated and extremely competitive bid could have lost out to FirstGroup but if even I could see that the bid they'd presented quite literally didn't add up, then there was clearly something terribly wrong with the government's decision.

It seemed to our team that the civil servants in charge of the process had either got their maths terribly wrong or simply hadn't done enough of it. They had clearly just looked at the highest bid without enough due diligence into FirstGroup's ability to deliver it. After fifteen years' experience running the route, we felt we knew better than anyone what was realistically achievable in terms of passenger numbers, fare levels and service expectations. We also believed the measure of our success was not just by the numbers but also by the quality of the customer service we were offering our passengers every day. This was borne out by the 180,000 signatures that were collected within a couple of weeks of FirstGroup's selection hitting the headlines. The petition was organised by our loyal passengers and sent to the government demanding that they reverse the FirstGroup decision and leave the service in our hands.

We tried to explain our concerns to the government but to no avail – all we got back was a wall of silence. But the clock was running and it was fast getting to the time for us to – as they say in the US – 'put up or shut up'. For the second time in my career I was going to take Freddie Laker's wise counsel and 'sue the bastards'. Last time we'd taken on British Airways and won, but this time it would be the British government!

Accordingly in late August of 2012 we threw down the legal gauntlet and filed an application before the high court of London requesting a judicial review of the decision to award FirstGroup the contract. Obviously our filing didn't seem to bother the Department for Transport too much, as they dismissively told the press that there would be 'no delays in awarding the franchise to FirstGroup'.

The court hearing was set for the middle of October, but with only a few weeks to go the government had still not disclosed any of the information we'd requested on how they had reached their decision to award the franchise to FirstGroup. Fearing things were not looking good for us, some of our senior team were starting to get cold feet and came to me to recommend that it was maybe time to withdraw from the legal proceedings. 'Let's forget the lawsuit,' they said. 'Nobody ever wins judicial reviews and if we get a bloody nose in court it will be very damaging to the brand as a whole.'

To address these apprehensions we hastily convened a war room meeting at our family home in Oxford where we discussed our options over cups of tea and several rounds of biscuits. Despite the concern that we might not prevail in court, Virgin Trains CEO Tony Collins was convinced that there was something akin to a smoking gun at the Department for Transport. Patrick McCall, my key adviser on Trains, confirmed the numbers did not make sense. Others including Nick Fox, our usually cautious PR director, felt it was better to go down with a fight than slink away at the eleventh hour.

I knew it was a big decision to pit the company's reputation against the might of the government, but something inside me just didn't sit well and, besides, it has never been the Virgin way to just lie down and play dead. The room that day was pretty well split down the middle, but knowing our long-term partner Sir Brian Souter (then chief executive of Stagecoach) and his right-hand man Martin Griffiths shared my views, I made my decision. We would stick with it – and if we went down at least it would be with all guns blazing!

The week before we were due to face down the Department for Transport in the high court, I was in New York on a business trip when my assistant Helen received a surprise telephone call from the Secretary for Transport's office in London, asking her to set up a call with me for 7 p.m. that evening – midnight in the UK. I agreed to take the call and immediately started agonising over what it could possibly be about: where our own people had failed was *he* now calling to try and talk me into throwing in the towel?

At 7 p.m. on the dot the phone rang and I found out. With little or no preamble, Patrick McLoughlin, the Secretary for Transport, got straight to the point, and pulling no punches he very apologetically told me the department had made some terrible mistakes and they would not be seeing us in court the next week. As my pulse quickened he went on to explain that they had uncovered several 'significant technical flaws' in the bidding process because of mistakes by Department for Transport staff and as a result they were cancelling the bidding process immediately.

I believe I may have been dancing a highland fling around the room as he continued to stress that we and FirstGroup had done nothing wrong and that 'the fault lies wholly and squarely with the Department of Transport' and there were likely going to be some suspensions of the staff involved. After we hung up – excited that our hard work had been vindicated – I immediately started to wake up our team in London. I even woke the chairman up to tell him the glad tidings, and while I did have to bite my tongue on a couple of occasions, the words 'I told you so' never passed my lips. Instead I sat down in my hotel room with our social media head Greg Rose and drafted a blog thanking all the staff at Virgin Trains and our customers for their incredible show of support. We had listened to their advice, we had acted and we had won!

Over the next few weeks, as more details emerged, we learned that what the Department for Transport had identified as 'the flaw' was exactly what we had been trying to tell them all along – they simply hadn't done their sums very well and had accepted some highly unrealistic assumptions about the growth of passenger numbers and inflation towards the back end of the franchise. Or more simply stated: they had failed to realise the level of risk they were taking on board by accepting the FirstGroup bid. Anyway, on the 'all's well that ends well' front, we have since been given approval to continue running the West Coast line until April 2017, so the decision to 'sue the bastards' would appear to have been the correct one. I am in no doubt that none of these 'flaws' would ever have seen the light of day had we not gone for the judicial review – the thing I was repeatedly told nobody ever wins.

I have to say, though, that I had nothing but admiration for the way the Secretary for Transport handled what was obviously a very embarrassing screw up by his department. First of all, he was recently appointed to the position and so the way the bidding system was set up hadn't happened on his watch. Secondly, as recently as a couple of weeks before the dramatic late-night volte-face, he had told the House of Commons that he was satisfied that the bidding had been handled fairly and with due diligence. As a latecomer to the scene he could only have done this based on the word of his people in the Department for Transport who had handled (or more accurately 'mishandled') the bidding. The Department for Transport could very easily have just issued a press statement with the news but Mr McLoughlin had instead decided to call me personally – probably not the easiest call he has ever made! He also didn't hide behind the fact that it was his predecessor's miscalculation or weasel-word his way around the situation. In addition to the mea culpa he'd given me during our phone conversation, in subsequent interviews he continued to use no-nonsense phrases like 'completely unacceptable mistakes' and 'deeply regrettable'.

Too often decision-makers, whether in business or politics, are happy to step up to the microphone or meet with the press when there is good news to dispense but, fearing it might damage their standing with the shareholders or voters, the same people can be conspicuously absent when the news is less palatable. This mentality of 'go to ground until the firestorm passes' seldom does either the leader or their company's reputations any favours and invariably only serves to add a secondary round of damages.

SHIP HAPPENS

In recent years the best (or should that be worst?) example of bad decision-making being compounded by more bad decisions could well be the peculiar behaviour of Carnival Corporation's billionaire chairman and CEO Micky Arison when his cruise lines suffered two major accidents in the space of a year. When his ship the *Costa Concordia* ran aground on a little Italian island (that it should not have been anywhere near) killing thirty-two and seriously disrupting the lives of thousands of passengers and their families, where was Micky? All that matters really is that for reasons unknown he made no attempt to get there. As soon as he was briefed as to the severity of the situation – all he had to do was turn on a TV set to see the disaster that the rest of the world was watching – he should have had his corporate jet fuelled up and been on his way to Italy. Instead Arison buried his head in the sand and went to a basketball game to watch the Miami Heat (the NBA team he owns). Amazingly, even after the lambasting he took for failing to make his way to Italy as soon as he heard of the *Costa Concordia* disaster, it seems he isn't one to learn from his mistakes.

Almost a year later another of Arison's huge cruise ships – the ironically named *Carnival Triumph* – was towed into Mobile Alabama after a fire had destroyed the ship's generators and left the passengers stranded at sea for five days in disgusting conditions with no power, refrigeration, water or toilet facilities. After his appallingly bad decision a year earlier, there was Micky (again) opting for basketball over comforting his customers. The day when he should have been dockside in Mobile handing out blankets and compensation cheques to angry passengers, he was instead tweeting that tickets were still available for an upcoming Miami Heat game!

When a CEO or president speeds to a disaster site there's really nothing tangible they can do to unravel or rewind what has taken place. Similarly, in ninety-nine per cent of cases they are unable to immediately answer the most common question of 'Who or what do you think was responsible for the accident?' The first thing one learns in any good crisis management training is not to offer opinions, speculation or hearsay until such time as the experts confirm the cause – something that usually takes months or even years. All a company's leaders can do is to show that they care enough to be there and demonstrate their sympathy for the victims and support for their own people who are handling the situation. When, on the other hand, a leader like Micky Arison decides to stay home and watch the story as it unfolds on the world's media, that sends a very different and equally clear message that is hard to interpret as anything other than 'I really don't give a damn.'

As the tragic tale of Malaysia Airlines' flight 370 demonstrated, no two emergency situations are ever quite the same. At the time of writing there is still no answer on the fate of the aircraft and everyone on board but the airline's handling of the incident has been the focus of some pretty damning criticism from despairing relatives and the media. While some say the airline's representatives were clearly unprepared to deal with the 24/7 demands of journalists from all around the world, the amount of contradictory information and speculative statements coming from them was quite extraordinary. In such awful and unprecedented circumstances my heart went out to everyone involved – including the embattled CEO of the airline. All I will say is that if, God forbid, such a situation were ever to happen to them again, I am sure they would handle it a lot more effectively.

Touching wood as I write this, for someone who has been in the transportation business for the last three decades with companies moving millions of passengers a year I am extremely fortunate to have been faced with only one serious accident resulting in a fatality. That came back in early 2007 when a Virgin train came off the tracks in the north-east of England. When it happened I was on a ski vacation in Zermatt, Switzerland with my family; a little after nine in the evening a text came in telling me there had been a 'code black' rail accident, which indicated it was serious. After a few hurried phone calls had established that the derailed carriages had plunged down a ravine, I was merely told to 'prepare myself for the worst'. I decided on the spot that there was only one thing for me to do and all I think I said was 'I'm on my way' – something I was about to discover was easier said than done. It was snowing heavily at the time, which meant that what would have been my first choice of transportation, a helicopter, was not an option. The snow had already closed our closest airport at Sion and Geneva was about to shut down as well. With no other alternatives, other than staying put, I rented a car and set off on a gruelling five-hour drive through the snowy night to the airport at Zurich – which I prayed would still be open. It was, and I managed to catch the first flight out at 6.30 a.m. to Manchester, where I was met by Tony Collins and our head of public affairs Will Whitehorn, who jointly updated me on the accident's status as we drove to the crash site.

I was greatly saddened to hear that Margaret Masson, an elderly female passenger, was confirmed as dead at the scene, and yet when I got to see the mangled wreckage I was also relieved that there had not been more fatalities. My decision to come without delay was certainly borne out as the right one when I made my way to the hospital where injured passengers were being treated. I met with as many of them as possible and then spent time with the clearly devastated Masson family, with whom I expressed my deep sorrow over their loss.

We learned a lot from the accident, which was quickly determined to have been down to a maintenance problem with the track – something completely outside of our control. Without knowing who or what was responsible, I never gave a moment's thought to anything other than getting myself to the scene as quickly as possible. Faced with such an unenviable situation, any senior corporate officer who decides to delay their arrival at a crisis scene can usually take credit for making a 'just in time' decision, as in when they eventually get there it will be just in time for the media to castigate them for not showing up earlier.

In the course of our lifetimes we will all make a multitude of decisions big and small, good and bad. In some cases they will be hailed as brilliant and in others condemned as wrong or questionable. When the going gets tough, though, as in the case of a major accident involving your company, as the leader your job is to gather as much reliable up-to-the minute information as is available, step up and take the bull by the horns. Whatever the situation, indecision is not an option, and as I believe Micky Arison might now agree, in most cases ninety per cent of life is just showing up.

Chapter 19

GOOD BUSINESS

... is good for business

As you will know by now, when I was sixteen, I dropped out of school to start up a small magazine called *Student*. It was the height of the turbulent 1960s when students were perpetually up in arms or having sit-ins over all kinds of stuff – from Vietnam to 'banning the bomb' to apartheid to... well, just about anything that was worthy of a demonstration. By creating *Student* my friends and I wanted to give our generation a stronger voice than they had on the placards they were shouldering around Hyde Park Corner on what seemed like every other weekend.

We didn't stop with the magazine. Following on from its reasonable success, we started a not-for-profit student advisory centre with a 24/7 hotline on which young people could get guidance on issues ranging from sexually transmitted diseases to birth control to mental health and anything else that was causing them strife. Looking back, it now seems clear that I've always believed that businesses – whether small or large – have the opportunity and the responsibility to do good things in their communities and beyond. While it came naturally to us back then and we have continued down the same path at Virgin ever since, unfortunately not everyone sees life and business in the same light.

Sadly, abuses of 'the system' are all too common, by individual, government and private sectors. Readers of my various newspaper and magazine articles as well as bloggers frequently send me questions, or in some cases desperate pleas for advice on how to deal with corruption and demands for kickbacks as they try to launch or keep small businesses afloat in countries where such practices are commonplace – as well as in a few places where you would not expect such problems. Over more than four decades of doing business all around the world, I have seen what happens when companies and corrupt officials conspire to serve their own selfish interests. They wreak havoc on our planet and its fragile ecosystems, destroy communities and perpetuate the cycle of poverty and despair. As a result, many people simply refuse to trust business and public institutions. And why wouldn't they?

Wherever you come across these abuses, whether a long-accepted way of doing business or not, such self-serving corrupt practices aren't only morally wrong, they are bad for business. Commerce should be a champion of good governance, taking a strong stand against corruption and lobbying for a better world. We should be fighting to build and support strong and healthy communities because the people who live in them are our employees and our customers, our suppliers and investors; with few exceptions, businesses and the communities they serve are one hundred per cent interdependent.

These days, Virgin has become a sizable operation – we have launched more than 400 enterprises over the years – and building on our small business roots and the lessons learned, we have also developed a strong understanding of the numerous ways that businesses big and small can lead in order to make a difference.

One is through sheer scale. Many large corporations control vast supply chains that involve thousands of smaller businesses operating in dozens of countries. It's known as 'clout'. Choices made by the management team at the top of the chain – anything from using more sustainable raw materials to improving gender diversity – trickle down through the entire system, and can often bring about change much faster than governments can. 'Change your ways or we will change our supplier' is a very straightforward demonstration of how money can talk – without it having to be passed below the counter.

Question – How many Wal-Marts does it take to change a light bulb?

Answer – 3,230

I was intrigued to read the story of what focused Wal-Mart's attention on their ability to fast forward one segment of the energy savings evolution while simultaneously doing their customers, the environment and themselves a huge favour.

Some time around 2008 a conversation started in Wal-Mart around the potential for the newest light bulb technology, CFL or Compact Fluorescent 'swirls', to save their customers money on utility bills. Somebody casually asked, 'Just out of interest, what difference would it make if we were to change the bulbs in all our ceiling-fan displays from incandescent to swirls?' It seems a typical US Wal-Mart has ten ceiling fan models on display, each of which has four bulbs – that made for a total of forty bulbs per store spread over their 3,230 stores. So someone did the maths on the back of an envelope and came up with the staggering sum of $6 million in electric bill savings – just by changing the incandescent bulbs to 'swirls' on ten ceiling fans in each of Wal-Mart's more than 3,000 stores. In a *Fast Company* magazine interview, Chuck Kerby, Wal-Mart's VP for hardware (which includes ceiling fans), stated, 'I couldn't believe we were paying $6 million more than we had to in order to light those fixtures. That, for me, was an "I got it" moment.'

So having seen what changing a few bulbs could do for their own energy bills, in the name of conservation and good corporate citizenship Wal-Mart embarked on a mission. In the next twelve months Wal-Mart decided it wanted to sell at least one swirl light bulb to every one of its regular customers – that would be 110 million in all. They calculated that if every one of these customers took a 'swirl' home and used it to replace an ordinary 60-watt bulb, the energy saved would be enough to power a city of 1.5 million people. Or even more incredibly, in terms of oil not burned, or greenhouse gases not exhausted into the atmosphere, that one bulb per person is equivalent to taking 1.3 million cars off the road.

In the process of reducing energy consumption and increasing public awareness of the benefits of something as simple as changing a light bulb, Wal-Mart also aimed to improve its own less than stellar reputation by showing how seriously it is taking its new positioning as an environmental activist.

As is almost always the story, one environmental improvement usually spawns a host of others. In this case, since every CFL bulb has a life span equivalent to that of between six and ten incandescent bulbs, if Wal-Mart alone sells 110 million swirls those eliminate the need for 110 million old-fashioned bulbs to be manufactured, packaged, shipped, bought and discarded next year and for the next six to eight years going forward. According to Wal-Mart those 110 million bulbs would fill almost 300 of their huge tractor trailer trucks per year and that's not counting the fleet of garbage trucks needed to cart 110 million burned-out incandescent bulbs to the dump and the fuel they burn in the process!

Of course over time Wal-Mart would appear to be shooting itself in the foot here as with swirl bulbs on a six-to-eight-year replacement cycle their revenue from light bulb sales is clearly going to plummet. Executives at Wal-Mart, however, claim to be looking forward to the day when the shelf space for light bulbs is cut by half. While this has the appearance of a negative commercial tactic, think again: Wal-Mart didn't get to be the world's largest retailer by getting such numbers wrong! CFL bulbs put out the same amount of light as classic incandescent bulbs but use up to eighty per cent less electricity and Wal-Mart is confident that the money their customers will save on their electric bills will eventually flow back in their direction – where there will be more well-priced things to buy on the shelves where there used to be light bulbs.

But don't get too used to using those fancy new CFL bulbs just yet! The same kind of fast-paced evolution we saw in the music business when we went from vinyl records to digital via cassette tapes and CDs seems to be happening in the long-stagnant world of light bulbs. The ten-year CFL's days as the market leader are already being threatened by LED technology – an LED bulb is much more expensive but can last as long as twenty-five years and their price is already dropping dramatically. So watch out, the decision to change a light bulb is nearly not as straightforward as it used to be!

THE LAW OF LARGE NUMBERS

This incredible light-bulb saga serves to ably demonstrate several arguments that others and I have been making for years.

First is the 'law of large numbers'. When told that by changing a single light bulb they can help the planet, the typical individual's reaction is one of, 'Come on! Get real – my doing that isn't going to change anything, except a light bulb!' But as Wal-Mart is very much aware, one small action, multiplied by tens or hundreds of millions can have some pretty astounding results. As the old saying goes, 'It takes lots of little things to make big things'. For example, if one person doesn't leave the tap running while brushing their teeth twice a day, it will save an astounding 7,000 litres of water per year – which is about the same amount of water that a resident of sub-Saharan Africa uses in a year for all purposes including drinking, bathing and cooking. So 'screw it in and let's do it' – with a few CFL bulbs and turning off that tap while brushing, you can become a one-person ecological tour de force!

Secondly, Wal-Mart's 'clout' demonstrates the ability of private enterprise and big business in particular to move mountains. Wal-Mart is by far and away General Electric's biggest customer for light bulbs. Consequently GE, which makes sixty per cent of the light bulbs in the US, agreed to work with Wal-Mart on keeping the cost of the new swirls as affordable as possible. The two companies also rolled out light bulb education centres in every Wal-Mart store to educate customers on the energy savings they can reap from switching to the new technology. By comparison, it took European legislators years to reach consensus on phasing out inefficient bulbs. While effective environmental regulations are necessary for sure, big business can lead the way and grease a lot of very creaky inefficient wheels.

As a postscript to this story I should perhaps note that in May 2013 Wal-Mart was fined $110 million for six counts of violating the US's federal Clean Water Act by illegally disposing of hazardous materials at its stores across the US, so while they are clearly making serious efforts in many areas, it would appear that in others they are not exactly a paragon of environmental virtue just yet!

GE WHIZZ

And last but by *no* means least, companies that commit to doing good for the planet almost always find it to be good for business as well. In 2005, long before they started to collaborate with Wal-Mart on the CFL drive, GE's CEO Jeffrey Immelt launched their 'Ecomagination' business push, which was neatly encapsulated by the slogan 'Green Can Be Green' (as in the 'greenback' dollar). Among a multitude of projects 'Ecomagination' has spawned programmes like 'Ecomagination Nation' a global power and water initiative designed to reduce GE's carbon footprint, energy and water use. To date eighteen global sites are participating, reducing water use in 2012 by 669 million gallons, the equivalent to shutting down Niagara Falls for seventy-seven minutes. Another GE programme has produced the natural gas-powered 'Flex Efficiency' power plant – the emissions reduction in a year from operating just one of these instead of a coal-powered unit is the equivalent to eliminating the annual CO_2 emissions of nearly three million cars in Japan.

Taking a stand on something you know to be right can lead to innovation and further business opportunities. Consider the leadership demonstrated by Safaricom and Vodafone in Kenya and Tanzania with 'M-Pesa'. This first of its kind mobile-phone-based 'branchless' banking service allows users with a national ID card or passport to deposit, withdraw and transfer money easily with a mobile device. Within four years of its launch in Kenya alone, M-Pesa had attracted seventeen million subscribers, many of whom had previously had little or no access to financial institutions. The system has provided millions with new opportunities, which is driving economic growth and reducing poverty.

Closer to home, a few years ago Virgin Unite and some great partners were instrumental in launching the Carbon War Room, an initiative to identify and scale up market-based solutions to climate change. The CWR team's research showed, for instance, that the global shipping industry could save up to $70 billion per year and reduce carbon emissions and other pollutants by up to thirty per cent if it shifted to more energy-efficient technologies and shipping vessels. Consequently, in cooperation with University College London, the Carbon War Room team started the ShIFT project (Shipping Innovation Fast Tracker) and is partnering with companies like Bermuda-based Magnuss Ltd that has developed a mechanical sail for cargo ships. Their VOSS (Vertically variable Ocean Sail System – don't you just love these acronyms!) saves fuel and reduces emissions by enabling a ship's main engines to be throttled back while maintaining cruise speed thereby achieving twenty to thirty-five per cent in fuel savings: all courtesy of Mother Nature!

Shipping is just one sector. The Carbon War Room's research team is constantly working to identify opportunities that have cost-negative, billion ton per annum carbon reduction potential over the next ten years and has to date found seven of them: industry, forestry, agriculture, waste management, transport, energy and construction. Across seventeen sub-sectors these seven sectors combined could account for a fourteen per cent reduction in the world's CO_2 annual emissions! If these numbers sound ambitious, they are. But Christopher Columbus was told the same thing when, with nothing but the courage of his own convictions, he went in search of the East Indies. And just look at what happened there – without any carbon footprint whatsoever!

All these huge numbers are very grand, I know, and a common question is what does all this mean for existing small businesses and entrepreneurs looking to start one? The simple answer is – a lot. In the long term, value or purpose-driven entrepreneurs stand a much better chance of succeeding in a global marketplace in which regulators everywhere are steadily tightening the compliance rules. In conjunction with this, consumers are beginning to rightfully demand more sustainable products and services, leaving global brands with no alternative but to attempt to find suppliers and partners who can demonstrate that they value people and the planet as much as they do profits and have a track record to prove it. I must confess that I am hugely encouraged to see that this is already starting to happen on so many fronts, which is great news for entre-preneurs determined to be a force for good in the world, and even better news for our society and the planet.

THERE IS A PLAN B

The old legacy business model – let's call it Plan A – that got the planet into today's perilous state, is clearly broken and needs to be rethought at every level. Plan A's playbook sees business leaders being forced to race from quarterly report to quarterly report. As a result almost all their efforts are focused on coming up with products and services that will profitably appeal to the masses and keep the investors happy. Elected officials, meanwhile, always seem to have one eye trained on the next election cycle and yet their campaign promises and their post-election actions often have little or no long-term relationship.

Up against these established Plan A patterns, it is surprising we are making any progress at all. But attitudes are changing and a new generation of social entrepreneurs and leaders are using strategies from the commercial world and employing technology to tackle all nature of tough social and environmental issues, even areas that used to be the exclusive domain of government agencies and charitable organisations. In an effort to help social entrepreneurs to tackle these challenges head-on and find new solutions, we recently were one of the principal movers in setting up a new not-for-profit initiative called 'The B Team'.

The B Team is a group of global business leaders in search of a 'Plan B' for business that balances the pursuit of enterprise with the needs of employees, societies and the environment. Our membership includes an amazing cross-section of global leaders such as Ratan Tata, chairman emeritus of the Tata Group, Arianna Huffington, chairman, president and editor in chief of the Huffington Post Media Group, Nobel Laureate Muhammad Yunus, Paul Polman, CEO of Unilever, Blake Mycoskie, founder and 'Chief Shoe Giver' at TOMS, Kathy Calvin, president and CEO of the UN Foundation and many, many more. At the risk of making this sound like an Oscar acceptance speech where I don't have time to list all the people involved, let me just show you our very short and precise mission statement:

'Our mission is to deliver a "Plan B" that puts people and planet alongside profit. Plan A – where companies have been driven by the profit motive alone – is no longer acceptable.'

Plan B is off to a good start, with plenty of great ideas and a growing community of like-minded colleagues, but we have a long road ahead us. The encouraging news is that so many of the young entrepreneurs we meet are already very much attuned to the B Team's call for a new way of doing business. Social, value-driven and purpose-driven enterprises are emerging in greater numbers than ever before, offering an amazing array of market-based solutions to some of the world's toughest challenges – from clean energy access to water scarcity and microfinance.

At a recent B Team meeting in New York, I joined Arianna Huffington, Blake Mycoskie and others to bring a group of founders and CEOs together who are focusing on 'People Innovation' as the core of their businesses. It was inspiring to be part of a group sharing innovative approaches to creating businesses that people love to be a part of. Some of the interesting ideas we heard about were the Netflix initiative of unlimited vacation days, meditation classes to combat stress, sleeping pods for afternoon naps and truly flexible working hours and locations. All of these innovations could and should be replicated by businesses all over the world and there's good reason to do so – it's good for business.

Today's twenty-four-hour work culture means it's more important than ever before to look after our people. Arianna Huffington has made 'wellness' integral to working life at the Huffington Post where she wants her team not just to succeed but also to thrive – so she's introduced healthy snacks, mindfulness training and, with the introduction of the Virgin Pulse Wellness Programme, Huffington Post employees are now fitter and more productive than ever before.

Of course, work is not just about productivity and the bottom line – it's about making a positive difference in our world. So it's important that we enable our people to experience their impact. TOMS sends its employees on 'shoe-giving trips' and Bridgeway Capital Management allows every one of its people to set up their own foundations while giving away a staggering fifty per cent of their profits – these are companies that are really going to make a difference in the world!

More businesses should be following the lead of all these fantastic companies and the B Team is working hard to encourage a better way of doing business for the well-being of people and the planet and changing work for good is an integral part of this.

OPENING CELLULAR DOORS

No matter what the structure of the company – whether it is for-profit, non-profit or some creative melding of the two – entrepreneurial solutions are now offering engagement, jobs and, just as importantly, they are kindling hope in areas where there used to be none. A great example of social entrepreneurship at work is the story of Zimbabwean Strive Masiyiwa – with a name like 'Strive' he was clearly destined to do great things! Strive is the founder and chairman of Econet Wireless Group. He first came to international prominence when he fought a landmark legal battle in his native Zimbabwe for the dissolution of the state's monopoly in telecommunications. After an arduous five-year battle, he won the day and this paved the way for opening the African telecommunications sector to private capital and a lot more. In the newly deregulated environment Econet was free to do things like distributing their patented 'Home Power Station', a solar charging station that supplies power for cell-phones, lights and other devices, transforming the lives of people living in rural African areas where the supply of electricity is either non existent or erratic at best.

By changing its business model to driving change for people and the planet, Econet also created all kinds of lucrative new revenue streams. This shift has opened up countless new avenues for the company, which is now using its charging stations to power everything from single light bulbs to refrigerators that can safely store vaccines for an entire community.

Business and government must encourage established entrepreneurs and young talent to focus on problem areas like health, education, climate change and social care. How can we speed up this process and make even more of an impact? There seem to be three key obstacles facing the next generation of business leaders who want to get social enterprises off the ground.

FUNDING – 'SHOW ME THE MONEY'

In 2012 the British Cabinet Office estimated that in the UK alone there were some 70,000 social enterprises working at helping people, communities and the environment. They further stated that these businesses and organisations contributed a staggering £54.9 billion to the economy while employing almost a million people. Unfortunately, as impressive as these numbers might sound, the fact is that they hardly begin to scratch the surface of the problems they are doing their best to address.

Entrepreneurs often struggle to raise seed money for any venture so it is invariably far tougher to get funding for social enterprises than their commercial counterparts – this despite the fact that the financial returns can be just as big or bigger. In the UK alone, for instance, if a start-up team is proposing to launch a social enterprise with the potential to radically change the nation's £87 billion social-care sector, they clearly should be deserving of a serious listen from those who are in a position to provide substantial funding, as opposed to just a little grant money.

We need to encourage more leadership initiatives and competitions such as Google's 2013 Global Impact Challenge, which set out to find four non-profits in the UK that would be awarded £500,000 each to help them tackle some of the world's toughest problems through technology. I was honoured to be one of the five judges and I have to say that the quality of the entrants was incredibly impressive. One winner was 'CDI [Change through Digital Inclusion] Apps for Good', which motivates schoolchildren to realise the potential of technology to empower them to change the world around them. CDI gives kids the tools to design, develop and even sell apps that deal with issues directly impacting their everyday lives. One such app that's made it to the 'Google Play Store' is Stop and Search UK, an app that enables users to instantaneously check out their rights when it comes to police searches, look up stop and search occurrences in their neighbourhood and anonymously share their experiences. In the last two years, in London alone, there have been close to 100,000 new tech job openings and yet fewer than 4,000 students in all of England have taken computing as an advanced-level subject in each of these years. Apps for Good plans to change that and CDI projects almost 200,000 students will have access to the programme over the next three years.

Another, and very different, winner of the Google Challenge was the Zoological Society of London (ZSL), which uses tracking devices to monitor and protect endangered species of wildlife. Wildlife crime is one of the largest illegal trades in the world, devastating not only threatened species but also the communities that depend on them for their livelihoods. Between 2011 and 2012, it is estimated that rhino poaching alone increased by more than forty per cent. The ZSL plans to put the $750,000 Global Impact Award funding to work with new hi-tech 'camera traps' equipped with automated sensors to help protect threatened wildlife: the sensors will instantaneously transmit alerts of gunfire, vehicle movement and human presence.

Over just two years, ZSL projects that this technology can reduce poaching incidents in just one threatened Kenyan protected area by fifty per cent by providing vastly improved protection for endangered rhinos, elephant, and other poacher-favoured species of wildlife. As awareness grows of the new systems and more effective patrols, it will not only deter poachers but also reduce threats, and increase security for local communities and wildlife rangers.

Google has to be praised for taking the lead with this wonderful initiative – I personally gave Larry Page a high five when I heard about the two stories above. Following the success of Google's social entrepreneurship awards, others are following suit. This is leadership in action – creating a force for good.

In yet another admirable UK initiative, 'Founders Forum For Good' started by Brent Hoberman and Jonnie Goodwin in partnership with social investor Nominet Trust has put up a £1 Million Challenge fund in order to inspire and encourage the brightest entrepreneurs to apply their technological talents to develop new ventures using digital solutions for social impact. Called Social Tech, Social Change, the programme will provide active investment and support to enable these social entrepreneurs to launch and develop their ideas. Within four months of its June 2013 launch, the programme had received 220 applications. Among the first ten ventures to each win a £50,000 share of the £1 million fund was MKS Solutions. Their set-top box is designed to combat the problem of isolation for the elderly by allowing video-calling via a TV set without the need to access the internet. Another was Specialisterne, whose technology creates a bridge between individuals with autism and organisations that have a need for their unique skills, thereby ensuring equal opportunity in the labour market. Two quite inspirational ventures that with some start-up capital and mentoring will now have a much greater chance of success.

In addition to helping social entrepreneurs directly, these kinds of initiatives also tend to attract significant amounts of media attention to the growing social enterprise sector that will hopefully encourage still more funding and in the process see even more great ideas spring to life. It has to be said, however, that to make an impact the awards don't have to be in seven figures. While bigger sums inevitably make for more media noise, if you or your company can see your way clear to offering a few thousand pounds or dollars to help launch worthy local social entrepreneurs, there's no telling what great oaks will grow from little acorns.

Now that's leadership!

EPILOGUE

START IT UP

Designing designers

Not so long ago, I experienced one of those fortunate chance encounters that help keep life interesting. By coincidence, right around the time that Virgin Produced, our entertainment division, was about to release the movie *Jobs*, which tells the story of Steve Jobs and the early years of Apple, I had dinner with a fascinating group of business leaders that included Twitter CEO Dick Costolo, Nest's Tony Fadell, Mike McCue of Flipboard and Dave Morin of the social network Path.

As someone who is a regular user of Flipboard and, for reasons I cannot begin to explain, has millions of followers on Twitter, this was a mindboggling group and they didn't disappoint – they all had great stories to share. Then I learned that Messrs Fadell and Morin had both worked at Apple earlier in their careers, and so couldn't resist the urge to cajole them into sharing a few insider impressions on Steve Jobs, who despite his well-documented character flaws – several of which are evident in the movie – is still one of the leaders I most admire. Jobs' extraordinary vision, attention to detail and commitment to form as well as function helped change the way we all live, work and communicate. As I write this I just heard a news item that the latest iteration of the iPhone has sold nine million units in its first three days on the market: a quite amazing statistic by any measure. Selling nine million of something in a decade would be an achievement for most companies, but in three days!

AN APPLE A DAY

Tony Fadell, I learned, was one of the key players in the development of Apple's revolutionary iPod. He told us how, early in his Apple career, he'd approached Jobs with the initial concept, then gone on to work on building and developing no fewer than eighteen generations of iPods and three generations of iPhones – gizmos that almost single-handedly turned the music and telecommunications industries on their heads. I had to laugh when Tony mentioned that, at Apple, any device that is over five years old is officially categorised as 'vintage'. I didn't want to say I'd been in the retail music business for almost forty years before I was rendered extinct by what they were brewing up at Apple. I mean, if five years is vintage, then forty must qualify me as what? Medieval or just plain ancient, I would guess.

I was, however, greatly intrigued to learn how Jobs' famously tough, aggressive and 'my way or the highway' style of leadership had affected the employees and corporate culture as a whole. It is well known that Jobs pushed his employees to their limits – both technically and emotionally – to achieve stunning results. He demanded, expected and accepted nothing short of perfection. He was quick to criticise and pulled no punches when things did not go right, but when his people did rise to the challenge then a lot of things went spectacularly right for Apple.

Fadell told the group that no matter how brilliant a new product in development might have been, if it fell even a tad short of Steve's vision of perfection, it was never quite good enough. As a by-product of this constant almost maniacal pursuit of perfection in function and design, Jobs could never bring himself to back down. According to Tony and Dave you could never hope to win an argument with Jobs unless you were able to back it up with cold, hard, irrefutable facts. If any argument boiled down to being a matter of opinion, there could be no possible winner other than Jobs. So if there were no mitigating facts to be found, and Tony and his team needed to win an opinion-based argument, they would always scheme together before conferring with Jobs, wait until the ideal moment presented itself during the meeting and when it did, one of them would proclaim 'now', at which point they'd all lean in and push back as a team. It sounded a bit like a lynching to me, but Tony said it usually worked and there were seldom any hard feelings from Steve – well, hardly ever!

An intrinsic abhorrence of the status quo and the belief that with a little or often a heck of a lot of thought everything in life can always be improved upon is what sets true entrepreneurs and great leaders apart. At the same time the skill set for the two is quite different. As the Steve Jobs' story clearly illustrates, whenever he got too involved in the day-to-day side of Apple, his people skills were sadly lacking. When, however, the board ousted Jobs and replaced him with John Scully, formerly president at Pepsico, they also sucked all the creative vision out of the company. Creators are never fully satisfied; they believe they can always do better. At the same time they need to recognise that any business needs a clear direction and a steady hand at the helm. And as great as it may be to be able to zig when the competition zags, incessant zig-zagging can make it very difficult to stay on any kind of a course.

Jobs' vision, drive and commitment to design perfection led the iPod team into the development of a huge range of variations on the theme before they felt they had attained their goal and were ready to launch it on an unsuspecting world. This is a long and lonely process at any company – as Morin said that evening, 'In today's euphoria, nobody remembers how at one stage we couldn't sell iPods and had to resort to giving a free one to every student at Duke University to get it going. It can be a long and often painful process to build a company.'

When we got to the topic of what projects we are working on now, Tony Fadell discussed his wonderful new company, Nest. Their product is an ingenious hi-tech variation on the good old home heating thermostat. Rather than just obeying pre-set timings, however, the Nest unit assimilates people's comings and goings from home and anticipates when to lower or raise the temperature.

This better intelligence can lead to reductions in carbon output and energy bills by up to twenty per cent. While some might think the home heating business a tad mundane after all the high-profile sexy stuff that Tony was involved with at Apple, Google obviously didn't agree with that assessment when in January 2014 (several months after my dinner with Tony), they paid a reported $3.2 billion in cash to acquire Nest. I suspect that what Google really wanted to get its hands on was not just a company that makes hi-tech thermostats but rather Tony and his entire team. The Nest team will remain within Google and become the core of a new focus on gadgets – as to what kind exactly, nobody is saying. Given Tony's iPod and iPhone background, however, with the creative might of Google suddenly at his disposal, watch this space – anything is possible!

Like all good entrepreneurs Tony is someone who starts each day asking, 'What's trending out there and how can I best reinvent my business to take advantage of it?' That's the classic sign of a chronic entrepreneur and good leader – they are always itching to move on to 'the next big thing'. I don't know about Tony Fadell or anyone else around the table that evening, but I've often been told I exhibit all the classic symptoms of suffering from ADD (Attention Deficit Disorder). There may be distinct similarities to ADD but I have always believed I am more likely to be suffering from a bad case of SERS – Serial Entrepreneurial Restlessness Syndrome.

As the Apple story so capably demonstrates, a company's culture is really the power behind the brand and feeds into everything it does. At Nest, using lessons learned from his time in Cupertino,

Tony Fadell told us he has worked at deliberately developing a more collegial and less dictatorial culture than that which Jobs fostered at Apple. Tony's style of leadership is to help everyone in the group to understand their vital role in its successes and to work towards realising those goals. It's more about nurturing, encouragement and praise than publicly bawling people out and demanding more.

On the other hand, Nest does share Apple's focus on brilliant design. Tony Fadell remarked that just like making practical, excellent products, 'You must look cool and do cool.' This gives customers both rational and irrational/emotional reasons to invest in a brand. 'Technology should be about more than just newest, loudest, prettiest – it should make a real difference.'

Dave Morin who spent time at Facebook as well as Apple before creating the critically acclaimed social-networking app Path, commented that the impetus for great design has got to come from the top. And having worked with both Steve Jobs and Mark Zuckerberg, he should certainly know! Dave believes that everyone at a company should care about how a product looks, feels and works — not just the people with the word 'design' in their job titles. He added that modern companies need CEOs with a taste for good design every bit as much as they need accountants who are great with numbers. This is a philosophy we have rigorously employed over the years at Virgin – on both design and accountants! We have always tried hard to ensure every level of the team is included in the design process. After all, who has more meaningful input than a flight attendant as to what works and doesn't work with an airline passenger, or a personal trainer on what members really want from a fitness club?

Good design is incredibly important. If the iPod or iPhone had functioned in exactly the same way but been clunky ugly ducklings, do you really think they would still have taken the planet by storm the way they have done? I seriously doubt it.

The Virgin way has always been to push sexy design to the forefront. Take our Galactic business, for instance: in essence it's all about the unique opportunity to travel into space and experience weightlessness while looking down on our planet from an altitude a dozen times higher than commercial flight levels. Accustomed to TV visions of ruggedly industrial NASA space capsule and space station interiors, I doubt if anyone would have balked at the chance to blast off because they didn't think the interior design of the Galactic cabin was quite right. Nevertheless we have spent vast amounts of time and effort getting the look and feel of everything from our Nevada New Mexico, Spaceport America to our astronaut uniforms and the cabin interiors in SpaceShipTwo to be every bit as sexy and cool as you'd expect to find in a new luxury sports car. Adam Wells who heads up the design team at Galactic is the person responsible for all the outstanding cabin innovations we have introduced on Virgin Atlantic and Virgin America in recent years and he has relished the design challenges of introducing the same but extremely disparate sizzle to an altogether different space – pun intended.

With Virgin Galactic, as with all our other businesses, one of my key roles has always been to continuously stir the pot by objectively listening to feedback and opinions from every possible source – or as someone once described me, 'sort of a shit-disturber in chief'. It is essential that this kind of listening, pro-active culture permeates the entire company at every level. Everyone has to be a leader and a hundred per cent comfortable in their own right to express their opinions freely and openly. How many times when you've complained about something have you heard the sad retort, 'Oh, I know! You're not the first person to say that and we've been telling *them* for years.' Employee and customer feedback has to have an unimpeded route to people who can act upon it or else nothing will ever get better. There is no room for the kind of departmental hubris that Dave Morin talks about. In short, you don't have to be a designer to have designs on improving your company's customer service, products and ultimately making everyone better off.

As our dinner wound to a close, we got around to discussing what would be the best advice we could take from our own varied experiences that might be useful for new entrepreneurs and leaders, whether with a new business or a new product. By the time we finished dessert we seemed to have a consensus that – to parody or perhaps mirror Nike's '*Just Do It*' slogan – our advice should be, '*Just Start It*'. In essence we agreed with the great advice I mentioned earlier that came from my mum: 'You're guaranteed to miss every shot you don't take.' So take that shot! Don't brood over one idea or another for two or three years as many people do – give it a go! Don't get lulled into the morass of perpetual paralysis by analysis: if your instinct is positive then go with it. You will learn so many more lessons by just doing than you ever will by mulling it over and over.

If music helps gets you going, then crank up the volume and let the Rolling Stones blast you into action with 'Start Me Up'. Trust the process, trust your instincts and trust your team. Don't start second-guessing yourself or worrying about a few mistakes along the way – you will only learn from them.

Just be sure that you don't make the same mistakes over and over – then you should worry!

AFTERWORD

As I said up front, no two people will ever do anything quite the same way, which is what keeps life and business interesting. The Virgin way probably isn't for everyone but it has worked well for us the majority of the time and so I hope you have managed to find the odd nugget or two of inspiration somewhere in the last couple of hundred pages.

If on the other hand you're the kind of person who (like I frequently did at school) likes to skip to the back of the book hoping to find a summary there, then I don't want to disappoint – here is my top ten.

1. FOLLOW YOUR DREAMS AND JUST DO IT

You will live a much better life if you 'just do it' and pursue your passions. People who have the courage to spend their time working on things they love are usually the ones enjoying life the most. They are also the ones who dared to take a risk and chase their dreams.

2. MAKE A POSITIVE DIFFERENCE AND DO SOME GOOD

If you aren't making a positive difference to other people's lives, then you shouldn't be in business. Companies have a responsibility to make a difference in the world, for their staff, their customers – everyone. The amazing part is that doing good is also good for business, so what are you waiting for?

3. BELIEVE IN YOUR IDEAS AND BE THE BEST

A passionate belief in your business and personal objectives can make all the difference between success and failure. If *you* aren't proud of what you're doing, why should anybody else be?

Don't get suckered into blindly pursuing profits and growth. Stay focused on being the best at everything you do and, if you want it to, the rest will follow.

4. HAVE FUN AND LOOK AFTER YOUR TEAM

Fun is one of the most important – and underrated – ingredients in any successful venture. If you're not having fun, then it's probably time to call it quits and try something else.

If your team members are engaged, having fun and genuinely care about other people, they will enjoy their work more and do a better job – it's really that simple. Find people who look for the best in others, lavish more praise than criticism, and love what they do.

5. DON'T GIVE UP

On every adventure I have undertaken – whether setting up a business, flying around the world in a balloon or racing across oceans in a boat – there have been moments when the easy thing to do would have been to throw in the towel and walk away.

By simply sticking with it, brushing yourself down and trying again, you'll be amazed what you can achieve.

6. LISTEN, TAKE LOTS OF NOTES AND KEEP SETTING NEW CHALLENGES

Listen more and talk less. Take notes – lots of notes. If you don't write down your own (and others') spontaneous ideas, they can be gone in the blink of an eye. Make lists to keep track of your goals.

You'll be amazed at the challenges a listening culture can overcome.

7. DELEGATE AND SPEND MORE TIME WITH YOUR FAMILY

The art of delegation is one of the key skills any entrepreneur must master. 'Hire your weaknesses' – if you find people who can take on tasks you aren't good at, it frees you up to plan for the future. It also gives you time to spend with your family, which is really the most important thing of all.

Oh yes, and don't forget to garner your family's input on the occasional big idea – like Virgin condoms, for instance!

8. TURN OFF THAT LAPTOP AND IPHONE AND GET YOUR DERRIÈRE OUT THERE

Rather than sitting in front of a screen all your life, try switching it all off on a regular basis and going out into the world. Start with your own backyard and then expand your field of vision.

'Life isn't a dress rehearsal'. With so many fascinating people to meet, exciting adventures to embark upon and rewarding challenges to undertake, there's no time to lose.

9. COMMUNICATE, COLLABORATE AND COMMUNICATE SOME MORE

Keep it simple, stupid, and above all else keep it coming. Mushrooms might grow when they are kept in the dark and fed a diet of dung but it doesn't work with people.

Remember Steve Jobs and the Pixar piazza: build open work environments that invite your people to intermingle and share their visions.

10. DO WHAT YOU LOVE AND HAVE A COUCH IN THE KITCHEN

As long as you are surrounded by the people you love and doing what you love, it really doesn't matter where you are. When we are on Necker we tend to spend most of our time in the kitchen. Add in a bedroom and a partner that you love, and you really don't need too much more.

Now I really must get back to my hammock and do some business – around here that's known as the Virgin Island Way!

ACKNOWLEDGEMENTS

Writing a book about listening, learning, laughing and leading has made me (again) acutely aware of how incredibly fortunate I have been over the years to have enjoyed such a seemingly endless stream of wonderful colleagues. There would never have been a 'Virgin Way' but for these tens of thousands of amazingly gifted and dedicated people.

I have spent my entire adult life listening to them and learning from them. Whenever we have entered a new business about which I had little or no first-hand knowledge – which is almost every time – it has almost always been a case of 'teaching the old dog (or perhaps "the older boss" sounds better) new tricks'. I frequently get way too much individual credit for the success of these companies when it is usually a case of the Virgin Way giving our people the freedom to express themselves by letting their imaginations take flight.

At every stop along the way, from *Student* magazine to Virgin Galactic and everything in between, we have certainly enjoyed great times together and laughed a lot – quite often at my expense, as with my night locked up in a London police station cell! Virgin is built on laughter and so again, this is a tribute to that indomitable communal sense of humour that has made forty plus years go by in the blink of an eye.

And when it comes to leading, on occasions too numerous to recall, I have often paused to wonder just who was leading who on any particular project. But whether I was leading or being led, what's important is that we get the job done and have fun getting there. That's really the core of the Virgin Way.

Finding the time to get my thoughts into manuscript form and eventually onto the pages of a book has always been a challenge for me. The process usually relies heavily on long, interruption-free flights, or those days when I can create a few free hours on Necker Island to peck away at my iPad or scribble in my trusty notebook.

The fact that this ever got started is very much down to the relentlessness of Ed Faulkner at Virgin Books – and that it got finished is again thanks to his incredibly forgiving spirit and tireless editing. As always, Nick Fox was an invaluable help, forever coaching, prodding and encouraging me with lines like, 'Hey, that's an idea you should develop for the book' or alternatively, 'I hope you're not thinking of putting *that* in the book!' Likewise my old friend (sorry, perhaps I should say 'long-time friend') and former colleague David Tait, who has been a tremendous resource in getting the contents spliced together. He not only revels in correcting my use of the language, but he's equally adept at gently nudging my recollections back on track with not so subtle comments like, 'Really Richard? I was there that day and that's not exactly how I remember it.'

Then there's my amazing mum, wonderful wife and kids, colleagues past and present, friends, competitors and others too numerous to list, that generously gave their time to refresh my memory on the finer points of the Virgin Way with pertinent examples of how it works in practice around our family of companies.

Thank you one and all.

Richard

INDEX